C-3258   CAREER EXAMINATION SERIES

This is your
PASSBOOK for...

Motor Vehicle Representative

Test Preparation Study Guide
Questions & Answers

NATIONAL LEARNING CORPORATION®

COPYRIGHT NOTICE

This book is SOLELY intended for, is sold ONLY to, and its use is RESTRICTED to individual, bona fide applicants or candidates who qualify by virtue of having seriously filed applications for appropriate license, certificate, professional and/or promotional advancement, higher school matriculation, scholarship, or other legitimate requirements of education and/or governmental authorities.

This book is NOT intended for use, class instruction, tutoring, training, duplication, copying, reprinting, excerption, or adaptation, etc., by:

1) Other publishers
2) Proprietors and/or Instructors of "Coaching" and/or Preparatory Courses
3) Personnel and/or Training Divisions of commercial, industrial, and governmental organizations
4) Schools, colleges, or universities and/or their departments and staffs, including teachers and other personnel
5) Testing Agencies or Bureaus
6) Study groups which seek by the purchase of a single volume to copy and/or duplicate and/or adapt this material for use by the group as a whole without having purchased individual volumes for each of the members of the group
7) Et al.

Such persons would be in violation of appropriate Federal and State statutes.

PROVISION OF LICENSING AGREEMENTS – Recognized educational, commercial, industrial, and governmental institutions and organizations, and others legitimately engaged in educational pursuits, including training, testing, and measurement activities, may address request for a licensing agreement to the copyright owners, who will determine whether, and under what conditions, including fees and charges, the materials in this book may be used them. In other words, a licensing facility exists for the legitimate use of the material in this book on other than an individual basis. However, it is asseverated and affirmed here that the material in this book CANNOT be used without the receipt of the express permission of such a licensing agreement from the Publishers. Inquiries re licensing should be addressed to the company, attention rights and permissions department.

All rights reserved, including the right of reproduction in whole or in part, in any form or by any means, electronic or mechanical, including photocopying, recording, or by any information storage and retrieval system, without permission in writing from the Publisher.

Copyright © 2024 by
National Learning Corporation

212 Michael Drive, Syosset, NY 11791
(516) 921-8888 • www.passbooks.com
E-mail: info@passbooks.com

PUBLISHED IN THE UNITED STATES OF AMERICA

PASSBOOK® SERIES

THE *PASSBOOK® SERIES* has been created to prepare applicants and candidates for the ultimate academic battlefield – the examination room.

At some time in our lives, each and every one of us may be required to take an examination – for validation, matriculation, admission, qualification, registration, certification, or licensure.

Based on the assumption that every applicant or candidate has met the basic formal educational standards, has taken the required number of courses, and read the necessary texts, the *PASSBOOK® SERIES* furnishes the one special preparation which may assure passing with confidence, instead of failing with insecurity. Examination questions – together with answers – are furnished as the basic vehicle for study so that the mysteries of the examination and its compounding difficulties may be eliminated or diminished by a sure method.

This book is meant to help you pass your examination provided that you qualify and are serious in your objective.

The entire field is reviewed through the huge store of content information which is succinctly presented through a provocative and challenging approach – the question-and-answer method.

A climate of success is established by furnishing the correct answers at the end of each test.

You soon learn to recognize types of questions, forms of questions, and patterns of questioning. You may even begin to anticipate expected outcomes.

You perceive that many questions are repeated or adapted so that you can gain acute insights, which may enable you to score many sure points.

You learn how to confront new questions, or types of questions, and to attack them confidently and work out the correct answers.

You note objectives and emphases, and recognize pitfalls and dangers, so that you may make positive educational adjustments.

Moreover, you are kept fully informed in relation to new concepts, methods, practices, and directions in the field.

You discover that you are actually taking the examination all the time: you are preparing for the examination by "taking" an examination, not by reading extraneous and/or supererogatory textbooks.

In short, this PASSBOOK®, used directedly, should be an important factor in helping you to pass your test.

MOTOR VEHICLE REPRESENTATIVE

Duties

As a Motor Vehicle Representative, you will have substantial in-person or telephone contact with members of the public seeking services or information regarding licenses, registrations, identification, testing, insurance, penalties, hearings, and related agency programs. You will be expected to effectively use a computer. You may be required to operate telecommunication consoles, cameras, cash drawer, photocopiers, fax machines, scanners, calculators, etc. You may be responsible for processing customer payments such as: cash, checks, credit card charges, and inventories of documents, license plates, registration stickers, and other security items. In an issuing office setting, the majority of your time will be spent assisting the public by greeting the public as they arrive in the office as well as in processing transactions by entering data on a personal computer using a keyboard and mouse. If assigned to a call center, you would wear a headset and would be expected to effectively answer telephone calls which are automatically and continuously distributed by a complex telephonic system. Telephone calls may be monitored for quality assurance.

Subject of Examination
The written test is designed to test for knowledge, skills, and/or abilities in such areas as:
1. **Arithmetic computation with calculator** - These questions test for the ability to use a calculator to do basic computations. Questions will involve addition, subtraction, multiplication and division. You may also be asked to calculate averages, to use percents, and to round an answer to the nearest whole number.
2. **Coding/decoding information** - These questions test for the ability to follow a set of coding rules. Some questions will require you to code information by converting certain information into letters or numbers. Other questions will require you to decode information by determining if the information that has already been converted into letters or numbers is correct. Complete directions will be provided; no previous knowledge of or training in any coding system is required.
3. **Evaluating conclusions in light of known facts** - These questions will consist of a set of factual statements and a conclusion. You must decide if the conclusion is proved by the facts, disproved by the facts or if the facts are not sufficient to prove or disprove the conclusion. The questions will not be specific to a particular field.
4. **Public contact principles and practices** - These questions test for knowledge of techniques used to interact with other people, to gather and present information, and to provide assistance, advice, and effective customer service in a courteous and professional manner. Questions will cover such topics as understanding and responding to people with diverse needs, perspectives, personalities, and levels of familiarity with agency operations, as well as acting in a way that both serves the public and reflects well on your agency.

HOW TO TAKE A TEST

I. YOU MUST PASS AN EXAMINATION

A. WHAT EVERY CANDIDATE SHOULD KNOW

Examination applicants often ask us for help in preparing for the written test. What can I study in advance? What kinds of questions will be asked? How will the test be given? How will the papers be graded?

As an applicant for a civil service examination, you may be wondering about some of these things. Our purpose here is to suggest effective methods of advance study and to describe civil service examinations.

Your chances for success on this examination can be increased if you know how to prepare. Those "pre-examination jitters" can be reduced if you know what to expect. You can even experience an adventure in good citizenship if you know why civil service exams are given.

B. WHY ARE CIVIL SERVICE EXAMINATIONS GIVEN?

Civil service examinations are important to you in two ways. As a citizen, you want public jobs filled by employees who know how to do their work. As a job seeker, you want a fair chance to compete for that job on an equal footing with other candidates. The best-known means of accomplishing this two-fold goal is the competitive examination.

Exams are widely publicized throughout the nation. They may be administered for jobs in federal, state, city, municipal, town or village governments or agencies.

Any citizen may apply, with some limitations, such as the age or residence of applicants. Your experience and education may be reviewed to see whether you meet the requirements for the particular examination. When these requirements exist, they are reasonable and applied consistently to all applicants. Thus, a competitive examination may cause you some uneasiness now, but it is your privilege and safeguard.

C. HOW ARE CIVIL SERVICE EXAMS DEVELOPED?

Examinations are carefully written by trained technicians who are specialists in the field known as "psychological measurement," in consultation with recognized authorities in the field of work that the test will cover. These experts recommend the subject matter areas or skills to be tested; only those knowledges or skills important to your success on the job are included. The most reliable books and source materials available are used as references. Together, the experts and technicians judge the difficulty level of the questions.

Test technicians know how to phrase questions so that the problem is clearly stated. Their ethics do not permit "trick" or "catch" questions. Questions may have been tried out on sample groups, or subjected to statistical analysis, to determine their usefulness.

Written tests are often used in combination with performance tests, ratings of training and experience, and oral interviews. All of these measures combine to form the best-known means of finding the right person for the right job.

II. HOW TO PASS THE WRITTEN TEST

A. NATURE OF THE EXAMINATION

To prepare intelligently for civil service examinations, you should know how they differ from school examinations you have taken. In school you were assigned certain definite pages to read or subjects to cover. The examination questions were quite detailed and usually emphasized memory. Civil service exams, on the other hand, try to discover your present ability to perform the duties of a position, plus your potentiality to learn these duties. In other words, a civil service exam attempts to predict how successful you will be. Questions cover such a broad area that they cannot be as minute and detailed as school exam questions.

In the public service similar kinds of work, or positions, are grouped together in one "class." This process is known as *position-classification*. All the positions in a class are paid according to the salary range for that class. One class title covers all of these positions, and they are all tested by the same examination.

B. FOUR BASIC STEPS

1) Study the announcement

How, then, can you know what subjects to study? Our best answer is: "Learn as much as possible about the class of positions for which you've applied." The exam will test the knowledge, skills and abilities needed to do the work.

Your most valuable source of information about the position you want is the official exam announcement. This announcement lists the training and experience qualifications. Check these standards and apply only if you come reasonably close to meeting them.

The brief description of the position in the examination announcement offers some clues to the subjects which will be tested. Think about the job itself. Review the duties in your mind. Can you perform them, or are there some in which you are rusty? Fill in the blank spots in your preparation.

Many jurisdictions preview the written test in the exam announcement by including a section called "Knowledge and Abilities Required," "Scope of the Examination," or some similar heading. Here you will find out specifically what fields will be tested.

2) Review your own background

Once you learn in general what the position is all about, and what you need to know to do the work, ask yourself which subjects you already know fairly well and which need improvement. You may wonder whether to concentrate on improving your strong areas or on building some background in your fields of weakness. When the announcement has specified "some knowledge" or "considerable knowledge," or has used adjectives like "beginning principles of…" or "advanced … methods," you can get a clue as to the number and difficulty of questions to be asked in any given field. More questions, and hence broader coverage, would be included for those subjects which are more important in the work. Now weigh your strengths and weaknesses against the job requirements and prepare accordingly.

3) Determine the level of the position

Another way to tell how intensively you should prepare is to understand the level of the job for which you are applying. Is it the entering level? In other words, is this the position in which beginners in a field of work are hired? Or is it an intermediate or advanced level? Sometimes this is indicated by such words as "Junior" or "Senior" in the class title. Other jurisdictions use Roman numerals to designate the level – Clerk I, Clerk II, for example. The word "Supervisor" sometimes appears in the title. If the level is not indicated by the title, check the description of duties. Will you be working under very close supervision, or will you have responsibility for independent decisions in this work?

4) Choose appropriate study materials

Now that you know the subjects to be examined and the relative amount of each subject to be covered, you can choose suitable study materials. For beginning level jobs, or even advanced ones, if you have a pronounced weakness in some aspect of your training, read a modern, standard textbook in that field. Be sure it is up to date and has general coverage. Such books are normally available at your library, and the librarian will be glad to help you locate one. For entry-level positions, questions of appropriate difficulty are chosen -- neither highly advanced questions, nor those too simple. Such questions require careful thought but not advanced training.

If the position for which you are applying is technical or advanced, you will read more advanced, specialized material. If you are already familiar with the basic principles of your field, elementary textbooks would waste your time. Concentrate on advanced textbooks and technical periodicals. Think through the concepts and review difficult problems in your field.

These are all general sources. You can get more ideas on your own initiative, following these leads. For example, training manuals and publications of the government agency which employs workers in your field can be useful, particularly for technical and professional positions. A letter or visit to the government department involved may result in more specific study suggestions, and certainly will provide you with a more definite idea of the exact nature of the position you are seeking.

III. KINDS OF TESTS

Tests are used for purposes other than measuring knowledge and ability to perform specified duties. For some positions, it is equally important to test ability to make adjustments to new situations or to profit from training. In others, basic mental abilities not dependent on information are essential. Questions which test these things may not appear as pertinent to the duties of the position as those which test for knowledge and information. Yet they are often highly important parts of a fair examination. For very general questions, it is almost impossible to help you direct your study efforts. What we can do is to point out some of the more common of these general abilities needed in public service positions and describe some typical questions.

1) General information

Broad, general information has been found useful for predicting job success in some kinds of work. This is tested in a variety of ways, from vocabulary lists to questions about current events. Basic background in some field of work, such as sociology or economics, may be sampled in a group of questions. Often these are principles which have become familiar to most persons through exposure rather than through formal training. It is difficult to advise you how to study for these questions; being alert to the world around you is our best suggestion.

2) Verbal ability

An example of an ability needed in many positions is verbal or language ability. Verbal ability is, in brief, the ability to use and understand words. Vocabulary and grammar tests are typical measures of this ability. Reading comprehension or paragraph interpretation questions are common in many kinds of civil service tests. You are given a paragraph of written material and asked to find its central meaning.

3) Numerical ability
Number skills can be tested by the familiar arithmetic problem, by checking paired lists of numbers to see which are alike and which are different, or by interpreting charts and graphs. In the latter test, a graph may be printed in the test booklet which you are asked to use as the basis for answering questions.

4) Observation
A popular test for law-enforcement positions is the observation test. A picture is shown to you for several minutes, then taken away. Questions about the picture test your ability to observe both details and larger elements.

5) Following directions
In many positions in the public service, the employee must be able to carry out written instructions dependably and accurately. You may be given a chart with several columns, each column listing a variety of information. The questions require you to carry out directions involving the information given in the chart.

6) Skills and aptitudes
Performance tests effectively measure some manual skills and aptitudes. When the skill is one in which you are trained, such as typing or shorthand, you can practice. These tests are often very much like those given in business school or high school courses. For many of the other skills and aptitudes, however, no short-time preparation can be made. Skills and abilities natural to you or that you have developed throughout your lifetime are being tested.

Many of the general questions just described provide all the data needed to answer the questions and ask you to use your reasoning ability to find the answers. Your best preparation for these tests, as well as for tests of facts and ideas, is to be at your physical and mental best. You, no doubt, have your own methods of getting into an exam-taking mood and keeping "in shape." The next section lists some ideas on this subject.

IV. KINDS OF QUESTIONS

Only rarely is the "essay" question, which you answer in narrative form, used in civil service tests. Civil service tests are usually of the short-answer type. Full instructions for answering these questions will be given to you at the examination. But in case this is your first experience with short-answer questions and separate answer sheets, here is what you need to know:

1) Multiple-choice Questions
Most popular of the short-answer questions is the "multiple choice" or "best answer" question. It can be used, for example, to test for factual knowledge, ability to solve problems or judgment in meeting situations found at work.
A multiple-choice question is normally one of three types—
- It can begin with an incomplete statement followed by several possible endings. You are to find the one ending which *best* completes the statement, although some of the others may not be entirely wrong.
- It can also be a complete statement in the form of a question which is answered by choosing one of the statements listed.

- It can be in the form of a problem – again you select the best answer.

Here is an example of a multiple-choice question with a discussion which should give you some clues as to the method for choosing the right answer:

When an employee has a complaint about his assignment, the action which will *best* help him overcome his difficulty is to
- A. discuss his difficulty with his coworkers
- B. take the problem to the head of the organization
- C. take the problem to the person who gave him the assignment
- D. say nothing to anyone about his complaint

In answering this question, you should study each of the choices to find which is best. Consider choice "A" – Certainly an employee may discuss his complaint with fellow employees, but no change or improvement can result, and the complaint remains unresolved. Choice "B" is a poor choice since the head of the organization probably does not know what assignment you have been given, and taking your problem to him is known as "going over the head" of the supervisor. The supervisor, or person who made the assignment, is the person who can clarify it or correct any injustice. Choice "C" is, therefore, correct. To say nothing, as in choice "D," is unwise. Supervisors have and interest in knowing the problems employees are facing, and the employee is seeking a solution to his problem.

2) True/False Questions

The "true/false" or "right/wrong" form of question is sometimes used. Here a complete statement is given. Your job is to decide whether the statement is right or wrong.

SAMPLE: A roaming cell-phone call to a nearby city costs less than a non-roaming call to a distant city.

This statement is wrong, or false, since roaming calls are more expensive.

This is not a complete list of all possible question forms, although most of the others are variations of these common types. You will always get complete directions for answering questions. Be sure you understand *how* to mark your answers – ask questions until you do.

V. RECORDING YOUR ANSWERS

Computer terminals are used more and more today for many different kinds of exams.
For an examination with very few applicants, you may be told to record your answers in the test booklet itself. Separate answer sheets are much more common. If this separate answer sheet is to be scored by machine – and this is often the case – it is highly important that you mark your answers correctly in order to get credit.
An electronic scoring machine is often used in civil service offices because of the speed with which papers can be scored. Machine-scored answer sheets must be marked with a pencil, which will be given to you. This pencil has a high graphite content which responds to the electronic scoring machine. As a matter of fact, stray dots may register as answers, so do not let your pencil rest on the answer sheet while you are pondering the correct answer. Also, if your pencil lead breaks or is otherwise defective, ask for another.

Since the answer sheet will be dropped in a slot in the scoring machine, be careful not to bend the corners or get the paper crumpled.

The answer sheet normally has five vertical columns of numbers, with 30 numbers to a column. These numbers correspond to the question numbers in your test booklet. After each number, going across the page are four or five pairs of dotted lines. These short dotted lines have small letters or numbers above them. The first two pairs may also have a "T" or "F" above the letters. This indicates that the first two pairs only are to be used if the questions are of the true-false type. If the questions are multiple choice, disregard the "T" and "F" and pay attention only to the small letters or numbers.

Answer your questions in the manner of the sample that follows:

32. The largest city in the United States is
    A. Washington, D.C.
    B. New York City
    C. Chicago
    D. Detroit
    E. San Francisco

1) Choose the answer you think is best. (New York City is the largest, so "B" is correct.)
2) Find the row of dotted lines numbered the same as the question you are answering. (Find row number 32)
3) Find the pair of dotted lines corresponding to the answer. (Find the pair of lines under the mark "B.")
4) Make a solid black mark between the dotted lines.

VI. BEFORE THE TEST

Common sense will help you find procedures to follow to get ready for an examination. Too many of us, however, overlook these sensible measures. Indeed, nervousness and fatigue have been found to be the most serious reasons why applicants fail to do their best on civil service tests. Here is a list of reminders:

- Begin your preparation early – Don't wait until the last minute to go scurrying around for books and materials or to find out what the position is all about.
- Prepare continuously – An hour a night for a week is better than an all-night cram session. This has been definitely established. What is more, a night a week for a month will return better dividends than crowding your study into a shorter period of time.
- Locate the place of the exam – You have been sent a notice telling you when and where to report for the examination. If the location is in a different town or otherwise unfamiliar to you, it would be well to inquire the best route and learn something about the building.
- Relax the night before the test – Allow your mind to rest. Do not study at all that night. Plan some mild recreation or diversion; then go to bed early and get a good night's sleep.
- Get up early enough to make a leisurely trip to the place for the test – This way unforeseen events, traffic snarls, unfamiliar buildings, etc. will not upset you.
- Dress comfortably – A written test is not a fashion show. You will be known by number and not by name, so wear something comfortable.

- Leave excess paraphernalia at home – Shopping bags and odd bundles will get in your way. You need bring only the items mentioned in the official notice you received; usually everything you need is provided. Do not bring reference books to the exam. They will only confuse those last minutes and be taken away from you when in the test room.
- Arrive somewhat ahead of time – If because of transportation schedules you must get there very early, bring a newspaper or magazine to take your mind off yourself while waiting.
- Locate the examination room – When you have found the proper room, you will be directed to the seat or part of the room where you will sit. Sometimes you are given a sheet of instructions to read while you are waiting. Do not fill out any forms until you are told to do so; just read them and be prepared.
- Relax and prepare to listen to the instructions
- If you have any physical problem that may keep you from doing your best, be sure to tell the test administrator. If you are sick or in poor health, you really cannot do your best on the exam. You can come back and take the test some other time.

VII. AT THE TEST

The day of the test is here and you have the test booklet in your hand. The temptation to get going is very strong. Caution! There is more to success than knowing the right answers. You must know how to identify your papers and understand variations in the type of short-answer question used in this particular examination. Follow these suggestions for maximum results from your efforts:

1) Cooperate with the monitor

The test administrator has a duty to create a situation in which you can be as much at ease as possible. He will give instructions, tell you when to begin, check to see that you are marking your answer sheet correctly, and so on. He is not there to guard you, although he will see that your competitors do not take unfair advantage. He wants to help you do your best.

2) Listen to all instructions

Don't jump the gun! Wait until you understand all directions. In most civil service tests you get more time than you need to answer the questions. So don't be in a hurry. Read each word of instructions until you clearly understand the meaning. Study the examples, listen to all announcements and follow directions. Ask questions if you do not understand what to do.

3) Identify your papers

Civil service exams are usually identified by number only. You will be assigned a number; you must not put your name on your test papers. Be sure to copy your number correctly. Since more than one exam may be given, copy your exact examination title.

4) Plan your time

Unless you are told that a test is a "speed" or "rate of work" test, speed itself is usually not important. Time enough to answer all the questions will be provided, but this does not mean that you have all day. An overall time limit has been set. Divide the total time (in minutes) by the number of questions to determine the approximate time you have for each question.

5) Do not linger over difficult questions

If you come across a difficult question, mark it with a paper clip (useful to have along) and come back to it when you have been through the booklet. One caution if you do this – be sure to skip a number on your answer sheet as well. Check often to be sure that you have not lost your place and that you are marking in the row numbered the same as the question you are answering.

6) Read the questions

Be sure you know what the question asks! Many capable people are unsuccessful because they failed to *read* the questions correctly.

7) Answer all questions

Unless you have been instructed that a penalty will be deducted for incorrect answers, it is better to guess than to omit a question.

8) Speed tests

It is often better NOT to guess on speed tests. It has been found that on timed tests people are tempted to spend the last few seconds before time is called in marking answers at random – without even reading them – in the hope of picking up a few extra points. To discourage this practice, the instructions may warn you that your score will be "corrected" for guessing. That is, a penalty will be applied. The incorrect answers will be deducted from the correct ones, or some other penalty formula will be used.

9) Review your answers

If you finish before time is called, go back to the questions you guessed or omitted to give them further thought. Review other answers if you have time.

10) Return your test materials

If you are ready to leave before others have finished or time is called, take ALL your materials to the monitor and leave quietly. Never take any test material with you. The monitor can discover whose papers are not complete, and taking a test booklet may be grounds for disqualification.

VIII. EXAMINATION TECHNIQUES

1) Read the general instructions carefully. These are usually printed on the first page of the exam booklet. As a rule, these instructions refer to the timing of the examination; the fact that you should not start work until the signal and must stop work at a signal, etc. If there are any *special* instructions, such as a choice of questions to be answered, make sure that you note this instruction carefully.

2) When you are ready to start work on the examination, that is as soon as the signal has been given, read the instructions to each question booklet, underline any key words or phrases, such as *least, best, outline, describe* and the like. In this way you will tend to answer as requested rather than discover on reviewing your paper that you *listed without describing*, that you selected the *worst* choice rather than the *best* choice, etc.

3) If the examination is of the objective or multiple-choice type – that is, each question will also give a series of possible answers: A, B, C or D, and you are called upon to select the best answer and write the letter next to that answer on your answer paper – it is advisable to start answering each question in turn. There may be anywhere from 50 to 100 such questions in the three or four hours allotted and you can see how much time would be taken if you read through all the questions before beginning to answer any. Furthermore, if you come across a question or group of questions which you know would be difficult to answer, it would undoubtedly affect your handling of all the other questions.

4) If the examination is of the essay type and contains but a few questions, it is a moot point as to whether you should read all the questions before starting to answer any one. Of course, if you are given a choice – say five out of seven and the like – then it is essential to read all the questions so you can eliminate the two that are most difficult. If, however, you are asked to answer all the questions, there may be danger in trying to answer the easiest one first because you may find that you will spend too much time on it. The best technique is to answer the first question, then proceed to the second, etc.

5) Time your answers. Before the exam begins, write down the time it started, then add the time allowed for the examination and write down the time it must be completed, then divide the time available somewhat as follows:
   - If 3-1/2 hours are allowed, that would be 210 minutes. If you have 80 objective-type questions, that would be an average of 2-1/2 minutes per question. Allow yourself no more than 2 minutes per question, or a total of 160 minutes, which will permit about 50 minutes to review.
   - If for the time allotment of 210 minutes there are 7 essay questions to answer, that would average about 30 minutes a question. Give yourself only 25 minutes per question so that you have about 35 minutes to review.

6) The most important instruction is to *read each question* and make sure you know what is wanted. The second most important instruction is to *time yourself properly* so that you answer every question. The third most important instruction is to *answer every question*. Guess if you have to but include something for each question. Remember that you will receive no credit for a blank and will probably receive some credit if you write something in answer to an essay question. If you guess a letter – say "B" for a multiple-choice question – you may have guessed right. If you leave a blank as an answer to a multiple-choice question, the examiners may respect your feelings but it will not add a point to your score. Some exams may penalize you for wrong answers, so in such cases *only*, you may not want to guess unless you have some basis for your answer.

7) Suggestions
   a. Objective-type questions
      1. Examine the question booklet for proper sequence of pages and questions
      2. Read all instructions carefully
      3. Skip any question which seems too difficult; return to it after all other questions have been answered
      4. Apportion your time properly; do not spend too much time on any single question or group of questions

5. Note and underline key words – *all, most, fewest, least, best, worst, same, opposite,* etc.
6. Pay particular attention to negatives
7. Note unusual option, e.g., unduly long, short, complex, different or similar in content to the body of the question
8. Observe the use of "hedging" words – *probably, may, most likely,* etc.
9. Make sure that your answer is put next to the same number as the question
10. Do not second-guess unless you have good reason to believe the second answer is definitely more correct
11. Cross out original answer if you decide another answer is more accurate; do not erase until you are ready to hand your paper in
12. Answer all questions; guess unless instructed otherwise
13. Leave time for review

   b. Essay questions
   1. Read each question carefully
   2. Determine exactly what is wanted. Underline key words or phrases.
   3. Decide on outline or paragraph answer
   4. Include many different points and elements unless asked to develop any one or two points or elements
   5. Show impartiality by giving pros and cons unless directed to select one side only
   6. Make and write down any assumptions you find necessary to answer the questions
   7. Watch your English, grammar, punctuation and choice of words
   8. Time your answers; don't crowd material

8) Answering the essay question

Most essay questions can be answered by framing the specific response around several key words or ideas. Here are a few such key words or ideas:

M's: manpower, materials, methods, money, management
P's: purpose, program, policy, plan, procedure, practice, problems, pitfalls, personnel, public relations
   a. Six basic steps in handling problems:
   1. Preliminary plan and background development
   2. Collect information, data and facts
   3. Analyze and interpret information, data and facts
   4. Analyze and develop solutions as well as make recommendations
   5. Prepare report and sell recommendations
   6. Install recommendations and follow up effectiveness

   b. Pitfalls to avoid
   1. *Taking things for granted* – A statement of the situation does not necessarily imply that each of the elements is necessarily true; for example, a complaint may be invalid and biased so that all that can be taken for granted is that a complaint has been registered

2. *Considering only one side of a situation* – Wherever possible, indicate several alternatives and then point out the reasons you selected the best one
3. *Failing to indicate follow up* – Whenever your answer indicates action on your part, make certain that you will take proper follow-up action to see how successful your recommendations, procedures or actions turn out to be
4. *Taking too long in answering any single question* – Remember to time your answers properly

IX. AFTER THE TEST

Scoring procedures differ in detail among civil service jurisdictions although the general principles are the same. Whether the papers are hand-scored or graded by machine we have described, they are nearly always graded by number. That is, the person who marks the paper knows only the number – never the name – of the applicant. Not until all the papers have been graded will they be matched with names. If other tests, such as training and experience or oral interview ratings have been given, scores will be combined. Different parts of the examination usually have different weights. For example, the written test might count 60 percent of the final grade, and a rating of training and experience 40 percent. In many jurisdictions, veterans will have a certain number of points added to their grades.

After the final grade has been determined, the names are placed in grade order and an eligible list is established. There are various methods for resolving ties between those who get the same final grade – probably the most common is to place first the name of the person whose application was received first. Job offers are made from the eligible list in the order the names appear on it. You will be notified of your grade and your rank as soon as all these computations have been made. This will be done as rapidly as possible.

People who are found to meet the requirements in the announcement are called "eligibles." Their names are put on a list of eligible candidates. An eligible's chances of getting a job depend on how high he stands on this list and how fast agencies are filling jobs from the list.

When a job is to be filled from a list of eligibles, the agency asks for the names of people on the list of eligibles for that job. When the civil service commission receives this request, it sends to the agency the names of the three people highest on this list. Or, if the job to be filled has specialized requirements, the office sends the agency the names of the top three persons who meet these requirements from the general list.

The appointing officer makes a choice from among the three people whose names were sent to him. If the selected person accepts the appointment, the names of the others are put back on the list to be considered for future openings.

That is the rule in hiring from all kinds of eligible lists, whether they are for typist, carpenter, chemist, or something else. For every vacancy, the appointing officer has his choice of any one of the top three eligibles on the list. This explains why the person whose name is on top of the list sometimes does not get an appointment when some of the persons lower on the list do. If the appointing officer chooses the second or third eligible, the No. 1 eligible does not get a job at once, but stays on the list until he is appointed or the list is terminated.

X. HOW TO PASS THE INTERVIEW TEST

The examination for which you applied requires an oral interview test. You have already taken the written test and you are now being called for the interview test – the final part of the formal examination.

You may think that it is not possible to prepare for an interview test and that there are no procedures to follow during an interview. Our purpose is to point out some things you can do in advance that will help you and some good rules to follow and pitfalls to avoid while you are being interviewed.

What is an interview supposed to test?

The written examination is designed to test the technical knowledge and competence of the candidate; the oral is designed to evaluate intangible qualities, not readily measured otherwise, and to establish a list showing the relative fitness of each candidate – as measured against his competitors – for the position sought. Scoring is not on the basis of "right" and "wrong," but on a sliding scale of values ranging from "not passable" to "outstanding." As a matter of fact, it is possible to achieve a relatively low score without a single "incorrect" answer because of evident weakness in the qualities being measured.

Occasionally, an examination may consist entirely of an oral test – either an individual or a group oral. In such cases, information is sought concerning the technical knowledges and abilities of the candidate, since there has been no written examination for this purpose. More commonly, however, an oral test is used to supplement a written examination.

Who conducts interviews?

The composition of oral boards varies among different jurisdictions. In nearly all, a representative of the personnel department serves as chairman. One of the members of the board may be a representative of the department in which the candidate would work. In some cases, "outside experts" are used, and, frequently, a businessman or some other representative of the general public is asked to serve. Labor and management or other special groups may be represented. The aim is to secure the services of experts in the appropriate field.

However the board is composed, it is a good idea (and not at all improper or unethical) to ascertain in advance of the interview who the members are and what groups they represent. When you are introduced to them, you will have some idea of their backgrounds and interests, and at least you will not stutter and stammer over their names.

What should be done before the interview?

While knowledge about the board members is useful and takes some of the surprise element out of the interview, there is other preparation which is more substantive. It *is* possible to prepare for an oral interview – in several ways:

1) Keep a copy of your application and review it carefully before the interview

This may be the only document before the oral board, and the starting point of the interview. Know what education and experience you have listed there, and the sequence and dates of all of it. Sometimes the board will ask you to review the highlights of your experience for them; you should not have to hem and haw doing it.

2) Study the class specification and the examination announcement

Usually, the oral board has one or both of these to guide them. The qualities, characteristics or knowledges required by the position sought are stated in these documents. They offer valuable clues as to the nature of the oral interview. For example, if the job involves supervisory responsibilities, the announcement will usually indicate that knowledge of modern supervisory methods and the qualifications of the candidate as a supervisor will be tested. If so, you can expect such questions, frequently in the form of a hypothetical situation which you are expected to solve. NEVER go into an oral without knowledge of the duties and responsibilities of the job you seek.

3) Think through each qualification required

Try to visualize the kind of questions you would ask if you were a board member. How well could you answer them? Try especially to appraise your own knowledge and background in each area, *measured against the job sought*, and identify any areas in which you are weak. Be critical and realistic – do not flatter yourself.

4) Do some general reading in areas in which you feel you may be weak

For example, if the job involves supervision and your past experience has NOT, some general reading in supervisory methods and practices, particularly in the field of human relations, might be useful. Do NOT study agency procedures or detailed manuals. The oral board will be testing your understanding and capacity, not your memory.

5) Get a good night's sleep and watch your general health and mental attitude

You will want a clear head at the interview. Take care of a cold or any other minor ailment, and of course, no hangovers.

What should be done on the day of the interview?

Now comes the day of the interview itself. Give yourself plenty of time to get there. Plan to arrive somewhat ahead of the scheduled time, particularly if your appointment is in the fore part of the day. If a previous candidate fails to appear, the board might be ready for you a bit early. By early afternoon an oral board is almost invariably behind schedule if there are many candidates, and you may have to wait. Take along a book or magazine to read, or your application to review, but leave any extraneous material in the waiting room when you go in for your interview. In any event, relax and compose yourself.

The matter of dress is important. The board is forming impressions about you – from your experience, your manners, your attitude, and your appearance. Give your personal appearance careful attention. Dress your best, but not your flashiest. Choose conservative, appropriate clothing, and be sure it is immaculate. This is a business interview, and your appearance should indicate that you regard it as such. Besides, being well groomed and properly dressed will help boost your confidence.

Sooner or later, someone will call your name and escort you into the interview room. *This is it.* From here on you are on your own. It is too late for any more preparation. But remember, you asked for this opportunity to prove your fitness, and you are here because your request was granted.

What happens when you go in?

The usual sequence of events will be as follows: The clerk (who is often the board stenographer) will introduce you to the chairman of the oral board, who will introduce you to the other members of the board. Acknowledge the introductions before you sit down. Do not be surprised if you find a microphone facing you or a stenotypist sitting by. Oral interviews are usually recorded in the event of an appeal or other review.

Usually the chairman of the board will open the interview by reviewing the highlights of your education and work experience from your application – primarily for the benefit of the other members of the board, as well as to get the material into the record. Do not interrupt or comment unless there is an error or significant misinterpretation; if that is the case, do not hesitate. But do not quibble about insignificant matters. Also, he will usually ask you some question about your education, experience or your present job – partly to get you to start talking and to establish the interviewing "rapport." He may start the actual questioning, or turn it over to one of the other members. Frequently, each member undertakes the questioning on a particular area, one in which he is perhaps most competent, so you can expect each member to participate in the examination. Because time is limited, you may also expect some rather abrupt switches in the direction the questioning takes, so do not be upset by it. Normally, a board member will not pursue a single line of questioning unless he discovers a particular strength or weakness.

After each member has participated, the chairman will usually ask whether any member has any further questions, then will ask you if you have anything you wish to add. Unless you are expecting this question, it may floor you. Worse, it may start you off on an extended, extemporaneous speech. The board is not usually seeking more information. The question is principally to offer you a last opportunity to present further qualifications or to indicate that you have nothing to add. So, if you feel that a significant qualification or characteristic has been overlooked, it is proper to point it out in a sentence or so. Do not compliment the board on the thoroughness of their examination – they have been sketchy, and you know it. If you wish, merely say, "No thank you, I have nothing further to add." This is a point where you can "talk yourself out" of a good impression or fail to present an important bit of information. Remember, *you close the interview yourself.*

The chairman will then say, "That is all, Mr. _____, thank you." Do not be startled; the interview is over, and quicker than you think. Thank him, gather your belongings and take your leave. Save your sigh of relief for the other side of the door.

How to put your best foot forward
Throughout this entire process, you may feel that the board individually and collectively is trying to pierce your defenses, seek out your hidden weaknesses and embarrass and confuse you. Actually, this is not true. They are obliged to make an appraisal of your qualifications for the job you are seeking, and they want to see you in your best light. Remember, they must interview all candidates and a non-cooperative candidate may become a failure in spite of their best efforts to bring out his qualifications. Here are 15 suggestions that will help you:

1) Be natural – Keep your attitude confident, not cocky

If you are not confident that you can do the job, do not expect the board to be. Do not apologize for your weaknesses, try to bring out your strong points. The board is interested in a positive, not negative, presentation. Cockiness will antagonize any board member and make him wonder if you are covering up a weakness by a false show of strength.

2) Get comfortable, but don't lounge or sprawl

Sit erectly but not stiffly. A careless posture may lead the board to conclude that you are careless in other things, or at least that you are not impressed by the importance of the occasion. Either conclusion is natural, even if incorrect. Do not fuss with your clothing, a pencil or an ashtray. Your hands may occasionally be useful to emphasize a point; do not let them become a point of distraction.

3) Do not wisecrack or make small talk

This is a serious situation, and your attitude should show that you consider it as such. Further, the time of the board is limited – they do not want to waste it, and neither should you.

4) Do not exaggerate your experience or abilities

In the first place, from information in the application or other interviews and sources, the board may know more about you than you think. Secondly, you probably will not get away with it. An experienced board is rather adept at spotting such a situation, so do not take the chance.

5) If you know a board member, do not make a point of it, yet do not hide it

Certainly you are not fooling him, and probably not the other members of the board. Do not try to take advantage of your acquaintanceship – it will probably do you little good.

6) Do not dominate the interview

Let the board do that. They will give you the clues – do not assume that you have to do all the talking. Realize that the board has a number of questions to ask you, and do not try to take up all the interview time by showing off your extensive knowledge of the answer to the first one.

7) Be attentive

You only have 20 minutes or so, and you should keep your attention at its sharpest throughout. When a member is addressing a problem or question to you, give him your undivided attention. Address your reply principally to him, but do not exclude the other board members.

8) Do not interrupt

A board member may be stating a problem for you to analyze. He will ask you a question when the time comes. Let him state the problem, and wait for the question.

9) Make sure you understand the question

Do not try to answer until you are sure what the question is. If it is not clear, restate it in your own words or ask the board member to clarify it for you. However, do not haggle about minor elements.

10) Reply promptly but not hastily

A common entry on oral board rating sheets is "candidate responded readily," or "candidate hesitated in replies." Respond as promptly and quickly as you can, but do not jump to a hasty, ill-considered answer.

11) Do not be peremptory in your answers

A brief answer is proper – but do not fire your answer back. That is a losing game from your point of view. The board member can probably ask questions much faster than you can answer them.

12) Do not try to create the answer you think the board member wants

He is interested in what kind of mind you have and how it works – not in playing games. Furthermore, he can usually spot this practice and will actually grade you down on it.

13) Do not switch sides in your reply merely to agree with a board member

Frequently, a member will take a contrary position merely to draw you out and to see if you are willing and able to defend your point of view. Do not start a debate, yet do not surrender a good position. If a position is worth taking, it is worth defending.

14) Do not be afraid to admit an error in judgment if you are shown to be wrong

The board knows that you are forced to reply without any opportunity for careful consideration. Your answer may be demonstrably wrong. If so, admit it and get on with the interview.

15) Do not dwell at length on your present job

The opening question may relate to your present assignment. Answer the question but do not go into an extended discussion. You are being examined for a *new* job, not your present one. As a matter of fact, try to phrase ALL your answers in terms of the job for which you are being examined.

Basis of Rating

Probably you will forget most of these "do's" and "don'ts" when you walk into the oral interview room. Even remembering them all will not ensure you a passing grade. Perhaps you did not have the qualifications in the first place. But remembering them will help you to put your best foot forward, without treading on the toes of the board members.

Rumor and popular opinion to the contrary notwithstanding, an oral board wants you to make the best appearance possible. They know you are under pressure – but they also want to see how you respond to it as a guide to what your reaction would be under the pressures of the job you seek. They will be influenced by the degree of poise you display, the personal traits you show and the manner in which you respond.

ABOUT THIS BOOK

This book contains tests divided into Examination Sections. Go through each test, answering every question in the margin. We have also attached a sample answer sheet at the back of the book that can be removed and used. At the end of each test look at the answer key and check your answers. On the ones you got wrong, look at the right answer choice and learn. Do not fill in the answers first. Do not memorize the questions and answers, but understand the answer and principles involved. On your test, the questions will likely be different from the samples. Questions are changed and new ones added. If you understand these past questions you should have success with any changes that arise. Tests may consist of several types of questions. We have additional books on each subject should more study be advisable or necessary for you. Finally, the more you study, the better prepared you will be. This book is intended to be the last thing you study before you walk into the examination room. Prior study of relevant texts is also recommended. NLC publishes some of these in our Fundamental Series. Knowledge and good sense are important factors in passing your exam. Good luck also helps. So now study this Passbook, absorb the material contained within and take that knowledge into the examination. Then do your best to pass that exam.

EXAMINATION SECTION

EXAMINATION SECTION
TEST 1

DIRECTIONS: Each question or incomplete statement is followed by several suggested answers or completions. Select the one that BEST answers the question or completes the statement. *PRINT THE LETTER OF THE CORRECT ANSWER IN THE SPACE AT THE RIGHT.*

Questions 1-5.

DIRECTIONS: Questions 1 through 5 consist of a sentence with an underlined word. For each question, select the choice that is CLOSEST in meaning to the underlined word.

EXAMPLE
This division reviews the fiscal reports of the agency.
In this sentence, the word *fiscal* means MOST NEARLY
    A. financial   B. critical   C. basic   D. personnel
The correct answer is A. "financial" because "financial" is closest to *fiscal*. Therefore, the answer is A.

1. Every good office worker needs basic skills.
   The word *basic* in this sentence means
       A. fundamental   B. advanced   C. unusual   D. outstanding

2. He turned out to be a good instructor.
   The word *instructor* in this sentence means
       A. student   B. worker   C. typist   D. teacher

3. The quantity of work in the office was under study.
   In this sentence, the word *quantity* means
       A. amount   B. flow   C. supervision   D. type

4. The morning was spent examining the time records.
   In this sentence, the word *examining* means
       A. distributing   B. collecting   C. checking   D. filing

5. The candidate filled in the proper spaces on the form.
   In this sentence, the word *proper* means
       A. blank   B. appropriate   C. many   D. remaining

Questions 6-8.

DIRECTIONS: Questions 6 through 8 are to be answered SOLELY on the basis of the information contained in the following paragraph.

The increase in the number of public documents in the last two centuries closely matches the increase in population in the United States. The great number of public documents has become a serious threat to their usefulness. It is necessary to have programs which will reduce the number of public documents that are kept and which will, at the same time, assure keeping those that have value. Such programs need a great deal of thought to have any success.

6. According to the above paragraph, public documents may be less useful if 6.____
   A. the files are open to the public
   B. the record room is too small
   C. the copying machine is operated only during normal working hours
   D. too many records are being kept

7. According to the above paragraph, the growth of the population in the United 7.____
   States has matched the growth in the quantity of public documents for a period of MOST NEARLY _____ years.
   A. 50   B. 100   C. 200   D. 300

8. According to the above paragraph, the increased number of public documents 8.____
   has made it necessary to
   A. find out which public documents are worth keeping
   B. reduce the great number of public documents by decreasing government services
   C. eliminate the copying of all original public documents
   D. avoid all new copying devices

Questions 9-10.

DIRECTIONS: Questions 9 and 10 are to be answered SOLELY on the basis of the information contained in the following paragraph.

The work goals of an agency can best be reached if the employees understand and agree with these goals. One way to gain such understanding and agreement is for management to encourage and seriously consider suggestions from employees in the setting of agency goals.

9. On the basis of the above paragraph, the BEST way to achieve the work goals 9.____
   of an agency is to
   A. make certain that employees work as hard as possible
   B. study the organizational structure of the agency
   C. encourage employees to think seriously about the agency's problems
   D. stimulate employee understanding of the work goals

10. On the basis of the above paragraph, understanding and agreement with agency   10._____
    goals can be gained by
    A. allowing the employees to set agency goals
    B. reaching agency goals quickly
    C. legislative review of agency operations
    D. employee participation in setting agency goals

Questions 11-15.

DIRECTIONS: Each of Questions 11 through 15 consists of a group of four words. One word in each group is incorrectly spelled. For each question, print the letter of the correct answer in the space at the right that is the same as the letter next to the word which is INCORRECTLY spelled.

EXAMPLE

    A. housing   B. certain   C. budgit   D. money

The word "budgit" is incorrectly spelled, because the correct spelling should be "budget." Therefore, the correct answer is C.

11. A. sentince   B. bulletin   C. notice   D. definition   11._____
12. A. appointment B. exactly   C. typest   D. light   12._____
13. A. penalty   B. suparvise   C. consider   D. division   13._____
14. A. schedule   B. accurate   C. corect   D. simple   14._____
15. A. suggestion   B. installed   C. proper   D. agincy   15._____

Questions 16-20.

DIRECTIONS: Each Question 16 through 20 consists of a sentence which may be
A. incorrect because of bad word usage, or
B. incorrect because of bad punctuation, or
C. incorrect because of bad spelling, or
D. correct
Read each sentence carefully. Then print in the space at the right A, B, C, or D, according to the answer you choose from the four choices listed above. There is only one type of error in each incorrect sentence. If there is no error, the sentence is correct.

EXAMPLE

George Washington was the father of his contry.
This sentence is incorrect because of bad spelling ("contry" instead of "country").
Therefore, the answer is C.

16. The assignment was completed in record time but the payroll for it has not yet been preparid. 16._____

17. The operator, on the other hand, is willing to learn me how to use the mimeograph. 17._____

18. She is the prettiest of the three sisters. 18._____

19. She doesn't know; if the mail has arrived. 19._____

20. The doorknob of the office door is broke. 20._____

21. A clerk can process a form in 15 minutes.
    How many forms can that clerk process in six hours?
    A. 10   B. 21   C. 24   D. 90 21._____

22. An office staff consists of 120 people. Sixty of them have been assigned to a special project. Of the remaining staff, 20 answer the mail, 10 handle phone calls, and the rest operate the office machines.
    The number of people operating the office machines is
    A. 20   B. 30   C. 40   D. 45 22._____

23. An office worker received 65 applications but on the first day had to return 26 of them for being incomplete and on the second day 25 had to be returned for being incomplete.
    How many applications did NOT have to be returned?
    A. 10   B. 12   C. 14   D. 16 23._____

24. An office worker answered 63 phone calls in one day and 91 phone calls the next day.
    For these 2 days, what was the average number of phone calls he answered per day?
    A. 77   B. 28   C. 82   D. 93 24._____

25. An office worker processed 12 vouchers of $8.50 each, 3 vouchers of $3.68 each, and 2 vouchers of $1.29 each.
    The TOTAL dollar amount of these vouchers is
    A. $116.04   B. $117.52   C. $118.62   D. $119.04 25._____

KEY (CORRECT ANSWERS)

1. A
2. D
3. A
4. C
5. B

6. D
7. C
8. A
9. D
10. D

11. A
12. C
13. B
14. C
15. D

16. C
17. A
18. D
19. B
20. A

21. C
22. B
23. C
24. A
25. C

TEST 2

DIRECTIONS: Each question or incomplete statement is followed by several suggested answers or completions. Select the one that BEST answers the question or completes the statement. *PRINT THE LETTER OF THE CORRECT ANSWER IN THE SPACE AT THE RIGHT.*

Questions 1-5.

DIRECTIONS: Each Question from 1 through 5 lists four names. The names may not be exactly the same. Compare the names in each question and mark your answer
    A if all the names are different
    B if only two names are exactly the same
    C if only three names are exactly the same
    D if all four names are exactly the same
EXAMPLE
Jensen, Alfred E.
Jensen, Alfred E.
Jensan, Alfred E.
Jensen, Fred E.

Since the name Jensen, Alfred E. appears twice and is exactly the same in both places, the correct answer is B.

1.   A. Riviera, Pedro S.   B. Rivers, Pedro S.   1.____
    C. Riviera, Pedro N.   D. Riviera, Juan S.

2.   A. Guider, Albert   B. Guidar, Albert   2.____
    C. Giuder, Alfred   D. Guider, Albert

3.   A. Blum, Rona   B. Blum, Rona   3.____
    C. Blum, Rona   D. Blum, Rona

4.   A. Raugh, John   B. Raugh, James   4.____
    C. Raughe, John   D. Raugh, John

5.   A. Katz, Stanley   B. Katz, Stanley   5.____
    C. Katze, Stanley   D. Katz, Stanley

Questions 6-10.

DIRECTIONS: Each Question 6 through 10 consists of numbers or letters in Columns I and II. For each question, compare each line of Column I with its corresponding line in Column II and decide how many lines in Column I are EXACTLY the same as their corresponding lines in Column II. In your answer space, mark your answer
    A if only ONE line in Column I is exactly the same as its corresponding line in Column II
    B if only TWO lines in Column I are exactly the same as their corresponding lines in Column II

2 (#2)

    C if only THREE lines in Column I are exactly the same as their corresponding lines in Column II
    D if all FOUR lines in Column I are exactly the same as their corresponding lines in Column II

EXAMPLE

Column I	Column II
1776	1776
1865	1865
1945	1945
1976	1978

Only three lines in Column I are exactly the same as their corresponding lines in Column II. Therefore, the correct answer is C.

	Column I	Column II	
6.	5653 8727 ZPSS 4952	5653 8728 ZPSS 9453	6.____
7.	PNJP NJPJ JNPN PNJP	PNPJ NJPJ JNPN PNPJ	7.____
8.	effe uWvw KpGj vmnv	eFfe uWvw KpGg vmnv	8.____
9.	5232 PfrC zssz rwwr	5232 PfrN zzss rwww	9.____
10.	czws cecc thrm lwtz	czws cece thrm lwtz	10.____

Questions 11-15.

DIRECTIONS: Questions 11 through 15 have lines of letters and numbers. Each letter should be matched with its number in accordance with the following table.

Letter	F	R	C	A	W	L	E	N	B	T
Matching Number	0	1	2	3	4	5	6	7	8	9

7

From the table you can determine that the letter F has the matching number 0 below it, the letter R has the matching number 1 below, etc.

For each question, compare each line of letters and numbers carefully to see if each letter has its correct matching number. If all the letters and numbers are matched correctly in

none of the lines of the question, mark your answer A
only *one* of the lines of the question, mark your answer B
only *two* of the lines of the question, mark your answer C
all three lines of the question, mark your answer D

EXAMPLE

WBCR	4826
TLBF	9580
ATNE	3986

There is a mistake in the first line because the letter R should have its matching number 1 instead of the number 6.

The second line is correct because each letter shown has the correct matching number.

There is a mistake in the third line because the letter N should have the matching number 7 instead of the number 8.

Since all the letters and numbers are correct matched in only one of the lines in the sample, the correct answer is B.

11. EBCT 6829
    ATWR 3961
    NLBW 7584

12. RNCT 1729
    LNCR 5728
    WAEB 5368

13. NTWB 7948
    RABL 1385
    TAEF 9360

14. LWRB 5417
    RLWN 1647
    CBWA 2843

15. ABTC 3792
    WCER 5261
    AWCN 3417

16. Your job often brings you into contact with the public.
    Of the following, it would be MOST desirable to explain the reasons for official actions to people coming into your office for assistance because such explanations
    A. help build greater understanding between the public and your agency
    B. help build greater self-confidence in city employees
    C. convince the public that nothing they do can upset a city employee
    D. show the public that city employees are intelligent

17. Assume that you strongly dislike one of your co-workers.
    You should FIRST
    A. discuss your feeling with the co-worker
    B. demand a transfer to another office
    C. suggest to your supervisor that the co-worker should be observed carefully
    D. try to figure out the reason for this dislike before you say or do anything

18. An office worker who has problems accepting authority is MOST likely to find it difficult to
    A. obey rules
    B. understand people
    C. assist other employees
    D. follow complex instructions

19. The employees in your office have taken a dislike to one person and frequently annoy her.
    Your supervisor should
    A. transfer this person to another unit at the first opportunity
    B. try to find out the reason for the staff's attitude before doing anything about it
    C. threaten to transfer the first person observed bothering this person
    D. ignore the situation

20. Assume that your supervisor has asked a worker in your office to get a copy of a report out of the files. You notice the worker as accidentally pulled out the wrong report.
    Of the following, the BEST way for you to handle this situation is to tell
    A. the worker about all the difficulties that will result from this error
    B. the worker about her mistake in a nice way
    C. the worker to ignore this error
    D. your supervisor that this worker needs more training in how to use the files

21. Filing systems differ in their efficiency.
    Which of the following is the BEST way to evaluate the efficiency of a filing system? A
    A. number of times used per day
    B. amount of material that is received each day for filing
    C. amount of time it takes to locate material
    D. type of locking system used

22. In planning ahead so that a sufficient amount of general office supplies is always available, it would be LEAST important to find out the
    A. current office supply needs of the staff
    B. amount of office supplies used last year
    C. days and times that office supplies can be ordered
    D. agency goals and objectives

23. The MAIN reason for establishing routine office work procedures is that once a routine is established
    A. work need not be checked for accuracy
    B. all steps in the routine will take an equal amount of time to perform
    C. each time the job is repeated, it will take less time to perform
    D. each step in the routine will not have to be planned all over again each time

24. When an office machine centrally located in an agency must be shut down for repairs, the bureaus and divisions using this machine should be informed of the
    A. expected length of time before the machine will be in operation again
    B. estimated cost of repairs
    C. efforts being made to avoid future repairs
    D. type of new equipment which the agency may buy in the future to replace the machine being repaired

25. If the day's work is properly scheduled, the MOST important result would be that the
    A. supervisor will not have to do much supervision
    B. employee will know what to do next
    C. employee will show greater initiative
    D. job will become routine

KEY (CORRECT ANSWERS)

1. A
2. B
3. D
4. B
5. C

6. B
7. B
8. B
9. A
10. C

11. C
12. B
13. D
14. B
15. A

16. A
17. D
18. A
19. B
20. B

21. C
22. D
23. D
24. A
25. B

EXAMINATION SECTION
TEST 1

DIRECTIONS: Each question or incomplete statement is followed by several suggested answers or completions. Select the one that BEST answers the question or completes the statement. *PRINT THE LETTER OF THE CORRECT ANSWER IN THE SPACE AT THE RIGHT.*

1. Assume that a few co-workers meet near your desk and talk about personal matters during working hours. Lately, this practice has interfered with your work. In order to stop this practice, the BEST action for you to take FIRST is to
   A. ask your supervisor to put a stop to the co-workers' meeting near your desk
   B. discontinue any friendship with this group
   C. ask your co-workers not to meet near your desk
   D. request that your desk be moved to another location

   1.____

2. In order to maintain office coverage during working hours, your supervisor has scheduled your lunch hour from 1 P.M. to 2 P.M. and your co-workers' lunch hour from 12 P.M. to 1 P.M. Lately, your co-worker has been returning late from lunch each day. As a result, you don't get a full hour since you must return to the office by 2 P.M.
   Of the following, the BEST action for you to take FIRST is to
   A. explain to your co-worker in a courteous manner that his lateness is interfering with your right to a full hour for lunch
   B. tell your co-worker that his lateness must stop or you will report him to your supervisor
   C. report your co-worker's lateness to your supervisor
   D. leave at 1 P.M. for lunch, whether your co-worker has returned or not

   2.____

3. Assume that, as an office worker, one of your jobs is to open mail sent to your unit, read the mail for content, and send the mail to the appropriate person to handle. You accidentally open and begin to read a letter marked *personal* to a co-worker.
   Of the following, the BEST action for you to take is to
   A. report to your supervisor that your co-worker is receiving personal mail at the office
   B. destroy the letter so that your co-worker does not know you saw it
   C. reseal the letter and place it on the co-worker's desk without saying anything
   D. bring the letter to your co-worker and explain that you opened it by accident

   3.____

11

4. Suppose that in evaluating your work, your supervisor gives you an overall rating, but states that you sometimes turn in work with careless errors.
   The BEST action for you to take would be to
   A. ask a co-worker who is good at details to proofread your work
   B. take time to do a careful job, paying more attention to detail
   C. continue working as usual since occasional errors are to be expected
   D. ask your supervisor if she would mind correcting your errors

4._____

5. Assume that you are taking a telephone message for a co-worker who is not in the office at the time.
   Of the following, the LEAST important item to write on the message is the
   A. length of the call   B. name of the caller
   C. time of the call   D. telephone number of the caller

5._____

Questions 6-13.

DIRECTIONS: Questions 6 through 13 each consist of a sentence which may or may not be an example of good English. The underlined parts of each sentence may be correct or incorrect. Examine each sentence, considering grammar, punctuation, spelling, and capitalization. If the English usage in the underlined parts of the sentence given is better than any of the changes in the underlined words suggested in Options B, C, or D, choose Option A. If the changes in the underlined words suggested in Options B, C, or D would make the sentence correct, choose the correct option. Do not choose an option that will change the meaning of the sentence.

6. This Fall, the office will be closed on Columbus Day, October 9th.
   A. Correct as is   B. fall...Columbus Day, October
   C. Fall...Columbus day, October   D. fall...Columbus Day, october

6._____

7. This manual discribes the duties performed by an Office Aide.
   A. Correct as is   B. describe the duties performed
   C. discribe the duties performed   D. describes the duties performed

7._____

8. There weren't no paper in the supply closet.
   A. Correct as is   B. weren't any
   C. wasn't any   D. wasn't no

8._____

9. The new employees left there office to attend a meeting.
   A. Correct as is   B. they're
   C. their   D. thier

9._____

10. The office worker started working at 8:30 a.m.
    A. Correct as is   B. 8:30 a.m.
    C. 8;30 a,m.   D. 8:30 am.

10._____

11. The alphabet, or A to Z sequence are the basis of most filing systems.
    A. Correct as is   B. alphabet, or A to Z sequence, is
    C. alphabet, or A to Z sequence are   D. alphabet, or A too Z sequence, is

11._____

12. Those file cabinets are five feet tall.   12._____
    A. Correct as is   B. Them...feet
    C. Those...foot   D. Them...foot

13. The Office Aide checked the register and finding the date of the meeting.   13._____
    A. Correct as is   B. regaster and finding
    C. register and found   D. regaster and found

Questions 14-21.

DIRECTIONS: Each of Questions 14 through 21 has two lists of numbers. Each list contains three sets of numbers. Check each of the three sets in the list on the right to see if they are the same as the corresponding set in the list on the left. Mark your answers
    A. if none of the sets in the right list are the same as those in the left list
    B. if only one of the sets in the right list are the same as those in the left list
    C. if only two of the sets in the right list are the same as those in the left list
    D. if all three sets in the right list are the same as those in the left list

14. 7354183476   7354983476   14._____
     4474747744   4474747774
     57914302311   57914302311

15. 7143592185   7143892185   15._____
     8344517699   8344518699
     9178531263   9178531263

16. 2572114731   257214731   16._____
     8806835476   8806835476
     8255831246   8255831246

17. 331476853821   331476858621   17._____
     6976658532996   6976655832996
     3766042113715   3766042113745

18. 8806663315   8806663315   18._____
     74477138449   74477138449
     211756663666   211756663666

19. 990006966996   99000696996   19._____
     53022219743   53022219843
     4171171117717   4171171177717

20. 24400222433004   24400222433004   20._____
     5300030055000355   5300030055500355
     20000075532002022   20000075532002022

21. 6111666406600011116   61116664066001116   21.____
    7111300117001100733   7111300117001100733
    26666446664476518   26666446664476518

Questions 22-25.

DIRECTIONS: Each of Questions 22 through 25 has two lists of names and addresses. Each
             list contains three sets of names and addresses. Check each of the three sets
             in the list on the right to see if they are the same as the corresponding set in
             the list on the left. Mark your answers
                A. if none of the sets in the right list are the same as those in the left list
                B. if only one of the sets in the right list are the same as those in the left list
                C. if only two of the sets in the right list are the same as those in the left list
                D. if all three sets in the right list are the same as those in the left list

22. Mary T. Berlinger   Mary T. Berlinger   22.____
     2351 Hampton St.   2351 Hampton St.
     Monsey, N.Y. 20117   Monsey, N.Y. 20117

     Eduardo Benes   Eduardo Benes
     473 Kingston Avenue   473 Kingston Avenue
     Central Islip, N.Y. 11734   Central Islip, N.Y. 11734

     Alan Carrington Fuchs   Alan Carrington Fuchs
     17 Gnarled Hollow Road   17 Gnarled Hollow Road
     Los Angeles, CA 91635   Los Angeles, CA 91685

23. David John Jacobson   David John Jacobson   23.____
     178 35 St. Apt. 4C   178 53 St. Apt. 4C
     New York, N.Y. 00927   New York, N.Y. 00927

     Ann-Marie Calonella   Ann-Marie Calonella
     7243 South Ridge Blvd.   7243 South Ridge Blvd.
     Bakersfield, CA 96714   Bakersfield, CA 96714

     Pauline M. Thompson   Pauline M. Thomson
     872 Linden Ave.   872 Linden Ave.
     Houston, Texas 70321   Houston, Texas 70321

24. Chester LeRoy Masterton   Chester LeRoy Masterson   24.____
     152 Lacy Rd.   152 Lacy Rd.
     Kankakee, Ill. 54532   Kankakee, Ill. 54532

     William Maloney   William Maloney
     S. LaCrosse Pla.   S. LaCross Pla.
     Wausau, Wisconsin 52146   Wausau, Wisconsin 52146

5 (#1)

Cynthia V. Barnes 16 Pines Rd. Greenpoint, Miss. 20376	Cynthia V. Barnes 16 Pines Rd. Greenpoint, Miss. 20376
25. Marcel Jean Frontenac 6 Burton On The Water Calender, Me. 01471	Marcel Jean Frontenac 25._____ 6 Burton On The Water Calender, Me. 01471
J. Scott Marsden 174 S. Tipton St. Cleveland, Ohio	J. Scott Marsden 174 Tipton St. Cleveland, Ohio
Lawrence T. Haney 171 McDonough St. Decatur, Ga. 31304	Lawrence T. Haney 171 McDonough St. Decatur, Ga. 31304

KEY (CORRECT ANSWERS)

1.	C		11.	B
2.	A		12.	A
3.	D		13.	C
4.	B		14.	B
5.	A		15.	B
6.	B		16.	C
7.	D		17.	A
8.	C		18.	D
9.	C		19.	A
10.	B		20.	C

21.	C
22.	C
23.	B
24.	B
25.	C

TEST 2

DIRECTIONS: Each question or incomplete statement is followed by several suggested answers or completions. Select the one that BEST answers the question or completes the statement. *PRINT THE LETTER OF THE CORRECT ANSWER IN THE SPACE AT THE RIGHT.*

Questions 1-6.

DIRECTIONS: Questions 1 through 6 are to be answered SOLELY on the basis of the information contained in the following passage.

Duplicating is the process of making a number of identical copies of letters, document, etc. from an original. Some duplicating processes make copies directly from the original document. Other duplicating processes require the preparation of a special master, and copies are then made from the master. Four of the most common duplicating processes are stencil, fluid, offset, and xerox.

In the stencil process, the typewriter is used to cut the words into a master called a stencil. Drawings, charts, or graphs can be cut into the stencil using a stylus. As many as 3,500 good-quality copies can be reproduced from one stencil. Various grades of finished paper from inexpensive mimeograph to expensive bond can be used.

The fluid process is a good method of copying from 50 to 125 good-quality copies from a master, which is prepared with a special dye. The master is placed on the duplicator, and special paper with a hard finish is moistened and then passed through the duplicator. Some of the dye on the master is dissolved, creating an impression on the paper. The impression becomes lighter as more copies are made; and once the dye on the master is used up, a new master must be made.

The offset process is the most adaptable office duplicating process because this process can be used for making a few copies or many copies. Masters can be made on paper or plastic for a few hundred copies, or on metal plates for as many as 75,000 copies. By using a special technique called photo-offset, charts, photographs, illustrations, or graphs can be reproduced on the master plate. The offset process is capable of producing large quantities of fine, top-quality copies on all types of finished paper.

The xerox process reproduces an exact duplicate from an original. It is the fastest duplicating method because the original material is placed directly on the duplicator, eliminating the need to make a special master. Any kind of paper can be used. The xerox process is the most expensive duplicating process; however, it is the best method of reproducing small quantities of good-quality copies of reports, letters, official documents, memos, or contracts.

1. Of the following, the MOST efficient method of reproducing 5,000 copies of a graph is 1.____
   A. stencil B. fluid C. offset D. xerox

2 (#2)

2. The offset process is the MOST adaptable office duplicating process because　　　2._____
   A. it is the quickest duplicating method
   B. it is the least expensive duplicating method
   C. it can produce a small number or large number of copies
   D. a softer master can be used over and over again

3. Which one of the following duplicating processes uses moistened paper?　　　3._____
   A. Stencil　　　B. Fluid　　　C. Offset　　　D. Xerox

4. The fluid process would be the BEST process to use for reproducing　　　4._____
   A. five copies of a school transcript
   B. fifty copies of a memo
   C. five hundred copies of a form letter
   D. five thousand copies of a chart

5. Which one of the following duplicating processes does NOT require a special master?　　　5._____
   A. Fluid　　　B. Xerox　　　C. Offset　　　D. Stencil

6. Xerox is NOT used for all duplicating jobs because　　　6._____
   A. it produces poor-quality copies
   B. the process is too expensive
   C. preparing the master is too time-consuming
   D. it cannot produce written reports

7. Assume a city agency has 775 office workers.　　　7._____
   If 2 out of 25 office workers were absent on a particular day, how many office workers reported to work on that day?
   A. 713　　　B. 744　　　C. 750　　　D. 773

Questions 8-11,

DIRECTIONS:　In Questions 8 through 11, select the choice that is CLOSEST in meaning to the underlined word.

SAMPLE:　This division reviews the fiscal reports of the agency.
In this sentence, the word *fiscal* means MOST NEARLY
A. financial　　　B. critical　　　C. basic　　　D. personnel

The correct answer is A, financial, because financial is closest to *fiscal*.

8. A central file eliminates the need to retain duplicate material.　　　8._____
   The word *retain* means MOST NEARLY
   A. keep　　　B. change　　　C. locate　　　D. process

9. Filing is a routine office task.　　　9._____
   Routine means MOST NEARLY
   A. proper　　　B. regular　　　C. simple　　　D. difficult

10. Sometimes a word, phrase, or sentence must be underlined to correct an error. 10.____
Deleted means MOST NEARLY
   A. removed   B. added   C. expanded   D. improved

11. Your supervisor will evaluate your work. 11.____
Evaluate means MOST NEARLY
   A. judge   B. list   C. assign   D. explain

Questions 12-19.

DIRECTIONS: The code table below shows 10 letters with matching numbers. For each Question 12 through 19, there are three sets of letters. Each set of letters is followed by a set of numbers which may or may not match their correct letter according to the code table. For each question, check all three sets of letters and numbers and mark your answer
   A. if no pairs are correctly matched
   B. if only one pair is correctly matched
   C. if only two pairs are correctly matched
   D. if all three pairs are correctly matched

CODE TABLE

T	M	V	D	S	P	R	G	B	H
1	2	3	4	5	6	7	8	9	0

SAMPLE QUESTION: TMVDSP   123456
                   RGBHTM   789011
                   DSPRGB   256789

In the sample question above, the first set of numbers correctly matches its set of letters. But the second and third pairs contain mistakes. In the second pair, M is incorrectly matched with number 1. According to the code table, letter M should be correctly matched with number 2. In the third pair, the letter D is incorrectly matched with number 2. According to the code table, letter D should be correctly matched with number 4. Since only one of the pairs is correctly matched, the answer to this sample question is B.

12. RSBMRM   759262   12.____
    GDSRVH   845730
    VDBRTM   349713

13. TGVSDR   183247   13.____
    SMHRDP   520647
    TRMHSR   172057

14. DSPRGM   456782   14.____
    MVDBHT   234902
    HPMDBT   062491

15.	BVPTRD	936184	15._____
	GDPHMB	807029	
	GMRHMV	827032	

16.	MGVRSH	283750	16._____
	TRDMBS	174295	
	SPRMGV	567283	

17.	SGBSDM	489542	17._____
	MGHPTM	290612	
	MPBMHT	269301	

18.	TDPBHM	146902	18._____
	VPBMRS	369275	
	GDMBHM	842902	

19.	MVPTBV	236194	19._____
	PDRTMB	647128	
	BGTMSM	981232	

Questions 20-25.

DIRECTIONS: In each of Questions 20 through 25, the names of four people are given. For each question, choose as your answer the one of the four names given which should be filed FIRST according to the usual system of alphabetical filing of names, as described in the following paragraph.

In filing names, you must start with the last name. Names are filed in order of the first letter of the last name, then the second letter, etc. Therefore, BAILY would be filed before BROWN, which would be filed before COLT. A name with fewer letters of the same type comes first; i.e., Smith before Smithe. If the last names are the same, the names are filed alphabetically by the first name. If the first name is an initial, a name with an initial would come before a first name that starts with the same letter as the initial. Therefore, I. BROWN would come before IRA BROWN. Finally, if both last name and first name are the same, the name would be filed alphabetically by the middle name, one again an initial coming before a middle name which starts with the same letter as the initial. If there is no middle name at all, the name would come before those with middle initials or names.

SAMPLE QUESTION: A. Lester Daniels
B. William Dancer
C. Nathan Danzig
D. Dan Lester

The last names beginning with D are filed before the last name beginning with L. Since DANIELS, DANCER, and DANZIG all begin with the same three letters, you must look at the fourth letter of the last name to determine which name should be filed first. C comes before I or Z in the alphabet, so DANCER is filed before DANIELS or DANZIG. Therefore, the answer to the above sample question is B.

20. A. Scott Biala   B. Mary Byala   20.____
    C. Martin Baylor   D. Francis Bauer

21. A. Howard J. Black B. Howard Black   21.____
    C. J. Howard Black D. John H. Black

22. A. Theodora Garth Kingston   B. Theadore Barth Kingston   22.____
    C. Thomas Kingston   D. Thomas T. Kingston

23. A. Paulette Mary Huerta   B. Paul M. Huerta   23.____
    C. Paulette L. Huerta   D. Peter A. Huerta

24. A. Martha Hunt Morgan   B. Martin Hunt Morgan   24.____
    C. Mary H. Morgan   D. Martine H. Morgan

25. A. James T. Meerschaum   B. James M. Mershum   25.____
    C. James F. Mearshaum   D. James N. Meshum

KEY (CORRECT ANSWERS)

1.	C		11.	A
2.	C		12.	B
3.	B		13.	B
4.	B		14.	C
5.	B		15.	A
6.	B		16.	D
7.	A		17.	A
8.	A		18.	D
9.	B		19.	A
10.	A		20.	D

21. B
22. B
23. B
24. A
25. C

TEST 3

DIRECTIONS: Each question or incomplete statement is followed by several suggested answers or completions. Select the one that BEST answers the question or completes the statement. *PRINT THE LETTER OF THE CORRECT ANSWER IN THE SPACE AT THE RIGHT.*

1. Which one of the following statements about proper telephone usage is NOT always correct?
   When answering the telephone, you should
   A. know whom you are speaking to
   B. give the caller your undivided attention
   C. identify yourself to the caller
   D. obtain the information the caller wishes before you do your other work

   1._____

2. Assume that, as a member of a worker's safety committee in your agency, you are responsible for encouraging other employees to follow correct safety practices. While you are working on your regular assignment, you observe an employee violating a safety rule.
   Of the following, the BEST action for you to take FIRST is to
   A. speak to the employee about safety practices and order him to stop violating the safety rule
   B. speak to the employee about safety practices and point out the safety rule he is violating
   C. bring the matter up in the next committee meeting
   D. report this violation of the safety rule to the employee's supervisor

   2._____

3. Assume that you have been temporarily assigned by your supervisor to do a job which you do not want to do.
   The BEST action for you to take is to
   A. discuss the job with your supervisor, explaining why you do not want to do it
   B. discuss the job with your supervisor and tell her that you will not do it
   C. ask a co-worker to take your place on this job
   D. do some other job that you like; your supervisor may give the job you do not like to someone else

   3._____

4. Assume that you keep the confidential personnel files of employees in your unit. A friend asks you to obtain some information from the file of one of your co-workers.
   The BEST action to take is to _____ to your friend.
   A. ask the co-worker if you can give the information
   B. ask your supervisor if you can give the information
   C. give the information
   D. refuse to give the information

   4._____

21

Questions 5-8.

DIRECTIONS: Questions 5 through 8 are to be answered SOLELY on the basis of the information contained in the following passage.

City government is committed to providing a safe and healthy work environment for all city employees. An effective agency safety program reduces accidents by educating employees about the types of careless acts which can cause accidents. Even in an office, accidents can happen. If each employee is aware of possible safety hazards, the number of accidents on the job can be reduced.

Careless use of office equipment can cause accidents and injuries. For example, file cabinet drawers which are filled with papers can be so heavy that the entire cabinet could tip over from the weight of one open drawer.

The bottom drawers of desks and file cabinets should never be left open since employees can easily trip over open drawers and injure themselves.

When reaching for objects on a high shelf, an employee should use a strong, sturdy object such as a stepstool to stand on. Makeshift platforms made out of books, papers, or boxes can easily collapse. Even chairs can slide out from under foot, causing serious injury.

Even at an employee's desk, safety hazards can occur. Frayed or cut wires should be repaired or replaced immediately. Computers which are not firmly anchored to the desk or table could fall, causing injury.

Smoking is one of the major causes of fires in the office. A lighted match or improperly extinguished cigarette thrown into a wastebasket filled with paper could cause a major fire with possible loss of life. Where smoking is permitted, ashtrays should be used. Smoking is particularly dangerous in offices were flammable chemicals are used.

5. The goal of an effective safety program is to
    A. reduce office accidents
    B. stop employees from smoking on the job
    C. encourage employees to continue their education
    D. eliminate high shelves in offices

6. Desks and file cabinets can become safety hazards when
    A. their drawers are left open
    B. they are used as wastebaskets
    C. they are makeshift
    D. they are not anchored securely to the floor

7. Smoking is especially hazardous when it occurs
    A. near exposed wires
    B. in a crowded office
    C. in an area where flammable chemicals are used
    D. where books and papers are stored

8. Accidents are likely to occur when
    A. employees' desks are cluttered with books and papers
    B. employees are not aware of safety hazards
    C. employees close desk drawers
    D. stepstools are used to reach high objects

9. Assume that part of your job as a worker in the accounting division of a city agency is to answer the telephone.
When you first answer the telephone, it is LEAST important to tell the caller
   A. your title
   B. your name
   C. the name of your unit
   D. the name of your agency

10. Assume that you are assigned to work as a receptionist, and your duties are to answer phones, greet visitors, and do other general office work. You are busy with a routine job when several visitors approach your desk.
The BEST action to take is to
   A. ask the visitors to have a seat and assist them after your work is completed
   B. tell the visitors that you are busy and they should return at a more convenient time
   C. stop working long enough to assist the visitors
   D. continue working and wait for the visitors to ask you for assistance

11. Assume that your supervisor has chosen you to take a special course during hours to learn a new payroll procedure. Although you know that you were chosen because of your good work record, a co-worker, who feels that he should have been chosen, has been telling everyone in your unit that the choice was unfair.
Of the following, the BEST way to handle this situation FIRST is to
   A. suggest to the co-worker that everything in life is unfair
   B. contact your union representative in case your co-worker presents a formal grievance
   C. tell your supervisor about your co-worker's complaints and let her handle the situation
   D. tell the co-worker that you were chosen because of your superior work record

12. Assume that while you are working on an assignment which must be completed quickly, a supervisor from another unit asks you to obtain information for her.
Of the following, the BEST way to respond to her request is to
   A. tell her to return in an hour since you are busy
   B. give her the names of some people in her own unit who could help her
   C. tell her you are busy and refer her to a co-worker
   D. tell her that you are busy and ask her if she could wait until you finish your assignment

13. A co-worker in your unit is often off from work because of illness. Your supervisor assigns the co-worker's work to you when she is not there. Lately, doing her work has interfered with your own job.
The BEST action for you to take FIRST is to
   A. discuss the problem with your supervisor
   B. complete your own work before starting your co-worker's work
   C. ask other workers in your unit to assist you
   D. work late in order to get the jobs done

14. During the month of June, 40,587 people attended a city-owned swimming pool. In July, 13,014 more people attended the swimming pool than the number that had attended in June. In August, 39,655 people attended the swimming pool. The TOTAL number of people who attended the swimming pool during the months of June, July, and August was 14.____
    A. 80,242   B. 93,256   C. 133,843   D. 210,382

Questions 15-22.

DIRECTIONS: Questions 15 through 22 test how well you understand what you read. It will be necessary for you to read carefully because your answers to these questions must be based ONLY on the information in the following paragraphs.

The telephone directory is made up of two books. The first book consists of the introductory section and the alphabetical listing of names section. The second book is the classified directory (also known as the yellow pages). Many people who are familiar with one book do not realize how useful the other can be. The efficient office worker should become familiar with both books in order to make the best use of this important source of information.

The introductory section gives general instructions for finding numbers in the alphabetical listing and classified directory. This section also explains how to use the telephone company's many services, including the operator and information services, gives examples of charges for local and long-distance calls, and lists area codes for the entire country. In addition, this section provides a useful zip code map.

The alphabetical listing of names section lists the names, addresses, and telephone numbers of subscribers in an area. Guide names, or *telltales*, are on the top corner of each page. These guide names indicate the first and last name to be found on that page. *Telltales* help locate any particular name quickly. A cross-reference spelling is also given to help locate names which are spelled several different ways. City, state, and federal government agencies are listed under the major government heading. For example, an agency of the federal government would be listed under *United States Government*.

The classified directory, or yellow pages, is a separate book. In this section are advertising services, public transportation line maps, shopping guides, and listings of businesses arranged by the type of product or services they offer. This book is most useful when looking for the name or phone number of a business when all that is known is the type of product offered and the address, or when trying to locate a particular type of business in an area. Businesses listed in the classified directory can usually be found in the alphabetical listing of names section. When the name of the business is known, you will find the address or phone number more quickly in the alphabetical listing of names section.

15. The introductory section provides 15.____
    A. shopping guides   B. government listings
    C. business listings   D. information services

16. Advertising services would be found in the 16.____
    A. introductory section   B. alphabetical listing of names section\
    C. classified directory   D. information services

17. According to the information in the above passage for locating government agencies, the Information Office of the Department of Consumer Affairs of New York City government would be alphabetically listed FIRST under
    A. *I* for Information Offices
    B. *D* for Department of Consumer Affairs
    C. *N* for New York City
    D. *G* for government

18. When the name of a business is known, the QUICKEST way to find the phone number is to look in the
    A. classified directory
    B. introductory section
    C. alphabetical listing of name section
    D. advertising service section

19. The QUICKEST way to find the phone number of a business when the type of service a business offers and its address is known is to look in the
    A. classified directory
    B. alphabetical listing of names section
    C. introductory section
    D. information service

20. What is a *telltale*?
    A. An alphabetical listing
    B. A guide name
    C. A map
    D. A cross-reference listing

21. The BEST way to find a postal zip code is to look in the
    A. classified directory
    B. introductory section
    C. alphabetical listing of names section
    D. government heading

22. To help find names which have several different spellings, the telephone directory provides
    A. cross-reference spelling
    B. *telltales*
    C. spelling guides
    D. advertising services

23. Assume that your agency has been given $2,025 to purchase file cabinets. If each file cabinet costs $135, how many file cabinet can your agency purchase?
    A. 8   B. 10   C. 15   D. 16

24. Assume that your unit ordered 14 staplers at a total cost of $30.20 and each stapler cost the same.
    The cost of one stapler was MOST NEARLY
    A. $1.02   B. $1.61   C. $2.16   D. $2.26

25. Assume that you are responsible for counting and recording licensing fees collected by your department. On a particular day, your department collected in fees 40 checks in the amount of $6 each, 80 checks in the amount of $4 each, 45 twenty dollar bills, 30 ten dollar bills, 42 five dollar bills, and 186 one dollar bills.
The TOTAL amount in fees collected on that day was
A. $1,406   B. $1,706   C. $2,156   D. $2,356

26. Assume that you are responsible for your agency's petty cash fund. During the month of February, you pay out 7 $2.00 subway fares and one taxi fare for $10.85. You pay out nothing else from the fund. At the end of February, you count the money left in the fund and find 3 one dollar bills, 4 quarters, 5 dimes, and 4 nickels.
The amount of money you had available in the petty cash fund at the BEGINNING of February was
A. $4.70   B. $16.35   C. $24.85   D. $29.55

27. You overhear your supervisor criticize a co-worker for handling equipment in an unsafe way. You feel that the criticism may be unfair.
Of the following, it would be BEST for you to
A. take your co-worker aside and tell her how you feel about your supervisor's comments
B. interrupt the discussion and defend your co-worker to your supervisor
C. continue working as if you had not overheard the discussion
D. make a list of other workers who have violated safety rules and give it to your supervisor

28. Assume that you have been assigned to work on a long-term project with an employee who is known for being uncooperative.
In beginning to work with this employee, it would be LEAST desirable for you to
A. understand why the person is uncooperative
B. act in a calm manner rather than an emotional manner
C. be appreciative of the co-worker's work
D. report the co-worker's lack of cooperation to your supervisor

29. Assume that you are assigned to sell tickets at a city-owned ice skating rink. An adult ticket costs $4.50, and a children's ticket costs $2.25. At the end of a day, you find that you have sold 36 adult tickets and 80 children's tickets.
The TOTAL amount of money you collected for that day was
A. $244.80   B. $318.00   C. $342.00   D. $348.00

30. If each office worker files 487 index cards in one hour, how many card can 26 office workers file in one hour?
A. 10,662   B. 12,175   C. 12,662   D. 14,266

KEY (CORRECT ANSWERS)

1.	D	11.	C	21.	B
2.	B	12.	D	22.	A
3.	A	13.	A	23.	C
4.	D	14.	C	24.	C
5.	A	15.	D	25.	C
6.	A	16.	C	26.	D
7.	C	17.	C	27.	C
8.	B	18.	C	28.	D
9.	A	19.	A	29.	C
10.	C	20.	B	30.	C

EFFECTIVELY INTERACTING WITH AGENCY STAFF AND MEMBERS OF THE PUBLIC

Test material will be presented in a multiple-choice question format.

Test Task: You will be presented with a variety of situations in which you must apply knowledge of how best to interact with other people.

SAMPLE QUESTION:

A person approaches you expressing anger about a recent action by your department.
Which one of the following should be your first response to this person?
    A. Interrupt to say you cannot discuss the situation until he calms down.
    B. Say you are sorry that he has been negatively affected by your department's action.
    C. Listen and express understanding that he has been upset by your department's action.
    D. Give him an explanation of the reasons for your department's action.

The CORRECT answer to this sample question is Choice C.
Solution:

Choice A is not correct. It would be inappropriate to interrupt. In addition, saying that you cannot discuss the situation until the person calms down will likely aggravate the person further.

Choice B is not correct. Apologizing for your department's action implies that the action was improper.

Choice C is the correct answer to this question. By listening and expressing understanding that your department's action has upset the person, you demonstrate that you have heard and understand the person's feelings and point of view.

Choice D is not correct. While an explanation of the reasons for the action may be appropriate at a later time, at this moment the person is angry and would not be receptive to such an explanation.

EXAMINATION SECTION

TEST 1

DIRECTIONS: Each question or incomplete statement is followed by several suggested answers or completions. Select the one that BEST answers the question or completes the statement. *PRINT THE LETTER OF THE CORRECT ANSWER IN THE SPACE AT THE RIGHT.*

1. Public organizations usually share each of the following customer-service problems with private organizations EXCEPT
    A. aversion to risk
    B. staff-heaviness
    C. provision of reverse incentives
    D. control-apportionment functions

    1.____

2. A service representative demonstrates interpersonal skills by
    A. identifying a customer's expectations
    B. learning how to use a new office telephone system
    C. studying a competitor's approach to service
    D. anticipating how a customer will react to certain situations

    2.____

3. Of the following, _____ is NOT generally considered to be a common reason for flaws in an organization's customer focus.
    A. commissioned employee compensation
    B. full problem-solving authority for front-line personnel
    C. inadequate hiring practices
    D. specific, case-oriented policy and procedural statements

    3.____

4. According to MOST research, approximately _____ of dissatisfied customers will actually complain or make their dissatisfaction with a product known to the organization.
    A. 5%
    B. 25%
    C. 50%
    D. 75%

    4.____

5. Which of the following is an example of an expected benefit associated with a product or service?
    A. Before buying a car, a customer believes she will not have to take the car in for repairs every few months.
    B. A customer in a sporting goods store tells a salesperson exactly what kind of trolling motor will meet the requirements of the lakes the customer wanted to fish.
    C. A supermarket shopper buys a loaf of bread, believing that the bread will remain fresh for a few days.
    D. An airline passenger discover that the meals served on board are good.

    5.____

6. During a meeting with a service representative, a customer makes an apparently reasonable request. However, the representative knows that satisfying the customer's request will violate a rule that is part of the organization's policy. Although the representative feels that an exception to the rule should be made in this case, she is not sure whether an exception can or should be made.

    6.____

31

The BEST course of action for the representative would be to
A. deny the request and apologize, explaining the company policy
B. rely on good judgment and allow the request
C. try to steer the customer toward a similar but clearly permissible request
D. contact a manager or more experienced peer to handle the request

7. While organizing an effective customer service department, it would be LEAST effective to 7.____
   A. create procedures for relaying reasons for complaints to other departments
   B. set up a clear chain-of-command for handling specific customer complaints
   C. continually monitor performance of front-line personnel
   D. give front-line people full authority to resolve all customer dissatisfaction

8. Of the following, _____ is an example of *tangible* service. 8.____
   A. an interior decorator telling his/her ideas to a potential client
   B. a salesclerk giving a written cost estimate to a potential buyer
   C. an automobile salesman telling a showroom customer about a car's performance
   D. a stockbroker offering investment advice over the telephone

9. As a rule, a customer service representative who handles telephones should always answer a call within no more than _____ ring(s). 9.____
   A. 1   B. 3   C. 5   D. 8

10. In order to be as useful as possible to an organization, feedback received from customers should NOT be 10.____
    A. portrayed on a line graph or similar device
    B. used to provide a general overview
    C. focused on end-use customers
    D. available upon demand

11. Of all the customers who switch to competing organizations approximately _____ percent do so because of poor service. 11.____
    A. 25   B. 40   C. 75   D. 95

12. When customers offer information that is incorrect in their complaints, a service representative should do each of the following EXCEPT 12.____
    A. assume that the customer is making an innocent mistake
    B. look for opportunities to educate the customer
    C. calmly state a reasonable argument that will correct the customer's mistake
    D. believe the customer until he/she is able to find proof of his/her error

13. In order to insure that a customer feels comfortable in a face-to-face meeting, a service representative should
    A. avoid discussing controversial issues
    B. use personal terms such as *dear* or *friend*
    C. address the customer by his/her first name
    D. tell a few jokes

14. Customer satisfaction is MOST effectively measured in terms of
    A. cost   B. benefit   C. convenience   D. value

15. Making a sale is NOT considered good service when
    A. there are no alternatives to the subject of the customer's complaint
    B. when the original product or service is outdated
    C. an add-in feature will forestall other problems
    D. the product or service the customer has been using is the wrong product

16. When dealing with an indecisive customer, the service representative should
    A. expand available possibilities
    B. offer a way out of unsatisfying decisions
    C. ask probing questions for understanding
    D. steer the customer toward one particular decision

17. Of the following, _____ would NOT be a source of direct organizational service promises.
    A. advertising materials
    B. published organizational policies
    C. contracts
    D. the customer's past experience with the organization

18. Generally, the only kind of organization that can validly circumvent the requirements of customer service is one that
    A. cannot afford to staff an entire service department
    B. relies solely on the sale of ten or fewer items per year
    C. has little or no competition
    D. serves clients that are separated from consumers

19. When using the problem-solving approach to solve the problem of an upset customer, the service representative should FIRST
    A. express respect for the customer
    B. identify the customer's expectations
    C. outline a solution or alternatives
    D. listen to understand the problem

20. During face-to-face meetings with strangers such as service personnel, most North Americans consider a comfortable proximity to be
    A. 6 inches - 1 foot   B. 8 inches - 1½ feet
    C. 1½ - 2 feet   D. 2-4 feet

21. When answering phone calls, a service representative should ALWAYS do each of the following EXCEPT
    A. state his/her name
    B. give the name of the organization or department
    C. ask probing questions
    D. offer assistance

21.____

22. If a customer appears to be emotionally neutral when lodging a complaint, it would be MOST appropriate for a service representative to demonstrate ____ in reaction to the complaint.
    A. urgency   B. empathy   C. nonchalance   D. surprise

22.____

23. When soliciting customer feedback, standard practice is to limit the number of questions asked to APPROXIMATELY
    A. 3-5   B. 5-10   C. 10-20   D. 15-40

23.____

24. A customer has purchased an item from a company and has been told that the item will be delivered in two weeks. However, a customer service representative later discovers that deliveries are running about three days behind schedule.
    The MOST appropriate course of action for the representative would be to
    A. call the customer immediately, apologize for the delay, and await the customer's response
    B. call the customer a few days before delivery is due and explain that the delay is the fault of the delivery company
    C. immediately sent out a *loaner* of the ordered item to the customer
    D. wait for the customer to note the delay and contact the organization

24.____

25. Most research show that ____% of what is communicated between people during face-to-face meetings is conveyed through words alone.
    A. 10   B. 30   C. 50   D. 80

25.____

KEY (CORRECT ANSWERS)

1. D
2. D
3. B
4. A
5. B

6. D
7. B
8. B
9. B
10. B

11. B
12. C
13. A
14. D
15. A

16. B
17. D
18. C
19. A
20. C

21. C
22. D
23. B
24. A
25. A

TEST 2

DIRECTIONS: Each question or incomplete statement is followed by several suggested answers or completions. Select the one that BEST answers the question or completes the statement. *PRINT THE LETTER OF THE CORRECT ANSWER IN THE SPACE AT THE RIGHT.*

1. When working cooperatively to identify specific internal service targets, personnel typically encounter each of the following obstacles EXCEPT
    A. rapidly-changing work environment
    B. philosophical differences about the nature of service
    C. specialized knowledge of certain personnel exceeds that of others
    D. a chain-of-command that isolates the end user

    1._____

2. Which of the following is an example of an external customer relationship?
    A. Baggage clerks to travelers
    B. Catering staff to flight attendants
    C. Managers to ticketing agents
    D. Maintenance workers to ground crew

    2._____

3. When a service representative puts a customer's complaint in writing, results will be produced more quickly than if the representative had merely told someone.
    Which of the following is NOT generally considered to be a reason for this?
    A. The complaint can be more easily routed to parties capable of solving the problem.
    B. Management will understand the problem more clearly.
    C. The representative can more clearly see the main aspects of the complaint.
    D. The complaint and response will become a part of a public record.

    3._____

4. A customer service representative creates a client file, which contains notes about what particular clients want, need, and expect.
    Which of the following basic areas of learning is the representative exercising?
    A. Interpersonal skills   B. Product and service knowledge
    C. Customer knowledge   D. Technical skills

    4._____

5. A customer complains that a desired product, which is currently on sale, is needed in at least two weeks, but the company is out of stock and the product will not be available for another four weeks.
    Of the following, the BEST example of a service *recovery* on the part of a representative would be to
    A. apologize for the company's inability to serve the customer while expressing a wish to deal with the customer in the future
    B. attempt to steer the customer's interest toward an unrelated product
    C. offer a comparable model at the same sale price

    5._____

6. Of the following, _____ is NOT generally considered to be a function of closed questioning when dealing with a customer.
   A. understanding requests
   B. getting the customer to agree
   C. clarifying what has been said
   D. summarizing a conversation

7. When dealing with a customer who speaks with a heavy foreign accent, a service representative should NOT
   A. speak loudly
   B. speak slowly
   C. avoid humor or witticism
   D. repeat what has been said

8. If a customer service representative is aware that time will be a factor in the delivery of service to a customer, the representative should FIRST
   A. warn the customer that the organization is under time constraints
   B. suggest that the customer return another time
   C. ask the customer to suggest a service deadline
   D. tell the customer when service can reasonably be expected

9. In relation to a customer service representative's view of an organization, the customer's view of the company tends to be
   A. more negative
   B. more objective
   C. broader in scope
   D. less forgiving

10. When asked to define the factors that determine whether they will do business with an organization, most customers maintain that _____ is the MOST important.
    A. friendly employees
    B. having their needs met
    C. convenience
    D. product pricing

11. While a customer is stating her service requirements, a service representative should do each of the following EXCEPT
    A. ask questions about complex or unclear information
    B. formulate a response to the customer's remarks
    C. repeat critical information
    D. attempt to roughly outline the customer's main points

12. If a customer service representative must deal with other member of a service team in order to resolve a problem, the representative should avoid
    A. conveying every single detail of a problem to others
    B. suggesting deadlines for problem resolution
    C. offering opinions about the source of the problem
    D. explaining the specifics concerning the need for resolution

13. Of the following, the LAST step in the resolution of a service problem should be
    A. the offer of an apology for the problem
    B. asking probing questions to understand and conform the nature of the problem
    C. listening to the customer's description of the problem
    D. determining and implementing a solution to the problem

14. _____ is a poor scheduling strategy for a customer service representative. 14.____
    A. Performing the easiest tasks first
    B. Varying work routines
    C. Setting deadlines that will allow some restful work periods
    D. Doing similar jobs at the same time

15. The MOST defensible reason for the avoidance of customer satisfaction 15.____
    guarantees is
    A. buyer remorse
    B. repeated customer contact
    C. high costs
    D. ability of buyers to take advantage of guarantees

16. A customer service representative demonstrates knowledge and courtesy to 16.____
    customers and is able to convey trust, competence, and confidence.
    Of the following service factors, the representative is demonstrating
    A. assurance   B. responsiveness
    C. empathy   D. reliability

17. If a service representative is involved in sales, _____ is NOT one of the primary 17.____
    pieces of information he/she will need to supply the customer.
    A. cost of product or service   B. how the product works
    C. how to repair the product   D. available payment plans

18. A customer appears to be experiencing extreme feelings of anger and 18.____
    frustration when loading a complaint.
    The MOST appropriate reaction for a service representative to demonstrate is
    A. urgency   B. empathy   C. nonchalance   D. surprise

19. Of the following obstacles to customer service, _____ is NOT generally 19.____
    considered to be unique to public organizations.
    A. ambivalence toward clients   B. limited competition
    C. a rule-based mission   D. clients who are not really customers

20. Most customers report that the MOST frustrating aspect of waiting in line 20.____
    for service is
    A. not knowing how long they will have to wait for service
    B. rudeness on the part of the service representatives
    C. being expected to wait for service at all
    D. unfair prioritizing on the part of service representatives

21. Which of the following is an example of an *assumed benefit* associated with a 21.____
    product or service?
    A customer
    A buys a sporty sedan and finds that its tight turning ratio makes it easy to
       park
    B. visits a fast-food restaurant because she is in a hurry to get dinner over
       with

C. buys a videotape and believes it will not cause damage to her VCR
D. tells a salesman that he wants to purchase a high-status automobile

22. On an average, for every complaint received by an organization, there are actually about _____ customers who have legitimate problems.
    A. 3 B. 5 C. 15 D. 25

23. Once a customer problem is identified, each of the following should become a part of the service recovery process EXCEPT
    A. apologizing
    B. an offer of compensation
    C. empathetic listening
    D. sympathy

24. As a rule, customers who telephone organizations should not be put on hold for any longer than
    A. 10 seconds
    B. 60 seconds
    C. 5 minutes
    D. 10 minutes

25. The LEAST effective way to make customers feel as if they are a part of a service team would be to ask them for
    A. information about similar products/services they have used
    B. opinions about how to solve problems
    C. personally contact the department that can best help them
    D. opinions about particular products and services

KEY (CORRECT ANSWERS)

1.	B	11.	B
2.	A	12.	C
3.	D	13.	A
4.	C	14.	A
5.	D	15.	B
6.	A	16.	A
7.	A	17.	C
8.	C	18.	B
9.	C	19.	B
10.	B	20.	A

21. C
22. D
23. D
24. B
25. C

EXAMINATION SECTION
TEST 1

DIRECTIONS: Each question or incomplete statement is followed by several suggested answers or completions. Select the one that BEST answers the question or completes the statement. *PRINT THE LETTER OF THE CORRECT ANSWER IN THE SPACE AT THE RIGHT.*

1. Companies with successful customer service organizations usually experience each of the following EXCEPT
    A. fewer customer complaints
    B. greater response to advertising
    C. lower marketing costs
    D. more repeat business

    1._____

2. To be most useful to an organization, feedback received from customers should be each of the following EXCEPT
    A. centered on internal customers
    B. orgoing
    C. focused on a limited number of indicators
    D. available to every employee in the organization

    2._____

3. Instead of directly saying *no* to a customer, service representatives will usually get BEST results with a reply that begins with the words:
    A. I'll try
    B. I don't believe
    C. You can
    D. It's not our policy

    3._____

4. Once a customer problem is identified, each of the following should become a part of the service recovery process EXCEPT
    A. following up on the problem resolution
    B. making whatever promises are necessary
    C. providing the customer with what was originally requested
    D. listening and responding to every complaint given by the customer

    4._____

5. The percentage of an organization's annual business that involves repeat customers is CLOSEST to
    A. 25%   B. 45%   C. 65%   D. 85%

    5._____

6. Of the following, the _____ is NOT generally considered to be a major source of *service promise*.
    A. customer service representative
    B. organization
    C. particular department that delivers product to the customer
    D. customer

    6._____

7. A customer appears to be mildly irritated when lodging a complaint. The MOST appropriate action for a service representative to take while attempting resolution is to
   A. allow venting of frustrations
   B. enlist the customer in generating solutions
   C. show emotional neutrality
   D. create calm

8. If an organization loses one customer who normally spends $50 per week, the projected result of reduction in sales for the following year will be APPROXIMATELY
   A. $2,600   B. $12,400   C. $124,000   D. $950,000

9. The majority of *service promises* originate from
   A. organizational management
   B. customer service professionals
   C. the customers' expectations
   D. organizational marketing

10. To arrive at a *fair fix* to a service problem, one should FIRSTS
    A. offer an apology for the problem
    B. ask probing questions to understand and confirm the nature of the problem
    C. listen to the customer's description of the problem
    D. determine and implement a solution to the problem

11. Which of the following is NOT generally considered to be a function of *open questioning* when dealing with a customer?
    A. Defining problems
    B. Confirming an order
    C. Getting more information
    D. Establishing customer needs

12. When dealing with a customer, service representatives should generally use the pronoun
    A. *they*, meaning the company as a whole
    B. *they*, meaning the department to whom the complaint will be referred
    C. *I*, meaning themselves, as representatives of the organization
    D. *we*, meaning themselves and the customer

13. A customer service representative demonstrates product and service knowledge by
    A. anticipating the changing needs of customers
    B. soliciting feedback from customers about customer service
    C. studying the capabilities of the office computer system
    D. knowing what questions are asked most by customers about a product or service

14. When listening to a customer during a face-to-face meeting, the MOST appropriate non-verbal gesture is
    A. clenched fists
    B. leaning slightly toward a customer
    C. hands casually in pockets
    D. standing with crossed arms

15. Before breaking or bending an existing service rule in order to better serve a customer, a representative should be aware of each of the following EXCEPT the
    A. reason for the rule
    B. location of a written copy of the rule and policy
    C. consequences of not following the rule
    D. situations in which the rule is applicable

16. The LEAST likely reason for a dissatisfied customer's failure to complain about a product or service is that the customer
    A. does not think the complaint will produce the desired results
    B. is unaware of the proper channels through which to voice his/her complaint
    C. does not believe he/she has the time to spend on the complaint
    D. does not believe anyone in the organization really cares about the complaint

17. Most research shows that _____% of what is communicated between people during face-to-face meetings is conveyed through entirely nonverbal cues.
    A. 10 B. 30 C. 50 D. 80

18. When a customer submits a written complaint, the representative should write a response that avoids
    A. addressing every single component of the customer's complaint
    B. a personal tone
    C. the use of a pre-formulated response structure
    D. mentioning future business transactions

19. A customer service representative spends several hours practicing with the various forms and paperwork required by the company for handling customer service situations.
    Which of the following basic areas of learning is the representative trying to improve upon?
    A. Interpersonal skills
    B. Product and service knowledge
    C. Customer knowledge
    D. Technical skills

20. If a customer service representative must deal with other members of a service team in order to resolve a problem, the representative should avoid
    A. developing personal relationships
    B. giving others credit for ideas that clearly were not theirs
    C. circumventing uncooperative team members by quietly contacting a superior
    D. involving customers in the resolution of a complaint

21. A customer service representative is willing to help customers promptly. Which of the following service factors is the representative able to demonstrate?
    A. Assurance
    B. Responsiveness
    C. Empathy
    D. Reliability

22. A service representative begins work in a specialized order entry job and son learns that many customers call in with orders at the last minute, causing her routine to be thrown out of balance and creating stress.
After studying the ordering patterns of all clients, the MOST effective resolution to the problem would be to
    A. mail reminder notices to habitually late customers in advance of typical ordering dates to establish lead time
    B. telephone habitually late customers a few days before their typical ordering dates to establish lead time
    C. place the orders of habitually late customers in advance, changing them later if necessary
    D. establish and enforce a rigid lead-time deadline to create more manageable client behavior

23. For BEST results, customer service representatives will improve service by considering themselves to be representative of
    A. the entire organization
    B. the department receiving the complaint
    C. the customer
    D. an adversary of the organization, who will fight along with the customer

24. Of all the customers who stop doing business with organizations, _____% do so because of product dissatisfaction.
    A. 15   B. 40   C. 65   D. 80

25. When using the *problem-solving* approach to solve the problem of a dissatisfied customer, the LAST step should be to
    A. double check for customer satisfaction
    B. identify the customer's expectations
    C. outline a solution or alternatives
    D. take action on the problem

KEY (CORRECT ANSWERS)

1.	B	11.	B
2.	A	12.	C
3.	C	13.	D
4.	B	14.	B
5.	C	15.	B
6.	C	16.	C
7.	B	17.	C
8.	A	18.	C
9.	B	19.	D
10.	C	20.	C

21. B
22. B
23. A
24. A
25. A

TEST 2

DIRECTIONS: Each question or incomplete statement is followed by several suggested answers or completions. Select the one that BEST answers the question or completes the statement. *PRINT THE LETTER OF THE CORRECT ANSWER IN THE SPACE AT THE RIGHT.*

1. Of the following, the LEAST likely reason for a customer to telephone an organization or department is to
   A. voice an objection
   B. make a statement
   C. offer praise
   D. ask a question

   1._____

2. Customer service usually requires each of the following EXCEPT
   A. product knowledge
   B. friendliness and approachability
   C. problem-solving skills
   D. company/organization knowledge

   2._____

3. According to research, a typical dissatisfied customer will tell about _____ people how dissatisfied he/she is with an organization's product or service.
   A. 3   B. 5   C. 10   D. 20

   3._____

4. When a service target is provided by manager, it is MOST important for a service representative to know the
   A. nature of the customer database associated with the target
   B. formula for achieving the target
   C. methods used by other service personnel for achieving the target
   D. purpose behind the target

   4._____

5. Typically, customers cause about _____ of the service and product problems they complain about.
   A. 1/5   B. 1/3   C. 1/2   D. 2/3

   5._____

6. When a dissatisfied customer complains to a service representative, making a sale is NOT considered to be good service when the
   A. customer appreciates being changed to a different service or product
   B. the original product or service is in need of additional parts or components to be complete
   C. the customer remains angry about the original complaint
   D. the original product or service is in need of repair

   6._____

7. As service representatives, personnel would be LEAST likely to be responsible for
   A. service
   B. marketing
   C. problem-solving
   D. sales

   7._____

8. When writing a memorandum on a customer complaint, _____ can be considered optional by a service representative.
   A. the date the complaint was filed and/or the problem occurred
   B. a summary of the customer's comments
   C. the address of the customer
   D. a suggestion for correcting the situation

   8._____

9. In most successful organizations, customer service is considered PRIMARILY to be the domain of the
    A. entire organization
    B. sales department
    C. complaint department
    D. service department

10. According to MOST research, the cost of attracting a new customer, in relation to the cost of retaining a current customer, is about
    A. half as much
    B. about the same
    C. twice as much
    D. five times as much

11. If a customer service representative is unable to do what a customer asks, the representative should avoid
    A. quoting organizational policy regarding the customer's request
    B. explaining why it cannot be done
    C. making specific statements
    D. offering alternatives

12. When a customer presents a service representative with a request, the representative's FIRST reaction should usually be a(n)
    A. apology
    B. friendly greeting
    C. statement of organizational policy regarding the request
    D. request for clarifying information

13. It is NOT a primary reason for written communication with customers to
    A. create documentation
    B. solidify relationships
    C. confirm understanding
    D. solicit business contact

14. Of the following, which would be LEAST frustrating for a customer to hear from a service representative?
    A. You will have to
    B. I will do my best
    C. Let me see what I can do
    D. He/she should be back any minute

15. A customer appears to be mildly irritated when lodging a complaint. It is MOST appropriate for a service representative to demonstrate _____ in reaction to the complaint.
    A. urgency
    B. empathy
    C. nonchalance
    D. surprise

16. The _____ would be indirectly served by an individual who takes customer orders at an organization's telephone center.
    A. customer
    B. management personnel
    C. billing agents
    D. warehouse staff

17. Based on the actions of a customer service representative, customers will be MOST likely to make judgments concerning each of the following EXCEPT the
    A. kind of people employed by the organization
    B. company's value system
    C. organization's commitment to advertised promises
    D. value of the organization's product

18. When dealing with customers, a service representative's apologies, if necessary, should NOT be
    A. immediate   B. official   C. sincere   D. personal

19. Of all the customers who stop doing business with organizations, approximately _____ do so because of indifferent treatment by employees.
    A. 20%   B. 45%   C. 70%   D. 95%

20. If a customer service representative is aware that the organization is not capable of meeting a customer's expectations, the representative's FIRST responsibility would be to
    A. tell the customer of the organization's inability to comply
    B. shape the customer's expectations to match what the organization can do as he/she asks
    C. encourage the customer to believe that the organization can do as he/she asks
    D. make the sale on the organization's product

21. The following is an example of a *bonus benefit* associated with a product or service:
    A customer
    A. buys a sporty sedan and finds that its tight turning ratio makes it easy to park
    B. buys bread specifically because he wants to receive a coupon for his next purchase
    C. purchases a car and discovers a strange smell in the upholstery
    D. buys a music audiotape and discovers that there are advertisements at the beginning and end of the tape

22. Approximately _____ of customers who voice complaints with an organization will continue to do business with the organization if the complaint is resolved promptly.
    A. 25   B. 40   C. 75   D. 95

23. Though necessary, a positive, proactive customer satisfaction policy will USUALLY be restricted by costs and
    A. volume of service problems
    B. limitations of management personnel authority
    C. unreasonable customer demands
    D. limitations of service policy

24. According to MOST customers, _____ prevents good listening on the part of a service representative when a customer is speaking.
    A. technological apparatus (e.g., voicemail)
    B. frequent interruptions by other staff or customers
    C. asking unnecessary questions
    D. background noise

25. The ability to provide the promised service or product dependably and accurately maybe defined as 25._____
    A. assurance
    B. responsiveness
    C. courtesy
    D. reliability

KEY (CORRECT ANSWERS)

1. C
2. B
3. C
4. D
5. B

6. C
7. B
8. C
9. A
10. D

11. A
12. D
13. D
14. C
15. A

16. B
17. D
18. B
19. C
20. B

21. A
22. D
23. D
24. B
25. D

EVALUATING CONCLUSIONS BASED ON FACTUAL INFORMATION

Test material will be presented in a multiple-choice question format.

Test Task: You will be given a set of statements and a conclusion based on the statements. You are to assume the statements are true. The conclusion is reached from these statements *only* not on what you may happen to know about the subject discussed. Each question has three possible answers. You must then select the correct answer in the following manner:

Select A, if the statements prove that the conclusion is true.
Select B, if the statements prove that the conclusion is false.
Select C, if the statements are inadequate to prove the conclusion either true or false.

SAMPLE QUESTION #1:

STATEMENTS: All uniforms are cleaned by the Conroy Company. Blue uniforms are cleaned on Mondays or Fridays; green or brown uniforms are cleaned on Wednesdays. Alan and Jean have blue uniforms, Gary has green uniforms, and Ryan has brown uniforms.

CONCLUSION: Jean's uniforms are cleaned on Wednesdays.
   A statements prove the conclusion TRUE
   B statements prove the conclusion FALSE
   C statements are INADEQUATE to prove the conclusion

The correct answer to this sample question is Choice B.

SOLUTION: The last sentence of the statements says that Jean has blue uniforms. The second sentence of the statements says that blue uniforms are cleaned on Monday or Friday. The conclusion says Jean's uniforms are cleaned on Wednesday. Wednesday is neither Monday nor Friday. Therefore, the conclusion must be false (choice B).

SAMPLE QUESTION #2

STATEMENTS: If Beth works overtime, the assignment will be completed. If the assignment is completed, then all unit employees will receive a bonus. Beth works overtime.

CONCLUSION: A bonus will be given to all employees in the unit.
   A. statements prove the conclusion TRUE.
   B. statements prove the conclusion FALSE.
   C. statements are INADEQUATE to prove the conclusion

The correct answer to this sample question is Choice A.

SOLUTION: The conclusion follows necessarily from the statements. Beth works overtime. The assignment is completed. Therefore, all unit employees will receive a bonus.

SAMPLE QUESTION #3

STATEMENTS: Bill is older than Wanda. Edna is older than Bill. Sarah is twice as old as Wanda.

CONCLUSION: Sarah is older than Edna.
  A. statements prove the conclusion TRUE
  B. statements prove the conclusion FALSE
  C. statements are INADEQUATE to prove the conclusion

The correct answer to this sample question is Choice C.

SOLUTION: We know from the statements that both Sarah and Edna are older than Wanda. We do not have any other information about Sarah and Edna. Therefore, no conclusion about whether or not Sarah is older than Edna can be made.

EVALUATING CONCLUSIONS IN LIGHT OF KNOWN FACTS
EXAMINATION SECTION
TEST 1

DIRECTIONS: Each question or incomplete statement is followed by several suggested answers or completions. Select the one that BEST answers the question or completes the statement. *PRINT THE LETTER OF THE CORRECT ANSWER IN THE SPACE AT THE RIGHT.*

Questions 1-9.

DIRECTIONS: In Questions 1 through 9, you will read a set of facts and a conclusion drawn from them. The conclusion may be valid or invalid, based on the facts—it's your task to determine the validity of the conclusion.

For each question, select the letter before the statement that BEST expresses the relationship between the given facts and the conclusion that has been drawn from them. Your choices are:
   A. The facts prove the conclusion;
   B. The facts disprove the conclusion; or
   C. The facts neither prove nor disprove the conclusion.

1. FACTS: If the supervisor retires, James, the assistant supervisor, will not be transferred to another department. James will be promoted to supervisor if he is not transferred. The supervisor retired.

    CONCLUSION: James will be promoted to supervisor.
       A. The facts prove the conclusion.
       B. The facts disprove the conclusion.
       C. The facts neither prove nor disprove the conclusion.

2. FACTS: In the town of Luray, every player on the softball team works at Luray National Bank. In addition, every player on the Luray softball team wear glasses.

    CONCLUSIONS: At least some of the people who work at Luray National Bank wear glasses.
       A. The facts prove the conclusion.
       B. The facts disprove the conclusion.
       C. The facts neither prove nor disprove the conclusion.

3. FACTS: The only time Henry and June go out to dinner is on an evening when they have childbirth classes. Their childbirth classes meet on Tuesdays and Thursdays.

CONCLUSION: Henry and June never go out to dinner on Friday or Saturday.
- A. The facts prove the conclusion.
- B. The facts disprove the conclusion.
- C. The facts neither prove nor disprove the conclusion.

4. FACTS: Every player on the field hockey team has at least one bruise. Everyone on the field hockey team also has scarred knees.

    CONCLUSION: Most people with both bruises and scarred knees are field hockey players.
    - A. The facts prove the conclusion.
    - B. The facts disprove the conclusion.
    - C. The facts neither prove nor disprove the conclusion.

4.____

5. FACTS: In the chess tournament, Lance will win his match against Jane if Jane wins her match against Mathias. If Lance wins his match against Jane, Christine will not win her match against Jane.

    CONCLUSION: Christine will not win her match against Jane if Jane wins her match against Mathias.
    - A. The facts prove the conclusion.
    - B. The facts disprove the conclusion.
    - C. The facts neither prove nor disprove the conclusion.

5.____

6. FACTS: No green lights on the machine are indicators for the belt drive status. Not all of the lights on the machine's upper panel are green. Some lights on the machine's lower panel are green.

    CONCLUSION: The green lights on the machine's lower panel may be indicators for the belt drive status.
    - A. The facts prove the conclusion.
    - B. The facts disprove the conclusion.
    - C. The facts neither prove nor disprove the conclusion.

6.____

7. FACTS: At a small, one-room country school, there are eight students: Amy, Ben, Carla, Dan, Elliot, Francine, Greg, and Hannah. Each student is in either the 6th, 7th, or 8th grade. Either two or three students are in each grade. Amy, Dan, and Francine are all in different grades. Ben and Elliot are both in the 7th grade. Hannah and Carl are in the same grade.

    CONCLUSION: Exactly three students are in the 7th grade.
    - A. The facts prove the conclusion.
    - B. The facts disprove the conclusion.
    - C. The facts neither prove nor disprove the conclusion.

7.____

8. FACTS: Two married couples are having lunch together. Two of the four people are German and two are Russian, but in each couple the nationality of the spouse is not necessarily the same as the other's. One person in the group is a teacher, the other a lawyer, one an engineer, and the other a writer. The teacher is a Russian man. The writer is Russian, and her husband is an engineer. One of the people, Mr. Stern, is German.

   CONCLUSION: Mr. Stern's wife is a writer.
   A. The facts prove the conclusion.
   B. The facts disprove the conclusion.
   C. The facts neither prove nor disprove the conclusion.

9. FACTS: The flume ride at the county fair is open only to children who are at least 36 inches tall. Lisa is 30 inches tall. John is shorter than Henry, but more than 10 inches taller than Lisa.

   CONCLUSION: Lisa is the only one who can't ride the flume ride.
   A. The facts prove the conclusion.
   B. The facts disprove the conclusion.
   C. The facts neither prove nor disprove the conclusion.

Questions 10-17.

DIRECTIONS: Questions 10 through 17 are based on the following reading passage. It is not your knowledge of the particular topic that is being tested, but your ability to reason based on what you have read. The passage is likely to detail several proposed courses of action and factors affecting these proposals. The reading passage is followed by a conclusion or outcome based on the facts in the passage, or a description of a decision taken regarding the situation. The conclusion is followed by a number of statements that have a possible connection to the conclusion. For each statement, you are to determine whether:
   A. The statement proves the conclusion.
   B. The statement supports the conclusion but does not prove it.
   C. The statement disproves the conclusion.
   D. The statement weakens the conclusion but does not disprove it.
   E. The statement has no relevance to the conclusion.

Remember that the conclusion after the passage is to be accepted as the outcome of what actually happened, and that you are being asked to evaluate the impact each statement would have had on the conclusion.

PASSAGE:

The Grand Army of Foreign Wars, a national veteran's organization, is struggling to maintain its National Home, where the widowed spouses and orphans of deceased members are housed together in a small village-like community. The Home is open to spouses and children who are bereaved for any reason, regardless of whether the member's death was related to military service, but a new global conflict has led to a dramatic surge in the number of members' deaths: many veterans who re-enlisted for the conflict have been killed in action.

The Grand Army of Foreign Wars is considering several options for handling the increased number of applications for housing at the National Home, which has been traditionally supported by membership due. At its national convention, it will choose only one of the following:

The first idea is a one-time $50 tax on all members, above and beyond the dues they pay already. Since the organization has more than a million member, this tax should be sufficient for the construction and maintenance of new housing for applicants on the existing grounds of the National Home. The idea is opposed, however, by some older members who live on fixed incomes. These members object in principle to the taxation of Grand Army members. The Grand Army has never imposed a tax on its members.

The second idea is to launch a national fundraising drive the public relations campaign that will attract donations for the National Home. Several national celebrities are members of the organization, and other celebrities could be attracted to the cause. Many Grand Army members are wary of this approach, however: in the past, the net receipts of some fundraising efforts have been relatively insignificant, given the costs of staging them.

A third approach, suggested by many of the younger members, is to have new applicants share some of the costs of construction and maintenance. The spouses and children would pay an up-front "enrollment" fee, based on a sliding scale proportionate to their income and assets, and then a monthly fee adjusted similarly to contribute to maintenance costs. Many older members are strongly opposed to this idea, as it is in direct contradiction to the principles on which the organization was founded more than a century ago.

The fourth option is simply to maintain the status quo, focus the organization's efforts on supporting the families who already live at the National Home, and wait to accept new applicants based on attrition.

CONCLUSION: At its annual national convention, the Grand Army of Foreign Wars votes to impose a one-time tax of $10 on each member for the purpose of expanding and supporting the National Home to welcome a larger number of applicants. The tax is considered to be the solution most likely to produce the funds needed to accommodate the growing number of applicants.

10. Actuarial studies have shown that because the Grand Army's membership consists mostly of older veterans from earlier wars, the organization's membership will suffer a precipitous decline in numbers in about five years.
    A. The statement proves the conclusion.
    B. The statement supports the conclusion but does not prove it.
    C. The statement disproves the conclusion.
    D. The statement weakens the conclusion but does not disprove it.
    E. The statement has no relevance to the conclusion.

10.____

11. After passage of the funding measure, a splinter group of older members appeals for the "sliding scale" provision to be applied to the tax, so that some members may be allowed to contribute less based on their income.
    A. The statement proves the conclusion.
    B. The statement supports the conclusion but does not prove it.
    C. The statement disproves the conclusion.
    D. The statement weakens the conclusion but does not disprove it.
    E. The statement has no relevance to the conclusion.

11.____

12. The original charter of the Grand Army of Foreign Wars specifically states that the organization will not levy taxes or duties on its members beyond its modest annual dues. It takes a super-majority of attending delegates at the national convention to make alterations to the charter.
    A. The statement proves the conclusion.
    B. The statement supports the conclusion but does not prove it.
    C. The statement disproves the conclusion.
    D. The statement weakens the conclusion but does not disprove it.
    E. The statement has no relevance to the conclusion.

12.____

13. Six months before Grand Army of Foreign Wars' national convention, the Internal Revenue Service rules that because it is an organization that engages in political lobbying, the Grand Army must no longer enjoy its own federal tax-exempt status.
    A. The statement proves the conclusion.
    B. The statement supports the conclusion but does not prove it.
    C. The statement disproves the conclusion.
    D. The statement weakens the conclusion but does not disprove it.
    E. The statement has no relevance to the conclusion.

13.____

14. Two months before the national convention, Dirk Rockwell, arguably the country's most famous film actor, announces in a nationally televised interview that he has been saddened to learn of the plight of the National Home, and that he is going to make it his own personal crusade to see that it is able to house and support a greater number of widowed spouses and orphans in the future.
    A. The statement proves the conclusion.
    B. The statement supports the conclusion but does not prove it.
    C. The statement disproves the conclusion.
    D. The statement weakens the conclusion but does not disprove it.
    E. The statement has no relevance to the conclusion.

14.____

15. The Grand Army's final estimate is that the cost of expanding the National Home to accommodate the increased number of applicants will be about $61 million.
    A. The statement proves the conclusion.
    B. The statement supports the conclusion but does not prove it.
    C. The statement disproves the conclusion.
    D. The statement weakens the conclusion but does not disprove it.
    E. The statement has no relevance to the conclusion.

15.____

16. Just before the national convention, the Federal Department of Veterans Affairs announces steep cuts in the benefits package that is currently offered to the widowed spouses and orphans of veterans.
    A. The statement proves the conclusion.
    B. The statement supports the conclusion but does not prove it.
    C. The statement disproves the conclusion.
    D. The statement weakens the conclusion but does not disprove it.
    E. The statement has no relevance to the conclusion.

16.____

6 (#1)

17. After the national convention, the Grand Army of Foreign Wars begins charging a modest "start-up" fee to all families who apply for residence at the national home.
    A. The statement proves the conclusion.
    B. The statement supports the conclusion but does not prove it.
    C. The statement disproves the conclusion.
    D. The statement weakens the conclusion but does not disprove it.
    E. The statement has no relevance to the conclusion.

17.____

Questions 18-25.

DIRECTIONS: Questions 18 through 25 each provide four factual statements and a conclusion based on these statements. After reading the entire question, you will decide whether:
    A. The conclusion is proved by statements I-IV;
    B. The conclusion is disproved by statements I-IV.
    C. The facts are not sufficient to prove or disprove the conclusion.

18. FACTUAL STATEMENTS:
    I. In the Field Day high jump competition, Martha jumped higher than Frank.
    II. Carl jumped higher than Ignacio.
    III. Ignacio jumped higher than Frank.
    IV. Dan jumped higher than Carl.

    CONCLUSION: Frank finished last in the high jump competition.
    A. The conclusion is proved by statements I-IV;
    B. The conclusion is disproved by statements I-IV.
    C. The facts are not sufficient to prove or disprove the conclusion.

18.____

19. FACTUAL STATEMENTS:
    I. The door to the hammer mill chamber is locked if light 6 is red.
    II. The door to the hammer mill chamber is locked only when the mill is operating.
    III. If the mill is not operating, light 6 is blue.
    IV. Light 6 is blue.

    CONCLUSION: The door to the hammer mill chamber is locked.
    A. The conclusion is proved by statements I-IV;
    B. The conclusion is disproved by statements I-IV.
    C. The facts are not sufficient to prove or disprove the conclusion.

19.____

20. FACTUAL STATEMENTS:
    I. Ziegfried, the lion tamer at the circus, has demanded ten additional minutes of performance time during each show.
    II. If Ziegfried is allowed his ten additional minutes per show, he will attempt to teach Kimba the tiger to shoot a basketball.
    III. If Kimba learns how to shoot a basketball, then Ziegfried was not given his ten additional minutes.
    IV. Ziegfried was given his ten additional minutes.

20.____

7 (#1)

CONCLUSION: Despite Ziegfried's efforts, Kimba did not learn how to shoot a basketball.
   A. The conclusion is proved by statements I-IV;
   B. The conclusion is disproved by statements I-IV.
   C. The facts are not sufficient to prove or disprove the conclusion.

21. FACTUAL STATEMENTS: 21._____
   I. If Stan goes to counseling, Sara won't divorce him.
   II. If Sara divorces Stan, she'll move back to Texas.
   III. If Sara doesn't divorce Stan, Irene will be disappointed.
   IV. Stan goes to counseling.

CONCLUSION: Irene will be disappointed.
   A. The conclusion is proved by statements I-IV;
   B. The conclusion is disproved by statements I-IV.
   C. The facts are not sufficient to prove or disprove the conclusion.

22. FACTUAL STATEMENTS: 22._____
   I. If Delia is promoted to district manager, Claudia will have to be promoted to team leader.
   II. Delia will be promoted to district manager unless she misses her fourth-quarter sales quota.
   III. If Claudia is promoted to team leader, Thomas will be promoted to assistant team leader.
   IV. Delia meets her fourth-quarter sales quota.

CONCLUSION: Thomas is promoted to assistant team leader.
   A. The conclusion is proved by statements I-IV;
   B. The conclusion is disproved by statements I-IV.
   C. The facts are not sufficient to prove or disprove the conclusion.

23. FACTUAL STATEMENTS: 23._____
   I. Clone D is identical to Clone B.
   II. Clone B is not identical to Clone A.
   III. Clone D is not identical to Clone C.
   IV. Clone E is not identical to the clones that are identical to Clone B.

CONCLUSION: Clone E is identical to Clone D.
   A. The conclusion is proved by statements I-IV;
   B. The conclusion is disproved by statements I-IV.
   C. The facts are not sufficient to prove or disprove the conclusion.

24. FACTUAL STATEMENTS: 24._____
   I. In the Stafford Tower, each floor is occupied by a single business.
   II. Big G Staffing is on a floor between CyberGraphics and MainEvent.
   III. Gasco is on the floor directly below CyberGraphics and three floors above Treehorn Audio.
   IV. MainEvent is five floors below EZ Tax and four floors below Treehorn Audio.

CONCLUSION: EZ Tax is on a floor between Gasco and MainEvent.
  A. The conclusion is proved by statements I-IV;
  B. The conclusion is disproved by statements I-IV.
  C. The facts are not sufficient to prove or disprove the conclusion.

25. FACTUAL STATEMENTS:
   I. Only county roads lead to Nicodemus.
   II. All the roads from Hill City to Graham County are federal highways.
   III. Some of the roads from Plainville lead to Nicodemus.
   IV. Some of the roads running from Hill City lead to Strong City.

   CONCLUSION: Some of the roads from Plainville are county roads.
     A. The conclusion is proved by statements I-IV;
     B. The conclusion is disproved by statements I-IV.
     C. The facts are not sufficient to prove or disprove the conclusion.

25.____

KEY (CORRECT ANSWERS)

1.	A	11.	A
2.	A	12.	D
3.	A	13.	E
4.	C	14.	D
5.	A	15.	B
6.	B	16.	B
7.	A	17.	C
8.	A	18.	A
9.	A	19.	B
10.	E	20.	A

21.	A
22.	A
23.	B
24.	A
25.	A

SOLUTIONS TO PROBLEMS

1. CORRECT ANSWER: A
Given Statement 3, we deduce that James will not be transferred to another department. By Statement 2, we can conclude that James will be promoted.

2. CORRECT ANSWER: A
Since every player on the softball team wears glasses, these individuals compose some of the people who work at the bank. Although not every person who works at the bank plays softball, those bank employees who do play softball wear glasses.

3. CORRECT ANSWER: A
If Henry and June go out to dinner, we conclude that it must be on Tuesday or Thursday, which are the only two days when they have childbirth classes. This implies that if it is not Tuesday or Thursday, then this couple does not go out to dinner.

4. CORRECT ANSWER: C
We can only conclude that if a person plays on the field hockey team, then he or she has both bruises and scarred knees. But there are probably a great number of people who have both bruises and scarred knees but do not play on the field hockey team. The given conclusion can neither be proven or disproven.

5. CORRECT ANSWER: A
From statement 1, if Jane beats Mathias, then Lance will beat Jane. Using statement 2, we can then conclude that Christine will not win her match against Jane.

6. CORRECT ANSWER: B
Statement 1 tells us that no green light can be an indicator of the belt drive status. Thus, the given conclusion must be false.

7. CORRECT ANSWER: A
We already know that Ben and Elliot are in the 7th grade. Even though Hannah and Carl are in the same grade, it cannot be the 7th grade because we would then have at least four students in this 7th grade. This would contradict the third statement, which states that either two or three students are in each grade. Since Amy, Dan, and Francine are in different grade, exactly one of them must be in the 7th grade. Thus, Ben, Elliot, and exactly one of Amy, Dan, and Francine are the three students in the 7th grade.

8. CORRECT ANSWER: A
One man is a teacher, who is Russian. We know that the writer is female and is Russian. Since her husband is an engineer, he cannot be the Russian teacher. Thus, her husband is of German descent, namely Mr. Stern. This means that Mr. Stern's wife is the writer. Note that one couple consists of a male Russian teacher and a female German lawyer. The other couple consists of a male German engineer and a female Russian writer.

10 (#1)

9. CORRECT ANSWER: A
Since John is more than 10 inches taller than Lisa, his height is at least 46 inches. Also, John is shorter than Henry, so Henry's height must be greater than 46 inches. Thus, Lisa is the only one whose height is less than 36 inches. Therefore, she is the only one who is not allowed on the flume ride.

18. CORRECT ANSWER: A
Dan jumped higher than Carl, who jumped higher than Ignacio, who jumped higher than Frank. Since Martha jumped higher than Frank, every person jumped higher than Frank. Thus, Frank finished last.

19. CORRECT ANSWER: B
If the light is red, then the door is locked. If the door is locked, then the mill is operating. Reversing the logical sequence of these statements, if the mill is not operating, then the door is not locked, which means that the light is blue. Thus, the given conclusion is disproved.

20. CORRECT ANSWER: A
Using the contrapositive of statement III, Ziegfried was given his ten additional minutes, then Kimba did not learn how to shoot a basketball. Since statement IV is factual, the conclusion is proved.

21. CORRECT ANSWER: A
From Statements IV and I, we conclude that Sara doesn't divorce Stan. Then statement III reveals that Irene will be disappointed. Thus, the conclusion is proved.

22. CORRECT ANSWER: A
Statement II can be rewritten as "Delia is promoted to district manager or she misses her sales quota." Furthermore, this statement is equivalent to "If Delia makes her sales quota, then she is promoted to district manager." From statement I, we conclude that Claudia is promoted to team leader. Finally, by statement III, Thomas is promoted to assistant team leader.

23. CORRECT ANSWER: B
By statement IV, Clone E is not identical to any clones identical to Clone B. Statement I tells us that Clones B and D are identical. Therefore, Clone E cannot be identical to Clone D. The conclusion is disproved.

24. CORRECT ANSWER: A
Based on all four statements, CyberGraphics is somewhere below MainEvent. Gasco is one floor below CyberGraphics. EZ Tax is two floors below Gasco. Treehorn Audio is one floor below EZ Tax. MainEvent is four floors below Treehorn Audio. Thus, EZ Tax is two floors below Gasco and five floors above MainEvent. The conclusion is proved.

25. CORRECT ANSWER: A
From statement III, we know that some of the roads from Plainville lead to Nicodemus. But statement I tells us that only county roads lead to Nicodemus. Therefore, some of the roads from Plainville must be county roads. The conclusion is proved.

TEST 2

DIRECTIONS: Each question or incomplete statement is followed by several suggested answers or completions. Select the one that BEST answers the question or completes the statement. *PRINT THE LETTER OF THE CORRECT ANSWER IN THE SPACE AT THE RIGHT.*

Questions 1-9.

DIRECTIONS: In Questions 1 through 9, you will read a set of facts and a conclusion drawn from them. The conclusion may be valid or invalid, based on the facts—it's your task to determine the validity of the conclusion.

For each question, select the letter before the statement that BEST expresses the relationship between the given facts and the conclusion that has been drawn from them. Your choices are:
- A. The facts prove the conclusion;
- B. The facts disprove the conclusion; or
- C. The facts neither prove nor disprove the conclusion.

1. FACTS: Some employees in the testing department are statisticians. Most of the statisticians who work in the testing department are projection specialists. Tom Wilks works in the testing department.

   CONCLUSION: Tom Wilks is a statistician.
   - A. The facts prove the conclusion.
   - B. The facts disprove the conclusion.
   - C. The facts neither prove nor disprove the conclusion.

   1.____

2. FACTS: Ten coins are split among Hank, Lawrence, and Gail. If Lawrence gives his coins to Hank, then Hank will have more coins than Gail. If Gail gives her coins to Lawrence, then Lawrence will have more coins than Hank.

   CONCLUSION: Hank has six coins.
   - A. The facts prove the conclusion.
   - B. The facts disprove the conclusion.
   - C. The facts neither prove nor disprove the conclusion.

   2.____

3. FACTS: Nobody loves everybody. Janet loves Ken. Ken loves everybody who loves Janet.

   CONCLUSION: Everybody loves Janet.
   - A. The facts prove the conclusion.
   - B. The facts disprove the conclusion.
   - C. The facts neither prove nor disprove the conclusion.

   3.____

4. FACTS: Most of the Torres family lives in East Los Angeles. Many people in East Los Angeles celebrate Cinco de Mayo. Joe is a member of the Torres family.

   CONCLUSION: Joe lives in East Los Angeles.
   A. The facts prove the conclusion.
   B. The facts disprove the conclusion.
   C. The facts neither prove nor disprove the conclusion.

   4.____

5. FACTS: Five professionals each occupy one story of a five-story office building. Dr. Kane's office is above Dr. Assad's. Dr. Johnson's office is between Dr. Kane's and Dr. Conlon's. Dr. Steen's office is between Dr. Conlon's and Dr. Assad's. Dr. Johnson is on the fourth story.

   CONCLUSION: Dr. Kane occupies the top story.
   A. The facts prove the conclusion.
   B. The facts disprove the conclusion.
   C. The facts neither prove nor disprove the conclusion.

   5.____

6. FACTS: To be eligible for membership in the Yukon Society, a person must be able to either tunnel through a snowbank while wearing only a T-shirt and short, or hold his breath for two minutes under water that is 50°F. Ray can only hold his breath for a minute and a half.

   CONCLUSION: Ray can still become a member of the Yukon Society by tunneling through a snowbank while wearing a T-shirt and shorts.
   A. The facts prove the conclusion.
   B. The facts disprove the conclusion.
   C. The facts neither prove nor disprove the conclusion.

   6.____

7. FACTS: A mark is worth five plunks. You can exchange four sharps for a tinplot. It takes eight marks to buy a sharp.

   CONCLUSION: A sharp is the most valuable.
   A. The facts prove the conclusion.
   B. The facts disprove the conclusion.
   C. The facts neither prove nor disprove the conclusion.

   7.____

8. FACTS: There are gibbons, as well as lemurs, who like to play in the trees at the monkey house. All those who like to play in the trees at the monkey house are fed lettuce and bananas.

   CONCLUSION: Lemurs and gibbons are types of monkeys.
   A. The facts prove the conclusion.
   B. The facts disprove the conclusion.
   C. The facts neither prove nor disprove the conclusion.

   8.____

9. FACTS: None of the Blackfoot tribes is a Salishan Indian tribe. Salishan Indians came from the northern Pacific Coast. All Salishan Indians live each of the Continental Divide.

9._____

CONCLUSION: No Blackfoot tribes live east of the Continental Divide.
   A. The facts prove the conclusion.
   B. The facts disprove the conclusion.
   C. The facts neither prove nor disprove the conclusion.

Questions 10-17.

DIRECTIONS: Questions 10 through 17 are based on the following reading passage. It is not your knowledge of the particular topic that is being tested, but your ability to reason based on what you have read. The passage is likely to detail several proposed courses of action and factors affecting these proposals. The reading passage is followed by a conclusion or outcome based on the facts in the passage, or a description of a decision taken regarding the situation. The conclusion is followed by a number of statements that have a possible connection to the conclusion. For each statement, you are to determine whether:
   A. The statement proves the conclusion.
   B. The statement supports the conclusion but does not prove it.
   C. The statement disproves the conclusion.
   D. The statement weakens the conclusion but does not disprove it.
   E. The statement has no relevance to the conclusion.

Remember that the conclusion after the passage is to be accepted as the outcome of what actually happened, and that you are being asked to evaluate the impact each statement would have had on the conclusion.

PASSAGE:

On August 12, Beverly Willey reported that she was in the elevator late on the previous evening after leaving her office on the 16th floor of a large office building. In her report, she states that a man got on the elevator at the 11th floor, pulled her off the elevator, assaulted her, and stole her purse. Ms. Willey reported that she had seen the man in the elevators and hallways of the building before. She believes that the man works in the building. Her description of him is as follows: he is tall, unshaven, with wavy brown hair and a scar on his left cheek. He walks with a pronounced limp, often dragging his left foot behind his right.

CONCLUSION: After Beverly Willey makes her report, the police arrest a 43-year-old man, Barton Black, and charge him with her assault.

10. Barton Black is a former Marine who served in Vietnam, where he sustained shrapnel wounds to the left side of his face and suffered nerve damage in his left leg.
    A. The statement proves the conclusion.
    B. The statement supports the conclusion but does not prove it.
    C. The statement disproves the conclusion.
    D. The statement weakens the conclusion but does not disprove it.
    E. The statement has no relevance to the conclusion.

    10._____

11. When they arrived at his residence to question him, detectives were greeted at the door by Barton Black, who was tall and clean-shaven.
    A. The statement proves the conclusion.
    B. The statement supports the conclusion but does not prove it.
    C. The statement disproves the conclusion.
    D. The statement weakens the conclusion but does not disprove it.
    E. The statement has no relevance to the conclusion.

    11._____

12. Barton Black was booked into the county jail several days after Beverly Willey's assault.
    A. The statement proves the conclusion.
    B. The statement supports the conclusion but does not prove it.
    C. The statement disproves the conclusion.
    D. The statement weakens the conclusion but does not disprove it.
    E. The statement has no relevance to the conclusion.

    12._____

13. Upon further investigation, detectives discover that Beverly Willey does not work at the office building.
    A. The statement proves the conclusion.
    B. The statement supports the conclusion but does not prove it.
    C. The statement disproves the conclusion.
    D. The statement weakens the conclusion but does not disprove it.
    E. The statement has no relevance to the conclusion.

    13._____

14. Upon further investigation, detectives discover that Barton Black does not work at the office building.
    A. The statement proves the conclusion.
    B. The statement supports the conclusion but does not prove it.
    C. The statement disproves the conclusion.
    D. The statement weakens the conclusion but does not disprove it.
    E. The statement has no relevance to the conclusion.

    14._____

15. In the spring of the following year, Barton Black is convicted of assaulting Beverly Willey on August 11.
    A. The statement proves the conclusion.
    B. The statement supports the conclusion but does not prove it.
    C. The statement disproves the conclusion.
    D. The statement weakens the conclusion but does not disprove it.
    E. The statement has no relevance to the conclusion.

    15._____

16. During their investigation of the assault, detectives determine that Beverly Willey 16.____
    was assaulted on the 12th floor of the office building.
    A. The statement proves the conclusion.
    B. The statement supports the conclusion but does not prove it.
    C. The statement disproves the conclusion.
    D. The statement weakens the conclusion but does not disprove it.
    E. The statement has no relevance to the conclusion.

17. The day after Beverly Willey's assault, Barton Black fled the area and was never 17.____
    seen again.
    A. The statement proves the conclusion.
    B. The statement supports the conclusion but does not prove it.
    C. The statement disproves the conclusion.
    D. The statement weakens the conclusion but does not disprove it.
    E. The statement has no relevance to the conclusion.

Questions 18-25.

DIRECTIONS: Questions 18 through 25 each provide four factual statements and a conclusion
              based on these statements. After reading the entire question, you will decide
              whether:
              A. The conclusion is proved by statements I-IV;
              B. The conclusion is disproved by statements I-IV.
              C. The facts are not sufficient to prove or disprove the conclusion.

18. FACTUAL STATEMENTS: 18.____
    I. Among five spice jars on the shelf, the sage is to the right of the parsley.
    II. The pepper is to the left of the basil.
    III. The nutmeg is between the sage and the pepper.
    IV. The pepper is the second spice from the left.

    CONCLUSION: The safe is the farthest to the right.
    A. The conclusion is proved by statements I-IV;
    B. The conclusion is disproved by statements I-IV.
    C. The facts are not sufficient to prove or disprove the conclusion.

19. FACTUAL STATEMENTS: 19.____
    I. Gear X rotates in a clockwise direction if Switch C is in the OFF position.
    II. Gear X will rotate in a counter-clockwise direction is Switch C is ON.
    III. If Gear X is rotating in a clockwise direction, then Gear Y will not be rotating
        at all.
    IV. Switch C is ON.

    CONCLUSION: Gear X is rotating in a counter-clockwise direction.
    A. The conclusion is proved by statements I-IV;
    B. The conclusion is disproved by statements I-IV.
    C. The facts are not sufficient to prove or disprove the conclusion.

20. FACTUAL STATEMENTS:
    I. Lane will leave for the Toronto meeting today only if Terence, Rourke, and Jackson all file their marketing reports by the end of the work day.
    II. Rourke will file her report on time only if Ganz submits last quarter's data.
    III. If Terence attends the security meeting, he will attend it with Jackson, and they will not file their marketing reports by the end of the work day.

    CONCLUSION: Lane will leave for the Toronto meeting today.
    A. The conclusion is proved by statements I-IV;
    B. The conclusion is disproved by statements I-IV.
    C. The facts are not sufficient to prove or disprove the conclusion.

21. FACTUAL STATEMENTS:
    I. Bob is in second place in the Boston Marathon.
    II. Gregory is winning the Boston Marathon.
    III. There are four miles to go in the race, and Bob is gaining on Gregory at the rate of 100 yards every minute.
    IV. There are 1760 yards in a mile and Gregory's usual pace during the Boston Marathon is one mile every six minutes.

    CONCLUSION: Bob wins the Boston Marathon.
    A. The conclusion is proved by statements I-IV;
    B. The conclusion is disproved by statements I-IV.
    C. The facts are not sufficient to prove or disprove the conclusion.

22. FACTUAL STATEMENTS:
    I. Four brothers are named Earl, John, Gary, and Pete.
    II. Earl and Pete are unmarried.
    III. John is shorter than the youngest of the four.
    IV. The oldest brother is married, and is also the tallest.

    CONCLUSION: Gary is the oldest brother.
    A. The conclusion is proved by statements I-IV;
    B. The conclusion is disproved by statements I-IV.
    C. The facts are not sufficient to prove or disprove the conclusion.

23. FACTUAL STATEMENTS:
    I. Brigade X is ten miles from the demilitarized zone.
    II. If General Woundwort gives the order, Brigade X will advance to the demilitarized zone, but not quickly enough to reach the zone before the conflict begins.
    III. Brigade Y, five miles behind Brigade X, will not advance unless General Woundwort gives the order.
    IV. Brigade Y advances.

7 (#2)

CONCLUSION: Brigade X reaches the demilitarized zone before the conflict begins.
- A. The conclusion is proved by statements I-IV;
- B. The conclusion is disproved by statements I-IV.
- C. The facts are not sufficient to prove or disprove the conclusion.

24. FACTUAL STATEMENTS:
   I. Jerry has decided to take a cab from Fullerton to Elverton.
   II. Chubby Cab charges $5 plus $3 a mile.
   III. Orange Cab charges $7.50 but gives free mileage for the first 5 miles.
   IV. After the first 5 miles, Orange Cab charges $2.50 a mile.

   CONCLUSION: Orange Cab is the cheaper fare from Fullerton to Elverton.
   - A. The conclusion is proved by statements I-IV;
   - B. The conclusion is disproved by statements I-IV.
   - C. The facts are not sufficient to prove or disprove the conclusion.

24.____

25. FACTUAL STATEMENTS:
   I. Dan is never in class when his friend Lucy is absent.
   II. Lucy is never absent unless her mother is sick.
   III. If Lucy is in class, Sergio is in class also.
   IV. Sergio is never in class when Dalton is absent.

   CONCLUSION: If Lucy is absent, Dalton may be in class.
   - A. The conclusion is proved by statements I-IV;
   - B. The conclusion is disproved by statements I-IV.
   - C. The facts are not sufficient to prove or disprove the conclusion.

25.____

KEY (CORRECT ANSWERS)

1.	C	11.	E
2.	B	12.	B
3.	B	13.	D
4.	C	14.	E
5.	A	15.	A
6.	A	16.	E
7.	B	17.	C
8.	C	18.	B
9.	C	19.	A
10.	B	20.	C

21.	C
22.	A
23.	B
24.	A
25.	B

9 (#2)

SOLUTIONS TO PROBLEMS

1. CORRECT ANSWER: C
   Statement 1 only tells us that some employees who work in the Testing Department are statisticians. This means that we need to allow the possibility that at least one person in this department is not a statistician. Thus, if a person works in the Testing Department, we cannot conclude whether or not this individual is a statistician.

2. CORRECT ANSWER: B
   If Hank had six coins, then the total of Gail's collection and Lawrence's collection would be four. Thus, if Gail gave all her coins to Lawrence, Lawrence would only have four coins. Thus, it would be impossible for Lawrence to have more coins than Hank.

3. CORRECT ANSWER: B
   Statement 1 tells us that nobody loves everybody. If everybody loved Janet, then Statement 3 would imply that Ken loves everybody. This would contradict statement 1. The conclusion is disproved.

4. CORRECT ANSWER: C
   Although most of the Torres family lives in East Los Angeles, we can assume that some members of this family do not live in East Los Angeles. Thus, we cannot prove or disprove that Joe, who is a member of the Torres family, lives in East Los Angeles.

5. CORRECT ANSWER: A
   Since Dr. Johnson is on the 4th floor, either (a) Dr. Kane is on the 5th floor and Dr. Conlon is on the 3rd floor, or (b) Dr. Kane is on the 3rd floor and Dr. Conlon is on the 5th floor. If option (b) were correct, then since Dr. Assad would be on the 1st floor, it would be impossible for Dr. Steen's office to be between Dr. Conlon and Dr. Assad's office. Therefore, Dr. Kane's office must be on the 5th floor. The order of the doctors' offices, from 5th floor down to the 1st floor is: Dr. Kane, Dr. Johnson, Dr. Conlon, Dr. Steen, Dr. Assad.

6. CORRECT ANSWER: A
   Ray does not satisfy the requirement of holding his breath for two minutes under water, since he can only hold is breath for one minute in that setting. But if he tunnels through a snowbank with just a T-shirt and shorts, he will satisfy the eligibility requirement. Note that the eligibility requirement contains the key word "or." So only one of the two clauses separated by "or" need to be fulfilled.

7. CORRECT ANSWER: B
   Statement 2 says that four sharps is equivalent to one tinplot. This means that a tinplot is worth more than a sharp. The conclusion is disproved. We note that the order of these items, from most valuable to least valuable are: tinplot, sharp, mark, plunk.

8. CORRECT ANSWER: C
   We can only conclude that gibbons and lemurs are fed lettuce and bananas. We can neither prove nor disprove that these animals are types of monkeys.

9. CORRECT ANSWER: C
We know that all Salishan Indians live east of the Continental Divide. But some non-members of this tribe of Indians may also live east of the Continental Divide. Since none of the members of the Blackfoot tribe belong to the Salishan Indian tribe, we cannot draw any conclusion about the location of the Blackfoot tribe with respect to the Continental Divide.

18. CORRECT ANSWER: B
Since the pepper is second from the left and the nutmeg is between the sage and the pepper, the positions 2, 3, and 4 (from the left) are pepper, nutmeg, sage. By statement II, the basil must be in position 5, which implies that the parsley is in position 1. Therefore, the basil, not the sage, is farthest to the right. The conclusion disproved.

19. CORRECT ANSWER: A
Statement II assures us that if switch C is ON, then Gear X is rotating in a counterclockwise direction. The conclusion is proved.

20. CORRECT ANSWER: C
Based on Statement IV, followed by Statement II, we conclude that Ganz and Rourke will file their reports on time. Statement III reveals that if Terence and Jackson attend the security meeting, they will fail to file their reports on time. We have no further information if Terence and Jackson attended the security meeting, so we are not able to either confirm or deny that their reports were filed on time. This implies that we cannot know for certain that Lane will leave for his meeting in Toronto.

21. CORRECT ANSWER: C
Although Bob is in second place behind Gregory, we cannot deduce how far behind Gregory he is running. At Gregory's current pace, he will cover four miles in 24 minutes. If Bob were only 100 yards behind Gregory, he would catch up to Gregory in one minute. But if Bob were very far behind Gregory, for example 5 miles, this is the equivalent of (5)(1760) = 8800 yards. Then Bob would need 8800/100 = 88 minutes to catch up to Gregory. Thus, the given facts are not sufficient to draw a conclusion.

22. CORRECT ANSWER: A
Statement II tells us that neither Earl nor Pete could be the oldest; also, either John or Gary is married. Statement IV reveals that the oldest brother is both married and the tallest. By Statement III, John cannot be the tallest. Since John is not the tallest, he is not the oldest. Thus, the oldest brother must be Gary. The conclusion is proved.

23. CORRECT ANSWER: B
By Statements III and IV, General Woundwort must have given the order to advance. Statement II then tells us that Brigade X will advance to the demilitarized zone, but not soon enough before the conflict begins. Thus, the conclusion is disproved.

11 (#2)

24. CORRECT ANSWER: A
If the distance is 5 miles or less, then the cost for the Orange Cab is only $7.50, whereas the cost for the Chubby Cab is $5 + 3x, where x represents the number of miles traveled. For 1 to 5 miles, the cost of the Chubby Cab is between $8 and $20. This means that for a distance of 5 miles, the Orange Cab costs $7.50, whereas the Chubby Cab costs $20. After 5 miles, the cost per mile of the Chubby Cab exceeds the cost per mile of the Orange Cab. Thus, regardless of the actual distance between Fullerton and Elverton, the cost for the Orange Cab will be cheaper than that of the Chubby Cab.

25. CORRECT ANSWER: B
It looks like "Dalton" should be replaced by "Dan" in the conclusion. Then by statement I, if Lucy is absent, Dan is never in class. Thus, the conclusion is disproved.

EXAMINATION SECTION
TEST 1

DIRECTIONS: Each question or incomplete statement is followed by several suggested answers or completions. Select the one that BEST answers the question or completes the statement. *PRINT THE LETTER OF THE CORRECT ANSWER IN THE SPACE AT THE RIGHT.*

Questions 1-9.

DIRECTIONS: Questions 1 through 9, inclusive, are based on the STATE MOTOR VEHICLE BUREAU'S POINT SYSTEM given below. Read this point carefully before answering these items.

STATE MOTOR VEHICLE BUREAU'S POINT SYSTEM

The newly revised point system was effective April 1. After that date, a driver having offenses resulting in an accumulation of eight points within two years, ten points within three years, or twelve points within four years, is to be summoned for a hearing which may result in the loss of his license. Under the point system, three points are charged for speeding, two points for passing a red light or crossing a double line or failing to stop at a stop sign, one and a half points for inoperative horn or insufficient lights, and one point for improper turn or failure to notify Bureau of change of address. The Commissioner of Motor Vehicles is required to revoke a driver's license if he has three speeding violations in a period of 18 months, or drives while intoxicated or leaves the scene of an accident or makes a false statement in his application for a driver's license. This system is necessary because studies show violations of traffic laws cause four out of five fatal accidents in the state.

1. The traffic offense which calls for license revocation if repeated three times within a period of 1½ years is
   A. passing a red light
   B. passing a stop sign
   C. crossing a double line
   D. speeding

2. The individual who has the power to revoke a driver's license is the
   A. traffic officer
   B. motor vehicle inspector
   C. Commissioner of Motor Vehicles
   D. Traffic Commissioner

3. Crossing a double line has a penalty of twice as many points as for
   A. making an improper turn
   B. speeding
   C. passing a red light
   D. an inoperative horn

4. Failure of a driver to properly notify the Bureau of Motor Vehicles of a change in his address carries a penalty of _____ point(s).
   A. ½   B. 1   C. 1½   D. 2

5. The point system is specifically designed to penalize the driver who
   A. is inexperienced
   B. repeatedly violates traffic laws
   C. is overage
   D. ignores parking violations

6. A false statement on a driver's license application calls for a penalty of 6.____
   A. 10 points B. 8 points
   C. license suspension D. license revocation

7. Insufficient lights carries a penalty of _____ point(s). 7.____
   A. ½ B. 1 C. 1½ D. 2

8. A driver is summoned for a hearing if, within a period of three years, he accumulates _____ points. 8.____
   A. 6 B. 8 C. 10 D. 12

9. The percentage of fatal accidents caused by traffic violations is 9.____
   A. 80% B. 70% C. 60% D. 50%

Questions 10-11.

DIRECTIONS: Questions 10 and 11 are to be answered ONLY according to the information given in the following passage.

The State Vehicle and Traffic law was changed effective October 1, 2005 to provide for all new driving licenses to be issued on a six-month probationary basis. The probationary license will be cancelled if during this six-month period the driver is found guilty of tailgating, speeding, reckless driving, or driving while his ability is impaired by alcohol. The license will also be cancelled if the driver is found guilty of two other moving violations. If a probationary license is cancelled, the driver must wait for sixty days after the date of cancellation before applying for another license; and if the application is approved, the applicant must meet certain additional requirements including a new road test before a new license will be issued.

10. It is MOST reasonable to assume that the main purpose of the change in the law referred to above was to 10.____
    A. find out who is responsible for most traffic accidents
    B. make the road tests more difficult for new drivers to pass
    C. make it harder to get a driver's license
    D. serve as a further check on the competence of new drivers

11. According to the above passage, we may assume that a probationary license will NOT be cancelled if a driver is found guilty of 11.____
    A. passing a red light and failing to keep to the right on a road
    B. following another vehicle too closely
    C. overtime parking at a meter on two or more occasions
    D. driving at 60 miles an hour on a road where the speed limit is 50 miles an hour

Questions 12-13.

DIRECTIONS: Questions 12 and 13 are to be answered ONLY on the basis of the following passage.

If a motor vehicle fails to pass inspection, the owner will be given a rejection notice by the inspection station. Repairs must be made within ten days after this notice is issued. It is not necessary to have the required adjustment or repairs made at the station where the inspection occurred. The vehicle may be taken to any other garage. Re-inspection after repairs may be made at any official inspection station, not necessarily the same station which made the initial inspection. The registration of any motor vehicle for which an inspection sticker has not been obtained as required, or which is not repaired and inspected within ten days after inspection indicates defects, is subject to suspension. A vehicle cannot be used on public highways while its registration is under suspension.

12. According to the above passage, the owner of a car which does NOT pass inspection must
    A. have repairs made at the same station which rejected this car
    B. take the car to another station and have it re-inspected
    C. have repairs made anywhere and then have the car re-inspected
    D. not use the car on a public highway until the necessary repairs have been made

13. According to the above passage, the one of the following which may be cause for suspension of the registration of a vehicle is that
    A. an inspection sticker was issued before the rejection notice had been in force for ten days
    B. it was not re-inspected by the station that rejected it originally
    C. it was not re-inspected either by the station that rejected it originally or by the garage which made the repairs
    D. it has not had defective parts repaired within ten days after inspection

Questions 14-18.

DIRECTIONS: Questions 14 through 18 are to be answered ONLY on the basis of the following passage.

Under the Vehicular Responsibility Law of a certain state, an insurance carrier who has previously furnished the Division of Roads and Vehicles with evidence of a vehicle registrant's financial responsibility (Form VR-1, VR-1A, VR-2B or VR-11) must, in case of termination of insurance, first notify the insured registrant at least 10 days in advance if the termination is due to failure to pay the insurance premium and at least 20 days if the termination is due to any other reason. The insurance carrier must then notify the Division not later than 30 days following the effective date of actual termination of insurance coverage. The only acceptable proof of such termination is Form VR-4.

Upon receipt of Form VR-4 by the Division, a search will be made for any superseding coverage or a record of voluntary surrender of plates and registration certificate on or prior to the effective date of termination. If such a record is found, no further action is taken by the

Division. If the Division finds no record of acceptable superseding coverage or timely surrender of plates and registration, Form Letter VR-7T is sent to the registrant with a photostatic copy of Form VR-4, providing him with an opportunity to invalidate the proceeding to cancel his registration by submitting additional evidence, which may take the form of proof of continuous financial responsibility, timely sale of the vehicle, or evidence of voluntary surrender of plates and registration certificate. Only after the registrant has failed to comply by one of the above three methods is an order to cancel registration (Form VR-8) issued.

Upon the issuance of a cancellation order, a copy of the order is mailed to the registrant directing him to immediately surrender his plates and registration certificate to a specified area office of the Division. At the same time, two copies of the cancellation order are sent to the area office, where they are held for 15 days. If the registrant complies with the order, he is issued a notice of compliance (Form VR-3). If he fails to comply within the 15 days, two more copies of the order are mailed to the Highway Patrol for enforcement of the cancellation order. No further action is taken for a period of 30 days. If no record of enforcement is received, another copy of the cancellation order is sent to the Police Department as a follow-up.

14. When the Division of Roads and Vehicles receives acceptable evidence that the insurance coverage on a particular registrant has been terminated, it is required FIRST to
    A. cancel the registration if the insurance was terminated because of failure to pay the insurance premium
    B. notify the registrant to voluntarily surrender his plates and registration certificate on or prior to a certain date
    C. determine whether the registrant has obtained other insurance for that vehicle
    D. send the registrant Form Letter VR-7T stating that he must submit evidence to prevent cancellation of his registration

15. In order to comply with the above procedure, the MINIMUM number of copies of the cancellation order that must be prepared, including one to be kept in the central Division of Roads and Vehicles file, is
    A. 3 B. 4 C. 5 d. 6

16. The one of the following which is required before steps
    A. the insurance carrier to notify the Division of Roads and Vehicles in writing (VR-11) that the insured registrant's premium payment is 30 days overdue
    B. the registrant to notify the Division of Roads and Vehicles that he either intends to sell or has sold his vehicle
    C. Form VR-8 to be sent to the insured registrant by the Division of Roads and Vehicles
    D. Form VR-4 to be sent by the insurance carrier to the Division of Roads and Vehicles

17. The MAXIMUM amount of time a vehicle registrant is allowed in which to comply with a cancellation order before the police are asked to enforce the order is _____ days.
    A. 30 B. 35 C. 40 D. 45

18. It would be MOST accurate to state with regard to the issuance of a certificate of compliance that the   18.____
    A. Division of Roads and Vehicles issues one to the registrant after he has submitted the additional evidence in response to Form Letter VR-7T
    B. Division of Roads and Vehicles may issue one to the registrant at any time after he has been mailed a copy of the cancellation order and before the Highway Patrol is notified
    C. Highway Patrol may issue one to the registrant if he surrenders his plates and registration to them during the 30 days following their receipt of the request for enforcement
    D. Highway Patrol may issue one to the registrant at any time before the Police Department is notified

Questions 19-22.

DIRECTIONS: Questions 19 through 22 are to be answered ONLY on the basis of the information given in the following passage.

All automotive accidents, no matter how slight, are to be reported to the Safety Division by the employee involved on Accident Report Form S-23 in duplicate. When the accident is of such a nature that it requires the filling out of the State Motor Vehicle Report Form MV-104, this form is also prepared by the employee in duplicate and sent to the Safety Division for comparison with Form S-23. The Safety Division forwards both copies of Form MV-104 to the Corporation Counsel, who sends one copy to the State Bureau of Motor Vehicles. When the information on the Form S-23 indicates that the employee may be at fault, an investigation is made by the Safety Division. If this investigation shows that the employee was at fault, the employee's dispatcher is asked to file a complaint on Form D-11. The foreman of mechanics prepares a damage report on Form D8 and an estimate of the cost of repairs on Form D-9. The dispatcher's complaint, the damage report, the repair estimate, and the employee's previous accident record are sent to the Safety Division where they are studied together with the accident report. The Safety Division then recommends whether or not disciplinary action should be taken against the employee.

19. According to the above passage, the Safety Division should be notified whenever an automotive accident has occurred by means of Form(s)   19.____
    A. S-23
    B. S-23 and MV-104
    C. S-23, MV-104, D-8, D-9, and D-11
    D. S-23, MV-104, D-8, D-9, D-11, and employee's accident report

20. According to the above passage, the forwarding of the Form MV-104 to the State Bureau of Motor Vehicles is done by the   20.____
    A. Corporation Counsel
    B. dispatcher
    C. employee involved in the accident
    D. Safety Division

21. According to the above passage, the Safety Division investigates an automotive accident if the
    A. accident is serious enough to be reported to the State Bureau of Motor Vehicles
    B. dispatcher files a complaint
    C. employee appears to have been at fault
    D. employee's previous accident report is poor

21.____

22. Of the forms mentioned in the above passage, the dispatcher is responsible for preparing the
    A. accident report form
    B. complaint form
    C. damage report
    D. estimate cost of repairs

22.____

Questions 23-25.

DIRECTIONS: Questions 23 through 25 are to be answered ONLY on the basis of the information given in the following passage.

One of the major problems in the control of city motor equipment, and especially passenger equipment, is keeping the equipment working for the city and for the city alone for as many hours of the day as is practical. Even when most city employees try to get the most out of the cars, a poor system of control will result in wasted car hours. Some city employees have a legitimate use for a car all day long while others use a car only a small part of the day and then let it stand. As a rule, trucks are easier to control than passenger cars because they are usually assigned to a specific job where a foreman continually oversees them. Even though trucks are usually fully utilized, there are times when the normal work assignment cannot be carried out because of weather conditions or seasonal changes. At such times, a control system could plan to make the trucks available for other uses.

23. According to the above passage, a problem connected with controlling the use of city motor equipment is
    A. increasing the life span of the equipment
    B. keeping the equipment working all hours of the day
    C. preventing the overuse of the equipment to avoid breakdowns
    D. preventing the private use of the equipment

23.____

24. According to the above passage, a good control system for passenger equipment will MOST likely lead to
    A. better employees being assigned to operate the cars
    B. fewer city employees using city cars
    C. fewer wasted car hours for city cars
    D. insuring that city cars are used for legitimate purposes

24.____

25. According to the above passage, a control system for trucks is useful because
    A. a foreman usually supervises each job
    B. special conditions sometimes prevent the planned use of a truck
    C. trucks are easier to control than passenger cars
    D. trucks are usually assigned to specific jobs where they cannot be fully utilized

25.____

Question 26.

DIRECTIONS: Question 26 is to be answered SOLELY on the basis of the following passage.

Whereas automobile travel in general corresponds to the general motor vehicles index, as represented by total gas usage. Traffic trends on one particular road may vary from average. Comparison of the records of various main arteries indicates that automobile travel on some highways has gone up much faster than the general trend of gas usage. The conclusion is that the bulk of local travel remains stable, but a very large share of the total increase in travel is concentrated on main highways. This would be especially true on new highways which provide better means of travel and foster trips which would not have been made if the new route has not been constructed.

26. According to the above passage, which one of the following is MOST likely to result in increased automobile travel?   26._____
    A. A new roadway
    B. Stable local conditions
    C. A choice of routes
    D. Traffic trends

Questions 27-30.

DIRECTIONS: Questions 27 through 30 are to be answered ONLY on the basis of the following passage.

Analysis of current data reveals that motor vehicle transportation actually requires less space than was used for other types of transportation in the pre-automobile era, even including the substantial area taken by freeways. The reason is that when the fast-moving through traffic is put on built-for-the-purpose arterial roads, then the amount of ordinary space needed for strictly local movement and for access to property drops sharply. Even the amount of land taken for urban expressways turns out to be surprisingly small in terms either of total urban acreage or of the volume of traffic they carry. No existing or contemplated urban expressway system requires as much as 3 percent of the land in the areas it serves, and this would be exceptionally high. The Los Angeles freeway system, when complete, will occupy only 2 percent of the available land; the same is true of the District of Columbia, where only 0.75 percent will be pavement, with the remaining 1.25 percent as open space. California studies estimate that, in a typical California urban community, 1.6 to 2 percent of the area should be devoted to freeways, which will handle 50 to 60 percent of all traffic needs, and about ten time as much land to the ordinary roads and streets that carry the rest of the traffic. By comparison, when John A. Sutter laid out Sacramento in 1850, he provided 38 percent of the area for street and sidewalks. The French architect, Pierre L'Enfant, proposed 59 percent of the area of the District of Columbia for roads and streets; urban renewal in Southwest Washington, incorporating a modern street network, reduced the acreage of space for pedestrian and vehicular traffic in the renewal area from 48.2 to 41.5 percent of the total. If we are to have a reasonable consideration of the impact of highway transportation on contemporary urban development, it would be well to understand these relationships.

27. The author of this passage says that
    A. modern transportation uses less space than was used for transportation before the auto age
    B. expressways require more space than streets in terms of urban acreage
    C. typical urban communities were poorly designed in terms of relationship between space used for traffic and that used for other purposes
    D. the need for local and access roads would increase if the number of expressways were increased

28. According to the above passage, it was originally planned that the percent of the area to be used for roads and streets in the District of Columbia should be MOST NEARLY
    A. 40%   B. 45%   C. 50%   D. 60%

29. The above passage states that the amount of space needed for local traffic
    A. *increases* when arterial highways are constructed
    B. *decreases* when arterial highways are constructed
    C. *decreases* when there is more land available
    D. *increases* when there is more land available

30. According to the above passage, studies estimate that, land devoted to in a typical California urban community, the amount of ordinary roads and streets as compared with that devoted to freeways should be MOST NEARLY as much.
    A. One-half   B. One-tenth   C. Twice   D. Ten times

KEY (CORRECT ANSWERS)

1.	D	11.	C	21.	C
2.	C	12.	C	22.	B
3.	A	13.	D	23.	D
4.	B	14.	C	24.	C
5.	B	15.	B	25.	B
6.	D	16.	D	26.	A
7.	C	17.	D	27.	A
8.	C	18.	B	28.	D
9.	A	19.	A	29.	B
10.	D	20.	A	30.	D

TEST 2

DIRECTIONS: Each question or incomplete statement is followed by several suggested answers or completions. Select the one that BEST answers the question or completes the statement. *PRINT THE LETTER OF THE CORRECT ANSWER IN THE SPACE AT THE RIGHT.*

Questions 1-5.

DIRECTIONS: Questions 1 through 5 are to be answered ONLY on the basis of information given in the following passage.

Fatigue can make a driver incompetent. He may become less vigilant. He may lose judgment as to the speed and distance of other cars. His reaction time is likely to be slowed down, and he is less able to resist glare. With increasing fatigue, driving efficiency falls. Finally, nodding at the wheel results, from which accidents follow almost invariably.

Accidents that occur with the driver asleep at the wheel are generally very serious. With the driver unconscious, no effort is made either to prevent the accident or to lessen its seriousness. Accidents increase as day wears on and reach their peak in the early evening and during the first half of the night. Driver fatigue undoubtedly plays a significant part in causing these frequent night accidents.

1. Among the results of fatigue, the passage does NOT indicate   1.____
   A. lessened hearing effectiveness   B. lessened vigilance
   C. loss of driving efficiency   D. increased reaction time

2. According to the passage, accidents almost always follow as a result of   2.____
   A. fatigue   B. slowed down reaction time
   C. nodding at the wheel   D. lessened vigilance

3. According to the passage, accidents that occur in the early evening and during   3.____
   the first half of the night are
   A. always caused by driver fatigue
   B. very frequently the result of lessened resistance to glare
   C. usually due to falling asleep at the wheel
   D. more frequent than accidents in the afternoon

4. According to the passage, very serious accidents result from   4.____
   A. falling asleep at the wheel   B. poor driving
   C. lack of judgment   D. poor vision

5. Referring to the passage, which of the following conclusions is NOT correct?   5.____
   A. There are only two paragraphs in the entire passage.
   B. One paragraph contains four sentences.
   C. There are six words in the first sentence.
   D. There is no sentence of less than six words.

Questions 6-8.

DIRECTIONS: Questions 6 through 8 are to be answered ONLY according to the information given in the following passage.

Drivers and pedestrians face additional traffic hazards during the fall months. Changing autumn weather conditions, longer hours of darkness, and the abrupt nightfall during the evening rush hour can mean more traffic deaths and injuries unless drivers and pedestrians exercise greater care and alertness. Drivers must adjust to changing light conditions; they cannot use the same driving habits and attitudes at dusk as they do during daylight. Moderate speed and continual alertness are imperative for safe city driving at this time of year.

6. According to the above passage, two new traffic risks which motorists face in the fall are
    A. changing weather conditions and more traffic during the evening rush hour
    B. fewer hours of daylight and sudden nightfall
    C. less care by pedestrians and a change in autumn weather conditions
    D. more pedestrians on the street and longer hours of darkness

6.____

7. According to the above passage, there may be more traffic deaths and injuries in the fall MAINLY because both pedestrians and drivers are
    A. distracted by car lights being turned on earlier
    B. hurrying to get home from work in the evening
    C. confronted with more traffic dangers
    D. using the streets in greater numbers

7.____

8. According to the above passage, an ESSENTIAL requirement of driving safely in the city in the fall is
    A. eyes down on the road at all times
    B. very slow speed
    C. no passing
    D. reasonable speed

8.____

Questions 9-11.

DIRECTIONS: Questions 9 through 11 are to be answered ONLY according to the information given in the following passage.

A traffic sign is a device mounted on a fixed or portable support through which a specific message is conveyed by means of words or symbols. It is erected through which a specific purpose of regulating, warning, or guiding traffic.

A regulatory sign is used to indicate the required method of traffic movement or the permitted use of a highway. It gives notice of traffic regulations that apply only at specific places or at specific times that would not otherwise be apparent.

A warning sign is used to call attention to conditions on or near a road that are actually or potentially hazardous to the safe movement of traffic.

A guide sign is used to direct traffic along a route or toward a destination, or to give directions, distances, or information concerning places or points of interest.

9. According to the above passage, which one of the following is NOT a *regulatory* sign?
    A. Right turn on red signal permitted
    B. Trucks use right lane
    C. Slippery when wet
    D. Speed limit 60

10. According to the above passage, which one of the following LEAST fits the description of a *warning* sign?
    A. No right turn
    B. Falling rock zone
    C. Low clearance, 12 ft. 6 in.
    D. Merging traffic

11. According to the above passage, which one of the following messages is LEAST likely to be conveyed by a *guide* sign?
    A. Southbound
    B. Signal ahead
    C. Bridge next exit
    D. Entering city

Questions 12-14.

DIRECTIONS: Questions 12 through 14 are to be answered ONLY on the basis of the information given in the following passage.

A National Safety Council study of 685,000 traffic accidents reveals that most accidents happen under *safe* conditions—in clear, dry weather, on straight roads, and when traffic volumes are low. The point is most accidents can be attributed to lapses on the part of the drivers rather than traffic or road conditions or deliberate law violations. Most drivers try to avoid accidents. Why, then, do so many get into trouble? A major cause is the average motorist's failure to recognize a hazard soon enough to avoid it entirely. He does not, by habit, notice the clues that are there for him to see. He takes constant risks in traffic without even knowing it. These faulty seeing habits plus the common distractions that all drivers must deal with, such as hurry, worry daydreaming, impatience, concentration on route problems, add up to a guaranteed answer—an accident.

12. According to a study by the National Safety Council, MOST accidents can be blamed on
    A. curving, hilly roads
    B. errors made by drivers
    C. heavy streams of traffic
    D. wet, foggy weather

13. According to the above passage, an IMPORTANT reason why the average motorist gets into an accident is that he
    A. does not see the danger of an accident soon enough
    B. does not try to avoid accidents
    C. drives at too great a speed
    D. purposely takes reckless chances

14. According to the above passage, it is NOT reasonable to say that drivers are distracted from their driving and possibly involved in an accident because they
    A. are impatient about something
    B. concentrate on the road ahead
    C. hurry to get to where they are going
    D. worry about some problem

14.____

Questions 15-18.

DIRECTIONS: Questions 15 through 18 are to be answered ONLY on the basis of the information given in the following passage.

If a good automobile road map is studied thoroughly before a trip is started, much useful information can be learned. This information may help to decrease the cost of and the time required for the trip and, at the same time, increase the safety and comfort of the trip. The legend found on the face of the map explains symbols and markings and the kind of roads on various routes. The legend also explains how to tell by width, color, or type of line whether the road is dual- or multiple-lane, and whether it is paved, all-weather, graded, earth, under construction, or proposed for construction. Federal routes are usually shown by a number within a shield, and state routes by a number within a circle. The legend also shows scale of miles on a bar marked to indicate the distance each portion of the bar represents on the earth's surface. Distances between locations on the map are shown by plain numerals beside the route lines; they indicate mileage between marked points or intersections. Add the mileage numbers shown along a route to determine distances.

15. According to the above passage, the markings on the road map will show
    A. a different color for a road proposed for construction than for one under construction
    B. a double line if a road is a dual-lane road
    C. what part of a road is damaged or being repaired
    D. which roads on state routes have more than two lanes

15.____

16. The above passage does NOT mention as a possible advantage of studying a good road map before beginning a trip the
    A. increase in interest of the trip
    B. reduction in the chance of an accident on the trip
    C. saving of money
    D. saving of time

16.____

17. According to the above passage, in order to find the total mileage of a certain route, a motorist should add the numbers
    A. on the bar scale in the legend
    B. between marked points beside the route lines
    C. inside a shield along the route
    D. within a circle along the route

17.____

18. According to the above passage, the legend on a road map includes information 18.____
    which a motorist could use to
    A. choose the best paved route   B. figure the toll charges
    C. find the allowable speed limits   D. learn the location of bridges

Questions 19-30.

DIRECTIONS: The following is an accident report similar to those used by departments for reporting accidents. Questions 19 through 30 are to be answered ONLY on the basis of the information contained in this accident report.

ACCIDENT REPORT

Date of Accident: April 12, _____
Place of Accident: 17th Ave. & 22nd St.
Time of Accident: 10:15 A.M.
City Vehicle:
Operator's Name: John Smith
Title: Motor Vehicle Operator
Badge No.: 17-5427
Operator License No.: S2874-7513-3984
Vehicle Code No.: B7-8213
License Plate No.: BK-4782
Damage to Vehicle: Left front fender dented; broken left front headlight and parking light; windshield wipers not operating

Date of Report: April 15, _____ Friday
Vehicle No. 2:
Operator's Name: James Jones
Operator's Address: 427 E. 198th St.
Operator License No.: J0837-0882-7851
Owner's Name: Michael Greene
Owner's Address: 582 E. 92nd St.
License Plate No.: 6Y-3916
Damage to Vehicle: Left front bumper bent inward; broken left front headlight; grille broken in three places

DESCRIPTION OF ACCIDENT: I was driving on 17th Avenue, a southbound one-way street and made a slow, wide turn west into 22nd Street, a two-way street, because a moving van was parked near the corner of 22nd Street. As I completed my turn, a station wagon going east on 22nd Street hit me. The driver of the station wagon said he put on his brakes but he skidded on some oil that was on the street. The driver of the van saw the accident from his cab and told me that the station wagon skidded as he put on his brakes. Patrolman Jack Reed, Badge #24578, who was at the southeast corner of the intersection, saw what happened and made some notes in his memo book.

   Persons Injured – Names and Addresses. If none, state NONE:
   Witnesses – Names and Addresses: If none, state NONE:
     Jack Reed, 33-47 83rd Drive
     Thomas Quinn: 527 Flatlands Avenue

                              Report prepared by: John Smith
                              Title: Motor Vehicle Operator

19. According to the report, the accident happened on
    A. Friday, between 6:00 A.M. and 12:00 Noon
    B. Friday, between 12:00 Noon and 6:00 P.M.
    C. Tuesday, between 6:00 A.M. and 12:00 Noon
    D. Monday, between 12:00 Noon and 6:00 P.M.

20. Which one of the following numbers is part of the driver's license of the operator of the city vehicle?
    A. 3984   B. 5247   C. 4782   D. 7851

21. The address of the driver of the city vehicle is
    A. not given in the report
    B. 427 E. 198th Street
    C. 582 E. 92nd Street
    D. 33-47 83rd Drive

22. A section of the report that is NOT properly filled out is
    A. Witnesses
    B. Description of Accident
    C. Persons Injured
    D. Damage to Vehicle

23. According to the accident report, if the only witnesses were the patrolman and the van driver, then the van driver's name is
    A. Reed   B. Quinn   C. Jones   D. Greene

24. According to the report, the diagram that would BEST show where the cars collided and where the moving van (v) was parked at the time of the accident is

25. According to the information in the report, it would be MOST correct to say that Michael Greene was
    A. the driver of the station wagon
    B. a passenger in the station wagon
    C. the owner of the moving van
    D. the owner of the station wagon

26. According to the information in the report, a factor which contributed to the accident was 26.____
    A. a slippery road condition
    B. bad brakes of one car
    C. obstructed view of traffic light caused by parked van
    D. windshield wipers on the city car not operating properly

27. When a driver makes a report such as this, it is MOST important that he 27.____
    A. print the information so that his supervisor can read it quickly
    B. keep it short because a long report makes it look as though he is hiding a mistake behind many words
    C. show clearly why the accident isn't his fault
    D. give all the facts accurately and completely

28. The first two letters or numbers in the City Vehicle Code Number indicate the type of vehicle. Two letters indicate an 8 passenger 8-cylinder car; two numbers indicates a 6 passenger, 8-cylinder car; a letter followed by a number indicates a 6 passenger 6-cylinder car; a number followed by a letter indicate an 8-cylinder station wagon. 28.____
    The city car involved in this accident is, therefore, a(n)
    A. 8-cylinder station wagon   B. 6 passenger 6-cylinder car
    C. 6 passenger 8-cylinder car   D. 8 passenger 8-cylinder car

29. From the information in the report, the driver of the city vehicle may have been partially at fault because he 29.____
    A. appears to have begun his turn from the wrong lane
    B. appears to have entered the wrong lane of traffic
    C. did not blow his horn as he made the turn
    D. should have braked as he made the turn

30. What evidence is there in the report that the two vehicles collided in front, driver's side? 30.____
    A. The description of the accident
    B. There is no such evidence
    C. The type of damage to the vehicles
    D. The van driver's statement

KEY (CORRECT ANSWERS)

1.	A	11.	B	21.	A
2.	C	12.	B	22.	C
3.	D	13.	A	23.	B
4.	A	14.	B	24.	D
5.	D	15.	D	25.	D
6.	B	16.	A	26.	A
7.	C	17.	B	27.	D
8.	D	18.	A	28.	B
9.	C	19.	C	29.	B
10.	A	20.	A	30.	C

TEST 3

DIRECTIONS: Each question or incomplete statement is followed by several suggested answers or completions. Select the one that BEST answers the question or completes the statement. *PRINT THE LETTER OF THE CORRECT ANSWER IN THE SPACE AT THE RIGHT.*

Questions 1-7.

DIRECTIONS: Questions 1 through 7, inclusive, are to be answered on the basis of the following passage.

DRINKING AND DRIVING

In fatal traffic accidents, a drinking driver is involved more than 30% of the time; on holiday weekends, more than 50% of the fatal accidents involve drinking drivers. Drinking to any extent reduces the judgment, self-control, and driving ability of any driver. Social drinkers, especially those who think they drive better after a drink, are a greater menace than commonly believed, and they outnumber the obviously intoxicated. Two cocktails may reduce visual acuity as much as wearing dark glasses at night. Alcohol is not a stimulant; it is classified medically as a depressant. Coffee or other stimulants will not offset the effects of alcohol; only time can eliminate alcohol from the bloodstream. It takes at least three hours to eliminate one ounce of pure alcohol from the bloodstream.

1. Alcohol is classified by doctors as a
   A. stimulant   B. sedative   C. depressant   D. medicine

2. Social drinkers
   A. never become obviously intoxicated
   B. always drink in large groups
   C. drive better after two cocktails
   D. are a greater menace than commonly believed

3. Alcohol will BEST be eliminated from the bloodstream by
   A. fresh air   B. a stimulant   C. coffee   D. time

4. More than half of the fatal accidents on holiday weekends involve _____ drivers.
   A. inexperienced   B. drinking   C. fast   D. slow

5. Drinking to any extent does NOT
   A. impair judgment
   B. decrease visual acuity
   C. reduce accident potential
   D. affect driving ability

6. In traffic accidents resulting in death, a drinking driver is involved
   A. about one-third of the time
   B. mainly at night
   C. more than 80% of the time
   D. practically all the time on weekends

7. After taking two alcoholic drinks, it is BEST not to drive until you have   7.____
   A. had a cup of black coffee   B. waited three hours
   C. eaten a full meal   D. taken a half-hour nap

Questions 8-12.

DIRECTIONS: Questions 8 through 12 are to be answered ONLY on the basis of the information contained in the following accident report.

REPORT OF ACCIDENT

Date of Accident: Nov. 27, ____   Time: 2:20 P.M.   Date of Report: 11/28

Department Vehicle   Vehicle No. 2
Operator's Name: John Doe   Operator's Name: Richard Roe
Title: Motor Vehicle Operator   Operator's Address: 983 E. 84th St.
Vehicle Code No.: 17-129   Owner's Name: Robert Roe
License Plate No.: IN-2345   Owner's Address: 983 E. 84th St.
Damage to Vehicle: Crumpled and   License Plate No.: 9Y-8765
torn front left fender, broken left headlight,   Damage to Vehicle: Crumpled right front
front bumper bent outward on left side,   fender, broken right headlight and parking
hubcap dented badly and torn off   light, right left front side of front bumper
                                                 badly bent

Place of Accident: 71st & 3rd Ave.

DESCRIPTION OF ACCIDENT: I was driving west on 71st St. and started to turn north into 3rd Avenue since the light was still green for me. I stopped at the crosswalk because a woman was in the middle of 3rd Avenue crossing from west to east. She had just cleared my car when a Ford sedan, going north, crashed into my left front fender. The light was green on 3rd Ave. when he hit me. The woman who had crossed the avenue in front of me, and whose name I got as a witness, was standing on the corner when I got out of the car.

Persons Injured

_____   _____
_____   _____
Mrs. Mary Brown   Witness   215 E. 71 St.

                                    Report prepared by: John Doe
                                    Title: Motor Vehicle Operator
                                    Badge #17832

3 (#3)

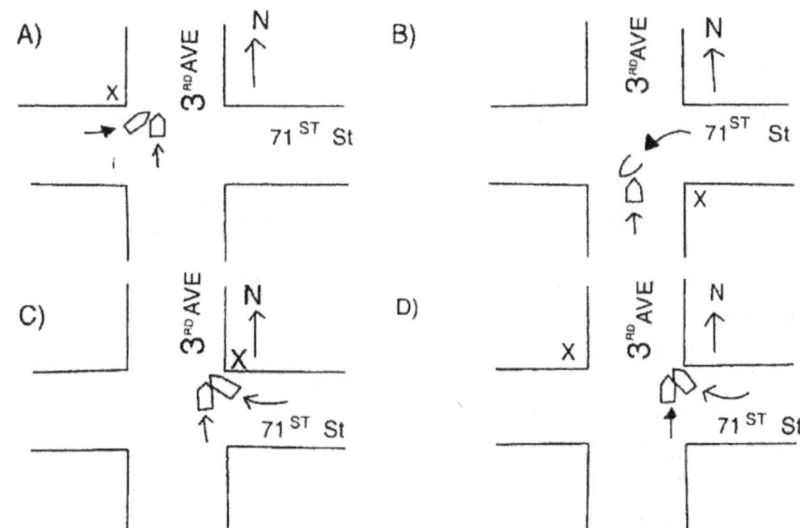

8. According to the description of the accident, the diagram that would BEST show how and where the vehicles crashed and the position of the witness (X) is
   A. A   B. B   C. C   D. D

9. The pedestrian mentioned in the description of the accident was
   A. an unknown woman   B. Mary Brown
   C. an unknown man   D. Robert Roe

10. According to the information in the report, the one of the following statements which is INCORRECT is:
    A. Both cars were moving when the accident happened
    B. One car was moving when the accident happened
    C. The Department car was headed northwest when the accident happened
    D. The traffic lights had changed just before the accident happened

11. From the description of the accident as given in the report, the accident would PROBABLY be classified as
    A. premeditated   B. calamitous   C. minor   D. fatal

12. From a reading of the accident report, it can be seen that
    A. the witness was completely unfamiliar with the neighborhood in which the accident took place
    B. the accident occurred in the early hours of the morning
    C. neither driver owned the vehicle he was driving
    D. it was raining when the accident took place

Questions 13-24.

DIRECTIONS: Questions 13 through 24 are based on the description of an automobile accident given below. Read the description carefully before answering these questions.

DESCRIPTION OF AUTOMOBILE ACCIDENT

Ten persons were injured, two critically, when a driverless auto—its accelerator jammed-up ran wild through the busy intersection at 8th Ave. and 42nd Street at 11:30 A.M. yesterday. The car struck a truck, overturned it, and mounted the sidewalk. Several persons were bowled over before the car was finally stopped by collision with a second truck. Police Officer Fred Black, Badge No. 82143, said that the freak accident occurred after the car's driver, Mrs. Mary Jones, 39, of Queens, got out of the car with her daughter, Gloria, aged 3, while the engine was still running. Mr. Herbert Field, 64, of the Bronx, a passenger in the car, accidentally stepped on the accelerator when he tried to get out. This caused the car to shoot forward because the shift was in *drive*, and 5 pedestrians were thrown to the ground.

13. This accident occurred
    A. late in the morning
    B. early in the morning
    C. early in the afternoon
    D. late in the evening

14. The number of persons who were injured, but not critically, is
    A. 2   B. 5   C. 8   D. 10

15. This accident occurred a block away from
    A. Grand Central Terminal
    B. Times Square
    C. Union Square
    D. Pennsylvania Station

16. The runaway car was finally stopped just after it
    A. mounted the sidewalk
    B. collided with a second truck
    C. crossed the intersection
    D. bowled over several persons

17. It can be inferred from the description that the driverless auto had
    A. power brakes
    B. power steering
    C. a turn indicator
    D. an automatic shift

18. The number on the police officer's badge is
    A. 82314   B. 82413   C. 82143   D. 82341

19. The first name of the driver of the car is
    A. Mary   B. Fred   C. Gloria   D. Herbert

20. According to the accident description, the adult passenger lives in
    A. the Bronx, and so does the driver
    B. Queens, and so does the driver
    C. the Bronx, and the driver in Queens
    D. Queens, and the driver in the Bronx

21. The number of pedestrians who were thrown to the ground is 21.____
 A. 2 B. 5 C. 7 D. 10

22. The person who made a statement about the runaway car was 22.____
 A. Herbert Field   B. Mary Jones
 C. Gloria Jones   D. Fred Black

23. Herbert Field is older than Mary Jones by about _____ years. 23.____
 A. 25 B. 35 C. 51 D. 61

24. The car shot forward immediately after 24.____
 A. Mrs. Jones placed the shift in *drive*
 B. Mr. Field stepped on the accelerator
 C. Mrs. Jones stepped out of the car
 D. Mr. Field got out of the car

Questions 25-28.

DIRECTIONS: Questions 25 through 28 are to be answered ONLY on the basis of the information given in the following passage.

ACCIDENT PRONESS

Accident proneness is a subject deserving much more attention than it has received. Studies have shown a high incidence of accidents to be associated with particular employees who are called accident prone. Such employees, according to these studies, behave on their jobs in ways which make them likely to have more accidents than would normally be expected.

It is important to point out the difference between the employee who is a *repeater* and the one who is truly accident prone. It is obvious that any person assigned to work about which he knows little will be liable to injury until he does learn the *how* of the job. Few workers left completely on their own will develop adequate safe practices. Therefore, they must be trained. Only those who fail to respond to proper training should be regarded as accident prone.

The dangers of an occupation should also be considered when judging an accident record. For a crane operator, a record of five accidents in a given period of time may not indicate accident proneness, while, in the case of a clerk, two accidents over the same period of time may be excessive. There are the reporters whose accident records can be explained by correctible physical defects, by correctible unsafe plant or machine conditions, or by assignment to work for which they are not suited because they cannot meet all the job's physical requirements. Such repeaters cannot be fairly called *accident prone*. A diagnosis of accident proneness should not be lightly made but should be based on all of these considerations.

25. According to the above passage, studies have shown that accident prone 25.____
 employees
 A. work under unsafe physical conditions
 B. act in unsafe ways on the job
 C. are not usually physically suited for their jobs
 D. work in the more dangerous occupations

26. According to the above passage, a person who is accident prone
    A. has received proper training which has not reduced his tendency toward accidents
    B. repeats the same accident several times over a short period of time
    C. experiences excessive anxiety about dangers in his occupation
    D. ignores unsafe but correctible machine conditions

27. According to the above passage, MOST persons who are given work they know little about
    A. will eventually learn on their own sufficient safety practices to follow
    B. work safely if they are not accident prone
    C. must be trained before they develop adequate safety methods
    D. should be regarded as accident prone until they become familiar with the job

28. According to the above passage, to effectively judge the accident record of an employee, one should consider
    A. the employee's age and physical condition
    B. that five accidents are excessive
    C. the type of dangers that are natural to his job
    D. the difficulty level of previous occupations held by the employee

Questions 29-30.

DIRECTIONS: Questions 29 and 30 are to be answered ONLY on the basis of the information given in the following passage.

When heavy rain beats on your windshield, it becomes hard for you to see ahead and even harder to see objects to the side—despite good windshield wipers. Also, the danger zone becomes longer when it is raining because the car takes longer to stop on wet streets. Remember that the danger zone of your car is the distance within which you can't stop after you have seen something on the road ahead of your car. The way to reduce the length of the danger zone of your car while driving is to reduce speed.

29. From the information in the above passage, you cannot tell if the danger zone of your car
    A. can be made smaller
    B. is greater on a rainy day
    C. is greater on cloudy days than on clear days
    D. is the distance in back of the car or in front of the car

30. According to the above passage, the danger zone of a moving car is affected by
    A. the condition of the street and the speed of the car
    B. many things which cannot be pinned down, in addition to the mechanical condition of the car
    C. the number of objects to the front and to the side
    D. visibility of the road and the reaction time of the driver

KEY (CORRECT ANSWERS)

1.	C	11.	C	21.	B
2.	D	12.	C	22.	D
3.	D	13.	A	23.	A
4.	B	14.	C	24.	B
5.	C	15.	B	25.	B
6.	A	16.	B	26.	A
7.	B	17.	D	27.	C
8.	C	18.	C	28.	C
9.	B	19.	A	29.	C
10.	A	20.	C	30.	A

CLERICAL ABILITIES TEST
EXAMINATION SECTION
TEST 1

DIRECTIONS: Each question or incomplete statement is followed by several suggested answers or completions. Select the one that BEST answers the question or completes the statement. *PRINT THE LETTER OF THE CORRECT ANSWER IN THE SPACE AT THE RIGHT.*

Questions 1-10.

DIRECTIONS: Questions 1 through 10 consist of lines of names, dates, and numbers. For each question, you are to choose the option (A, B, C, or D) in Column II which EXACTLY matches the information in Column I. *PRINT THE LETTER OF THE CORRECT ANSWER IN THE SPACE AT THE RIGHT.*

SAMPLE QUESTION

Column I
Schneider 11/16/75 581932

Column II
A. Schneider 11/16/75 518932
B. Schneider 11/16/75 581932
C. Schnieder 11/16/75 581932
D. Shnieder 11/16/75 518932

The correct answer is B. Only Option B shows the name, date, and number exactly as they are in Column I. Option A has a mistake in the number. Option C has a mistake in the name. Option D has a mistake in the name and in the number. Now answer Questions 1 through 10 in the same manner.

Column I
1. Johnston 12/26/74 659251

Column II
A. Johnson 12/23/74 659251
B. Johston 12/26/74 659251
C. Johnston 12/26/74 695251
D. Johnston 12/26/74 659251

1.____

2. Allison 1/26/75 9939256

A. Allison 1/26/75 9939256
B. Alisson 1/26/75 9939256
C. Allison 1/26/76 9399256
D. Allison 1/26/75 9993356

2.____

3. Farrell 2/12/75 361251

A. Farell 2/21/75 361251
B. Farrell 2/12/75 361251
C. Farrell 2/21/75 361251
D. Farrell 2/12/75 361151

3.____

4. Guerrero 4/28/72 105689
   A. Guererro 4/28/72 105689
   B. Guererro 4/28/72 105986
   C. Guerrero 4/28/72 105869
   D. Guerrero 4/28/72 105689

   4.____

5. McDonnell 6/05/73 478215
   A. McDonnell 6/15/73 478215
   B. McDonnell 6/05/73 478215
   C. McDonnell 6/05/73 472815
   D. MacDonell 6/05/73 478215

   5.____

6. Shepard 3/31/71 075421
   A. Sheperd 3/31/71 075421
   B. Shepard 3/13/71 075421
   C. Shepard 3/31/71 075421
   D. Shepard 3/13/71 075241

   6.____

7. Russell 4/01/69 031429
   A. Russell 4/01/69 031429
   B. Russell 4/10/69 034129
   C. Russell 4/10/69 031429
   D. Russell 4/01/69 034129

   7.____

8. Phillips 10/16/68 961042
   A. Philipps 10/16/68 961042
   B. Phillips 10/16/68 960142
   C. Phillips 10/16/68 961042
   D. Philipps 10/16/68 916042

   8.____

9. Campbell 11/21/72 624856
   A. Campbell 11/21/72 624856
   B. Campbell 11/21/72 624586
   C. Campbell 11/21/72 624686
   D. Campbel 11/21/72 624856

   9.____

10. Patterson 9/18/71 76199176
    A. Patterson 9/18/72 76191976
    B. Patterson 9/18/71 76199176
    C. Patterson 9/18/72 76199176
    D. Patterson 9/18/71 76919176

    10.____

Questions 11-15.

DIRECTIONS: Questions 11 through 15 consist of groups of numbers and letters which you are to compare. For each question, you are to choose the option (A, B, C, or D) in Column I which EXACTLY matches the group of numbers and letters given in Column I.

SAMPLE QUESTION

Column I
B92466

Column II
A. B92644
B. B94266
C. A92466
D. B92466

3 (#1)

The correct answer is D. Only Option D in Column II shows the group of numbers and letters EXACTLY as it appears in Column I. Now answer Questions 11 through 15 in the same manner.

	Column I		Column II	
11.	925AC5	A.	952CA5	11._____
		B.	925AC5	
		C.	952AC5	
		D.	925CA6	
12.	Y006925	A.	Y060925	12._____
		B.	Y006295	
		C.	Y006529	
		D.	Y006925	
13.	J236956	A.	J236956	13._____
		B.	J326965	
		C.	J239656	
		D.	J932656	
14.	AB6952	A.	AB6952	14._____
		B.	AB9625	
		C.	AB9652	
		D.	AB6925	
15.	X259361	A.	X529361	15._____
		B.	X259631	
		C.	X523961	
		D.	X259361	

Questions 16-25.

DIRECTIONS: Each of questions 16 through 25 consists of three lines of code letters and three lines of numbers. The numbers on each line should correspond with the code letters on the same line in accordance with the table below.

Code Letter	S	V	W	A	Q	M	X	E	G	K
Corresponding Number	0	1	2	3	4	5	5	7	8	9

On some of the lines, an error exists in the coding. Compare the letters and numbers in each question carefully. If you find an error or errors on:
    only one of the lines in the question, mark your answer A;
    any two lines in the question, mark your answer B;
    all three lines in the question, mark your answer C;
    none of the lines in the question, mark your answer D.

4 (#1)

SAMPLE QUESTION

WQGKSXG	2489068
XEKVQMA	6591453
KMAESXV	9527061

In the above sample, the first line is correct since each code letter listed has the correct corresponding number. On the second line, an error exists because code letter E should have the number 7 instead of the number 5. On the third line, an error exists because the code letter A should have the number 3 instead of the number 2. Since there are errors in two of the three lines, the correct answer is B. Now answer Questions 16 through 25 in the same manner.

16. SWQEKGA   0247983   16.____
     KEAVSXM   9731065
     SSAXGKQ   0036894

17. QAMKMVS   4259510   17.____
     MGGEASX   5897306
     KSWMKWS   9125920

18. WKXQWVE   2964217   18.____
     QKXXQVA   4966413
     AWMXGVS   3253810

19. GMMKASE   8559307   19.____
     AWVSKSW   3210902
     QAVSVGK   4310189

20. XGKQSMK   6894049   20.____
     QSVKEAS   4019730
     GSMXKMV   8057951

21. AEKMWSG   3195208   21.____
     MKQSVQK   5940149
     XGQAEVW   6843712

22. XGMKAVS   6858310   22.____
     SKMAWEQ   0953174
     GVMEQSA   8167403

23. VQSKAVE   1489317   23.____
     WQGKAEM   2489375
     MEGKAWQ   5689324

24. XMQVSKG   6541098   24.____
     QMEKEWS   4579720
     KMEVGKG   9571983

102

5 (#1)

25. GKVAMEW   88912572   25.____
    AXMVKAE   3651937
    KWAGMAV   9238531

Questions 26-35.

DIRECTIONS: Each of Questions 26 through 35 consists of a column of figures. For each question, add the column of figures and choose the correct answer from the four choices given.

26. 5,665.43   26.____
     2,356.69
     6,447.24
     7,239.65

     A. 20,698.01   B. 21,709.01
     C. 21,718.01   D. 22,609.01

27. 817,209.55   27.____
     264,354.29
      82,368.76
     849,964.89

     A. 1,893.977.49   B. 1,989,988.39
     C. 2,009,077.39   D. 2,013,897.49

28. 156,366.89   28.____
     249,973.23
     823,229.49
      56,869.45

     A. 1,286,439.06   B. 1,287,521.06
     C. 1,297,539.06   D. 1,296,421.06

29.   23,422.15   29.____
     149,696.24
     238,377.53
      86,289.79
     505,533.63

     A. 989,229.34   B. 999,879.34
     C. 1,003,330.34   D. 1,023,329.34

103

30. 2,468,926.70
　　　656,842.28
　　　　49,723.15
　　　832,369.59

　　A. 3,218,062.72　　　　　B. 3,808,092.72
　　C. 4,007,861.72　　　　　D. 4,818,192.72

31. 　　524,201.52
　　7,775,678.51
　　8,345,299.63
　　40,628,898.08
　　31,374,670.07

　　A. 88,646,647.81　　　　B. 88,646,747.91
　　C. 88,648,647.91　　　　D. 88,648,747.81

32. 6,824,829.40
　　　682,482.94
　　5,542,015.27
　　　775,678.51
　　7,732,507.25

　　A. 21,557,513.37　　　　B. 21,567,513.37
　　C. 22,567,503.37　　　　D. 22,567,513.37

33. 22,109,405.58
　　6,097,093.43
　　5,050,073.99
　　8,118,050.05
　　4,313,980.82

　　A. 45,688,593.87　　　　B. 45,688,603.87
　　C. 45,689,593.87　　　　D. 45,689,603.87

34. 79,324,114.19
　　99,848,129.74
　　43,331,653.31
　　41,610,207.14

　　A. 264,114,104.38　　　　B. 264,114,114.38
　　C. 265,114,114.38　　　　D. 265,214,104.38

30.____

31.____

32.____

33.____

34.____

35. 33,729,653.94
    5,959,342.58
    26,052,715.47
    4,452,669.52
    7,079,953.59

    A. 76,374,334.10   B. 76,375,334.10
    C. 77,274,335.10   D. 77,275,335.10

35._____

Questions 36-40.

DIRECTIONS: Each of Questions 36 through 40 consists of a single number in Column I and four options in Column II. For each question, you are to choose the option (A, B, C, or D) in Column II which EXACTLY matches the number in Column I.

SAMPLE QUESTION

Column I   Column II
5965121   A. 5956121
                B. 5965121
                C. 5966121
                D. 5965211

The correct answer is B. Only Option B shows the number EXACTLY as it appears in Column I. Now answer Questions 36 through 40 in the same manner.

Column I   Column II
36. 9643242   A. 9643242   36._____
                              B. 9462342
                              C. 9642442
                              D. 9463242

37. 3572477   A. 3752477   37._____
                              B. 3725477
                              C. 3572477
                              D. 3574277

38. 5276101   A. 5267101   38._____
                              B. 5726011
                              C. 5271601
                              D. 5276101

39. 4469329   A. 4496329   39._____
                              B. 4469329
                              C. 4496239
                              D. 4469239

40. 2326308   A. 2236308
              B. 2233608
              C. 2326308
              D. 2323608

40.____

KEY (CORRECT ANSWERS)

1.	D	11.	B	21.	A	31.	D
2.	A	12.	D	22.	C	32.	A
3.	B	13.	A	23.	B	33.	B
4.	D	14.	A	24.	D	34.	A
5.	B	15.	D	25.	A	35.	C
6.	C	16.	D	26.	B	36.	A
7.	A	17.	C	27.	D	37.	C
8.	C	18.	A	28.	A	38.	D
9.	A	19.	D	29.	C	39.	B
10.	B	20.	B	30.	C	40.	C

TEST 2

DIRECTIONS: Each question or incomplete statement is followed by several suggested answers or completions. Select the one that BEST answers the question or completes the statement. *PRINT THE LETTER OF THE CORRECT ANSWER IN THE SPACE AT THE RIGHT.*

Questions 1-5.

DIRECTIONS: Each of Questions 1 through 5 consists of a name and a dollar amount. In each question, the name and dollar amount in Column II should be an EXACT copy of the name and dollar amount in Column I. If there is:
    a mistake only in the name, mark your answer A;
    a mistake only in the dollar amount, mark your answer B;
    a mistake in both the name and the dollar amount, mark your answer C;
    no mistake in either the name or the dollar amount, mark your answer D.

SAMPLE QUESTION

Column I	Column II
George Peterson	George Petersson
$125.50	$125.50

Compare the name and dollar amount in Column II with the name and dollar amount in Column I. The name *Petersson* in Column II is spelled *Peterson* in Column I. The amount is the same in both columns. Since there is a mistake only in the name, the answer to the sample question is A. Now answer Questions 1 through 5 in the same manner.

	Column I	Column II	
1.	Susanne Shultz $3440	Susanne Schultz $3440	1.____
2.	Anibal P. Contrucci $2121.61	Anibel P. Contrucci $2112.61	2.____
3.	Eugenio Mendoza $12.45	Eugenio Mendozza $12.45	3.____
4.	Maurice Gluckstadt $4297	Maurice Gluckstadt $4297	4.____
5.	John Pampellonne $4656.94	John Pammpellonne $4566.94	5.____

Questions 6-11.

DIRECTIONS: Each of Questions 6 through 11 consist of a set of names and addresses, which you are to compare. In each question, the name and addresses in Column II should be an EXACT copy of the name and address in Column I. If there is:
- a mistake only in the name, mark your answer A;
- a mistake only in the address, mark your answer B;
- a mistake in both the name and address, mark your answer C;
- no mistake in either the name or address, mark your answer D.

SAMPLE QUESTION

Column I
Michael Filbert
456 Reade Street
New York, N.Y. 10013

Column II
Michael Filbert
645 Reade Street
New York, N.Y. 10013

Since there is a mistake only in the address (the street number should be 456 instead of 645), the answer to the sample question is B. Now answer Questions 6 through 11 in the same manner.

	Column I	Column II	
6.	Hilda Goettelmann 55 Lenox Rd. Brooklyn, N.Y. 11226	Hilda Goettelman 55 Lenox Ave. Brooklyn, N.Y. 11226	6.____
7.	Arthur Sherman 2522 Batchelder St. Brooklyn, N.Y. 11235	Arthur Sharman 2522 Batcheder St. Brooklyn, N.Y. 11253	7.____
8.	Ralph Barnett 300 West 28 Street New York, New York 10001	Ralph Barnett 300 West 28 Street New York, New York 10001	8.____
9.	George Goodwin 135 Palmer Avenue Staten Island, New York 10302	George Godwin 135 Palmer Avenue Staten Island, New York 10302	9.____
10.	Alonso Ramirez 232 West 79 Street New York, N.Y. 10024	Alonso Ramirez 223 West 79 Street New York, N.Y. 10024	10.____
11.	Cynthia Graham 149-34 83 Street Howard Beach, N.Y. 11414	Cynthia Graham 149-35 83 Street Howard Beach, N.Y. 11414	11.____

Questions 12-20.

DIRECTIONS: Questions 12 through 20 are problems in subtraction. For each question do the subtraction and select your answer from the four choices given.

12. 232,921.85
    -179,587.68

    A. 52,433.17   B. 52,434.17
    C. 53,334.17   D. 53,343,17

    12.____

13. 5,531,876.29
    -3,897,158.36

    A. 1,634,717.93   B. 1,644,718.93
    C. 1,734,717.93   D. 1,7234,718.93

    13.____

14. 1,482,658.22
    -937,925.76

    A. 544,633.46   B. 544,732.46
    C. 545,632.46   D. 545,732.46

    14.____

15. 937,828.17
    -259,673.88

    A. 678,154.29   B. 679,154.29
    C. 688,155.39   D. 699,155.39

    15.____

16. 760,412.38
    -263,465.95

    A. 496,046.43   B. 496,946.43
    C. 496,956.43   D. 497,046.43

    16.____

17. 3,203,902.26
    -2,933,087.96

    A. 260,814.30   B. 269,824.30
    C. 270,814.30   D. 270,824.30

    17.____

18. 1,023,468.71
    -934,678.88

    A. 88,780.83   B. 88,789.83
    C. 88,880.83   D. 88,889.83

    18.____

19. 831,549.47
     -772,814.78

   A. 58,734.69   B. 58,834.69
   C. 59,735.69   D. 59,834.69

20. 6,306,181.74
     -3,617,376.99

   A. 2,687,904.99   B. 2,688,904.99
   C. 2,689,804.99   D. 2,799,905.99

Questions 21-30.

DIRECTIONS: Each of Questions 21 through 30 consists of three lines of code letters and three lines of numbers. The numbers on each line should correspond with the code letters on the same line in accordance with the table below.

Code Letter	J	U	B	T	Y	D	K	R	L	P
Corresponding Number	0	1	2	3	4	5	5	7	8	9

On some of the lines, an error exists in the coding. Compare the letters and numbers in each question carefully. If you find an error or errors on:
  only *one* of the lines in the question, mark your answer A;
  any *two* lines in the question, mark your answer B;
  all *three* lines in the question, mark your answer C;
  none of the lines in the question, mark your answer D.

SAMPLE QUESTION

BJRPYUR   2079417
DTBPYKJ   5328460
YKLDBLT   4685283

In the above sample, the first line is correct since each code letter listed has the correct corresponding number. On the second line, an error exists because code letter P should have the number 9 instead of the number 8. The third line is correct since each code letter listed has the correct corresponding number. Since there is an error in *one* of the three lines, the correct answer is A. Now answer Questions 21 through 30 in the same manner.

21. BYPDTJL   2495308
    PLRDTJU   9815301
    DTJRYLK   5207486

22. RPBYRJK   7934706
    PKTYLBU   9624821
    KDLPJYR   6489047

5 (#2)

23.	TPYBUJR	3942107	23.____
	BYRKPTU	2476931	
	DUKPYDL	5169458	
24.	KBYDLPL	6345898	24.____
	BLRKBRU	2876261	
	JTULDYB	0318542	
25.	LDPYDKR	8594567	25.____
	BDKDRJL	2565708	
	BDRPLUJ	2679810	
26.	PLRLBPU	9858291	26.____
	LPYKRDJ	88936750	
	TDKPDTR	3569527	
27.	RKURPBY	7617924	27.____
	RYUKPTJ	7426930	
	RTKPTJD	7369305	
28.	DYKPBJT	5469203	28.____
	KLPJBTL	6890238	
	TKPLBJP	3698209	
29.	BTPRJYL	2397148	29.____
	LDKUTYR	8561347	
	YDBLRPJ	4528190	
30.	ULPBKYT	1892643	30.____
	KPDTRBJ	6953720	
	YLKJPTB	4860932	

KEY (CORRECT ANSWERS)

1.	A	11.	D	21.	B
2.	C	12.	C	22.	C
3.	A	13.	A	23.	D
4.	D	14.	B	24.	B
5.	C	15.	A	25.	A
6.	C	16.	B	26.	C
7.	C	17.	C	27.	A
8.	D	18.	B	28.	D
9.	A	19.	A	29.	B
10.	B	20.	B	30.	D

CLERICAL ABILITIES
EXAMINATION SECTION
TEST 1

DIRECTIONS: Each question or incomplete statement is followed by several suggested answers or completions. Select the one that BEST answers the question or completes the statement. *PRINT THE LETTER OF THE CORRECT ANSWER IN THE SPACE AT THE RIGHT.*

Questions 1-4.

DIRECTIONS: Questions 1 through 4 are to be answered on the basis of the information given below.

The most commonly used filing system and the one that is easiest to learn is alphabetical filing. This involves putting records in an A to Z order, according to the letters of the alphabet. The name of a person is filed by using the following order: first, the surname or last name; second, the first name; third, the middle name or middle initial. For example, *Henry C. Young* is filed under *Y* and thereafter under *Young, Henry C.* The name of a company is filed in the same way. For example, *Long Cabinet Co.* is filed under *L* while *John T. Long Cabinet Co.* is filed under *L* and thereafter under *Long, John T. Cabinet Co.*

1. The one of the following which lists the names of persons in the CORRECT alphabetical order is:
    A. Mary Carrie, Helen Carrol, James Carson, John Carter
    B. James Carson, Mary Carrie, John Carter, Helen Carrol
    C. Helen Carrol, James Carson, John Carter, Mary Carrie
    D. John Carter, Helen Carrol, Mary Carrie, James Carson

1.____

2. The one of the following which lists the names of persons in the CORRECT alphabetical order is:
    A. Jones, John C.; Jones, John A.; Jones, John P.; Jones, John K.
    B. Jones, John P.; Jones, John K.; Jones, John C.; Jones, John A.
    C. Jones, John A.; Jones, John C.; Jones, John K.; Jones, John P.
    D. Jones, John K.; Jones, John C.; Jones, John A.; Jones, John P.

2.____

3. The one of the following which lists the names of the companies in the CORRECT alphabetical order is:
    A. Blane Co., Blake Co., Block Co., Blear Co.
    B. Blake Co., Blane Co., Blear Co., Block Co.
    C. Block Co., Blear Co., Blane Co., Blake Co.
    D. Blear Co., Blake Co., Blane Co., Block Co.

3.____

4. You are to return to the file an index card on *Barry C. Wayne Materials and Supplies Co.*
   Of the following, the CORRECT alphabetical group that you should return the index card to is
   A. A to G B. H to M C. N to S D. T to Z

Questions 5-10.

DIRECTIONS: In each of Questions 5 through 10, the names of four people are given. For each question, choose as your answer the one of the four names given which should be filed FIRST according to the usual system of alphabetical filing of names, as described in the following paragraph.

In filing names, you must start with the last name. Names are filed in order of the first letter of the last name, then the second letter, etc. Therefore, BAILY would be filed before BROWN, which would be filed before COLT. A name with fewer letters of the same type comes first, i.e., Smith before Smithe. If the last names are the same, the names are filed alphabetically by the first name. If the first name is an initial, a name with an initial would come before a first name that starts with the same letter as the initial. Therefore, I. BROWN would come before IRA BROWN. Finally, if both last name and first name are the same, the name would be filed alphabetically by the middle name, once again an initial coming before a middle name which starts with the same letter as the initial. If there is no middle name at all, the name would come before those with middle initials or names.

SAMPLE QUESTION:
A. Lester Daniels
B. William Dancer
C. Nathan Danzig
D. Dan Lester

The last names beginning with D are filed before the last name beginning with L. Since DANIELS, DANCER, and DANZIG all begin with the same three letters, you must look at the fourth letter of the last name to determine which name should be filed first. C comes before I or Z in the alphabet, so DANCER is filed before DANIELS or DANZIG. Therefore, the answer to the above sample question is B.

5. A. Scott Biala
   B. Mary Byala
   C. Martin Baylor
   D. Francis Bauer

6. A. Howard J. Black
   B. Howard Black
   C. J. Howard Black
   D. John H. Black

7. A. Theodora Garth Kingston
   B. Theadore Barth Kingston
   C. Thomas Kingston
   D. Thomas T. Kingston

8. A. Paulette Mary Huerta
    B. Paul M. Huerta
    C. Paulette L. Huerta
    D. Peter A. Huerta

9. A. Martha Hunt Morgan
    B. Martin Hunt Morgan
    C. Mary H. Morgan
    D. Martine H. Morgan

10. A. James T. Meerschaum
    B. James M. Mershum
    C. James F. Mearshaum
    D. James N. Meshum

Questions 11-14.

DIRECTIONS: Questions 11 through 14 are to be answered SOLELY on the basis of the following information.

You are required to file various documents in file drawers which are labeled according to the following pattern:

DOCUMENTS

MEMOS		LETTERS	
File	Subject	File	Subject
84PM1	(A-L)	84PC1	(A-L)
84PM2	(M-Z)	84PC2	(M-Z)

REPORTS		INQUIRIES	
File	Subject	File	Subject
84PR1	(A-L)	84PQ1	(A-L)
84PR2	(M-Z)	84PQ2	(M-Z)

11. A letter dealing with a burglary should be filed in the drawer labeled
    A. 84PM1   B. 84PC1   C. 84PR1   D. 84PQ2

12. A report on Statistics should be found in the drawer labeled
    A. 84PM1   B. 84PC2   C. 84PR2   D. 84PQS

13. An inquiry is received about parade permit procedures. It should be filed in the drawer labeled
    A. 84PM2   B. 84PC1   C. 84PR1   D. 84PQ2

14. A police officer has a question about a robbery report you filed. You should pull this file from the drawer labeled
    A. 84PM1   B. 84PM2   C. 84PR1   D. 84PR2

Questions 15-22.

DIRECTIONS: Each of Questions 15 through 22 consists of four or six numbered names. For each question, choose the option (A, B, C, or D) which indicates the order in which the names should be filed in accordance with the following filing instructions:
- File alphabetically according to last name, then first name, then middle initial.
- File according to each successive letter within a name.
- When comparing two names in which the letters in the longer name are identical to the corresponding letters in the shorter name, the shorter name is filed first.
- When the last names are the same, initials are always filed before names beginning with the same letter.

15. I. Ralph Robinson
    II. Alfred Ross
    III. Luis Robles
    IV. James Roberts

The CORRECT filing sequence for the above names should be
A. IV, II, I, III   B. I, IV, III, II   C. III, IV, I, II   D. IV, I, III, II

16. I. Irwin Goodwin
    II. Inez Gonzalez
    III. Irene Goodman
    IV. Ira S. Goodwin
    V. Ruth I. Goldstein
    VI. M.B. Goodman

The CORRECT filing sequence for the above names should be
A. V, II, I, IV, III, VI   B. V, II, VI, III, IV, I
C. V, II, III, VI, IV, I   D. V, II, III, VI, I, IV

17. I. George Allan
    II. Gregory Allen
    III. Gary Allen
    IV. George Allen

The CORRECT filing sequence for the above names should be
A. IV, III, I, II   B. I, IV, II, III   C. III, IV, I, II   D. I, III, IV, II

18.
   I. Simon Kauffman
   II. Leo Kaufman
   III. Robert Kaufmann
   IV. Paul Kauffmann

   The CORRECT filing sequence for the above names should be
   A. I, IV, II, III   B. II, IV, III, I   C. III, II, IV, I   D. I, II, III, IV

   18.____

19.
   I. Roberta Williams
   II. Robin Wilson
   III. Roberta Wilson
   IV. Robin Williams

   The CORRECT filing sequence for the above names should be
   A. III, II, IV, I   B. I, IV, III, II   C. I, II, III, IV   D. III, I, II, IV

   19.____

20.
   I. Lawrence Shultz
   II. Albert Schultz
   III. Theodore Schwartz
   IV. Thomas Schwarz
   V. Alvin Schultz
   VI. Leonard Shultz

   The CORRECT filing sequence for the above names should be
   A. II, V, III, IV, I, VI
   B. IV, III, V, I, II, VI
   C. II, V, I, VI, III, IV
   D. I, VI, II, V, III, IV

   20.____

21.
   I. McArdle
   II. Mayer
   III. Maletz
   IV. McNiff
   V. Meyer
   VI. MacMahon

   The CORRECT filing sequence for the above names should be
   A. I, IV, VI, III, II, V
   B. II, I, IV, VI, III, V
   C. VI, III, II, I, IV, V
   D. VI, III, II, V, I, IV

   21.____

22.
   I. Jack E. Johnson
   II. R.H. Jackson
   III. Bertha Jackson
   IV. J.T. Johnson
   V. Ann Johns
   VI. John Jacobs

   The CORRECT filing sequence for the above names should be
   A. II, III, VI, V, IV, I
   B. III, II, VI, V, IV, I
   C. VI, II, III, I, V, IV
   D. III, II, VI, IV, V, I

   22.____

Questions 23-30.

DIRECTIONS: The code table below shows 10 letters with matching numbers. For each question, there are three sets of letters. Each set of letters is followed by a set of numbers which may or may not match their correct letter according to the code table. For each question, check all three sets of letters and numbers and mark your answer:
   A. if no pairs are correctly matched
   B. if only one pair is correctly matched
   C. if only two pairs are correctly matched
   D. if all three pairs are correctly matched

CODE TABLE

T	M	V	D	S	P	R	G	B	H
1	2	3	4	5	6	7	8	9	0

SAMPLE QUESTION: TMVDSP – 123456
RGBHTM – 789011
DSPRGB – 256789

In the sample question above, the first set of numbers correctly match its set of letters. But the second and third pairs contain mistakes. In the second pair, M is correctly matched with number 1. According to the code table, letter M should be correctly matched with number 2. In the third pair, the letter D is incorrectly matched with number 2. According to the code table, letter D should be correctly matched with number 4. Since only one of the pairs is correctly matched, the answer to this sample question is B.

23. RSBMRM – 759262
    GDSRVH – 845730
    VDBRTM - 349713

24. TGVSDR – 183247
    SMHRDP – 520647
    TRMHSR - 172057

25. DSPRGM – 456782
    MVDBHT – 234902
    HPMDBT - 062491

26. BVPTRD – 936184
    GDPHMB – 807029
    GMRHMV - 827032

27. MGVRSH – 283750
    TRDMBS – 174295
    SPRMGV - 567283

23.____

24.____

25.____

26.____

27.____

28. SGBSDM – 489542
    MGHPTM – 290612
    MPBMHT - 269301

    28.____

29. TDPBHM – 146902
    VPBMRS – 369275
    GDMBHM - 842902

    29.____

30. MVPTBV – 236194
    PDRTMB – 47128
    BGTMSM - 981232

    30.____

KEY (CORRECT ANSWERS)

1.	A	11.	B	21.	C		
2.	C	12.	C	22.	B		
3.	B	13.	D	23.	B		
4.	D	14.	D	24.	B		
5.	D	15.	D	25.	C		
6.	B	16.	C	26.	A		
7.	B	17.	D	27.	D		
8.	B	18.	A	28.	A		
9.	A	19.	B	29.	D		
10.	C	20.	A	30.	A		

TEST 2

DIRECTIONS: Each question or incomplete statement is followed by several suggested answers or completions. Select the one that BEST answers the question or completes the statement. *PRINT THE LETTER OF THE CORRECT ANSWER IN THE SPACE AT THE RIGHT.*

Questions 1-10.

DIRECTIONS: Questions 1 through 10 each consists of two columns, each containing four lines of names, numbers and/or addresses. For each question, compare the lines in Column I with the lines in Column II to see if they match exactly, and mark your answer A, B, C, or D, according to the following instructions:
- A. all four lines match exactly
- B. only three lines match exactly
- C. only two lines match exactly
- D. only one line matches exactly

	COLUMN I	COLUMN II	
1.	I. Earl Hodgson II. 1409870 III. Shore Ave. IV. Macon Rd.	Earl Hodgson 1408970 Schore Ave. Macon Rd.	1.____
2.	I. 9671485 II. 470 Astor Court III. Halprin, Phillip IV. Frank D. Poliseo	9671485 470 Astor Court Halperin, Phillip Frank D. Poliseo	2.____
3.	I. Tandem Associates II. 144-17 Northern Blvd. III. Alberta Forchi IV. Kings Park, NY 10751	Tandom Associates 144-17 Northern Blvd. Albert Forchi Kings Point, NY 10751	3.____
4.	I. Bertha C. McCormack II. Clayton, MO III. 976-4242 IV. New City, NY 10951	Bertha C. McCormack Clayton, MO 976-4242 New City, NY 10951	4.____
5.	I. George C. Morill II. Columbia, SC 29201 III. Louis Ingham IV. 3406 Forest Ave.	George C. Morrill Columbia, SD 29201 Louis Ingham 3406 Forest Ave.	5.____
6.	I. 506 S. Elliott Pl. II. Herbert Hall III. 4712 Rockaway Pkway IV. 169 E. 7 St.	506 S. Elliott Pl. Hurbert Hall 4712 Rockaway Pkway 169 E. 7 St.	6.____

2 (#2)

7.
   I. 345 Park Ave. 345 Park Pl. 7.____
   II. Colman Oven Corp. Coleman Oven Corp.
   III. Robert Conte Robert Conti
   IV. 6179846 6179846

8.
   I. Grigori Schierber Grigori Schierber 8.____
   II. Des Moines, Iowa Des Moines, Iowa
   III. Gouverneur Hospital Gouverneur Hospital
   IV. 91-35 Cresskill Pl. 91-35 Cresskill Pl.

9.
   I. Jeffery Janssen Jeffrey Janssen 9.____
   II. 8041071 8041071
   III. 40 Rockefeller Plaza 40 Rockafeller Plaza
   IV. 407 6 St. 406 7 St.

10.
    I. 5971996 5871996 10.____
    II. 3113 Knickerbocker Ave. 31123 Knickerbocker Ave.
    III. 8434 Boston Post Rd. 8424 Boston Post Rd.
    IV. Penn Station Penn Station

Questions 11-14.

DIRECTIONS: Questions 11 through 14 are to be answered by looking at the four groups of names and addresses listed below (I, II, III, and IV), and then finding out the number of groups that have their corresponding numbered lies exactly the same.

GROUP I   GROUP II
Line 1. Richmond General Hospital   Richman General Hospital
Line 2. Geriatric Clinic   Geriatric Clinic
Line 3. 3975 Paerdegat St.   3975 Peardegat St.
Line 4. Loudonville, New York 11538   Londonville, New York 11538

GROUP III   GROUP IV
Line 1. Richmond General Hospital   Richmend General Hospital
Line 2. Geriatric Clinic   Geriatric Clinic
Line 3. 3795 Paerdegat St.   3975 Paerdegat St.
Line 4. Loudonville, New York 11358   Loudonville, New York 11538

1. In how many groups is line one exactly the same? 11.____
   A. Two   B. Three   C. Four   D. None

12. In how many groups is line two exactly the same? 12.____
    A. Two   B. Three   C. Four   D. None

13. In how many groups is line three exactly the same? 13.____
    A. Two   B. Three   C. Four   D. None

14. In how many groups is line four exactly the same? 14.____
    A. Two   B. Three   C. Four   D. None

Questions 15-18.

DIRECTIONS: Each of Questions 15 through 18 has two lists of names and addresses. Each list contains three sets of names and addresses. Check each of the three sets in the list on the right to see if they are the same as the corresponding set in the list on the left. Mark your answers:
    A. if none of the sets in the right list are the same as those in the left list
    B. if only one of the sets in the right list is the same as those in the left list
    C. if only two of the sets in the right list are the same as those in the left list
    D. if all three sets in the right list are the same as those in the left list

15. Mary T. Berlinger   Mary T. Berlinger   15.____
    2351 Hampton St.   2351 Hampton St.
    Monsey, N.Y. 20117   Monsey, N.Y. 20117

    Eduardo Benes   Eduardo Benes
    483 Kingston Avenue   473 Kingston Avenue
    Central Islip, N.Y. 11734   Central Islip, N.Y. 11734

    Alan Carrington Fuchs   Alan Carrington Fuchs
    17 Gnarled Hollow Road   17 Gnarled Hollow Road
    Los Angeles, CA 91635   Los Angeles, CA 91685

16. David John Jacobson   David John Jacobson   16.____
    178 34 St. Apt. 4C   178 53 St. Apt. 4C
    New York, N.Y. 00927   New York, N.Y. 00927

    Ann-Marie Calonella   Ann-Marie Calonella
    7243 South Ridge Blvd.   7243 South Ridge Blvd.
    Bakersfield, CA 96714   Bakersfield, CA 96714

    Pauline M. Thompson   Pauline M. Thomson
    872 Linden Ave.   872 Linden Ave.
    Houston, Texas 70321   Houston, Texas 70321

17. Chester LeRoy Masterton   Chester LeRoy Masterson   17.____
    152 Lacy Rd.   152 Lacy Rd.
    Kankakee, Ill. 54532   Kankakee, Ill. 54532

    William Maloney   William Maloney
    S. LaCrosse Pla.   S. LaCross Pla.
    Wausau, Wisconsin 52136 Wausau, Wisconsin 52146

    Cynthia V. Barnes   Cynthia V. Barnes
    16 Pines Rd.   16 Pines Rd.
    Greenpoint, Miss. 20376   Greenpoint,, Miss. 20376

4 (#2)

18. Marcel Jean Frontenac
8 Burton On The Water
Calender, Me. 01471

J. Scott Marsden
174 S. Tipton St.
Cleveland, Ohio

Lawrence T. Haney
171 McDonough St.
Decatur, Ga. 31304

Marcel Jean Frontenac
6 Burton On The Water
Calender, Me. 01471

J. Scott Marsden
174 Tipton St.
Cleveland, Ohio

Lawrence T. Haney
171 McDonough St.
Decatur, Ga. 31304

18.____

Questions 19-26.

DIRECTIONS: Each of Questions 19 through 26 has two lists of numbers. Each list contains three sets of numbers. Check each of the three sets in the list on the right to see if they are the same as the corresponding set in the list on the left. Mark your answers:
- A. if none of the sets in the right list are the same as those in the left list
- B. if only one of the sets in the right list is the same as those in the left list
- C. if only two of the sets in the right list are the same as those in the left list
- D. if all three sets in the right list are the same as those in the left lists

19. 7354183476
4474747744
5791430231

7354983476
4474747774
57914302311

19.____

20. 7143592185
8344517699
9178531263

7143892185
8344518699
9178531263

20.____

21. 2572114731
8806835476
8255831246

257214731
8806835476
8255831246

21.____

22. 331476853821
6976658532996
3766042113715

331476858621
6976655832996
3766042113745

22.____

23. 8806663315
74477138449
211756663666

88066633115
74477138449
211756663666

23.____

123

24. 990006966996   99000696996   24.____
     53022219743   53022219843
     4171171117717   4171171177717

25. 24400222433004   24400222433004   25.____
     5300030055000355   5300030055500355
     20000075532002022   20000075532002022

26. 6111666406600001116   61116664066001116   26.____
     7111300117001100733   7111300117001100733
     26666446664476518   26666446664476518

Questions 27-30.

DIRECTIONS: Questions 27 through 30 are to be answered by picking the answer which is in the correct numerical order, from the lowest number to the highest number, in each question.

27. A. 44533, 44518, 44516, 44547   27.____
    B. 44516, 44518, 44533, 44547
    C. 44547, 44533, 44518, 44516
    D. 44518, 44516, 44547, 44533

28. A. 95587, 95593, 95601, 95620   28.____
    B. 95601, 95620, 95587, 95593
    C. 95593, 95587, 95601. 95620
    D. 95620, 95601, 95593, 95587

29. A. 232212, 232208, 232232, 232223   29.____
    B. 232208, 232223, 232212, 232232
    C. 232208, 232212, 232223, 232232
    D. 232223, 232232, 232208, 232208

30. A. 113419, 113521, 113462, 113462   30.____
    B. 113588, 113462, 113521, 113419
    C. 113521, 113588, 113419, 113462
    D. 113419, 113462, 113521, 113588

KEY (CORRECT ANSWERS)

1.	C	11.	A	21.	C
2.	B	12.	C	22.	A
3.	D	13.	A	23.	D
4.	A	14.	A	24.	A
5.	C	15.	C	25.	C
6.	B	16.	B	26.	C
7.	D	17.	B	27.	B
8.	A	18.	B	28.	A
9.	D	19.	B	29.	C
10.	C	20.	B	30.	D

CODING

EXAMINATION SECTION

TEST 1

COMMENTARY

An ingenious question-type called coding, involving elements of alphabetizing, filing, name and number comparison, and evaluative judgment and application, has currently won wide acceptance in testing circles for measuring clerical aptitude and general ability, particularly on the senior (middle) grades (levels).

While the directions for this question-type usually vary in detail, the candidate is generally asked to consider groups of names, codes, and numbers, and, then, according to a given plan, to arrange codes in alphabetic order; to arrange these in numerical sequence; to rearrange columns of names and numbers in correct order; to espy errors in coding; to choose the correct coding arrangement in consonance with the given directions and examples, etc.

This question-type appears to have few parameters in respect to form, substance, or degree of difficulty.

Accordingly, acquaintance with, and practice in the coding question is recommended for the serious candidate.

DIRECTIONS: Column I consists of serial numbers of dollar bills. Column II shows different ways of arranging the corresponding serial numbers.
The serial numbers of dollar bills in Column I begin and end with a capital letter and have an eight-digit number in between. The serial numbers in Column I are to be arranged according to the following rules:
First: In alphabetical order according to the first letter.
Second: When two or more serial numbers have the same first letter, in alphabetical order according to the last letter.
Third: When two or more serial numbers have the same first and last letters, in numerical order, beginning with the lowest number.

The serial numbers in Column I are numbered (1) through (5) in the order in which they are listed. In Column II, the numbers (1) through (5) are arranged in four different ways to show different arrangements of the corresponding serial numbers. Choose the answer in Column II in which the serial numbers are arranged according to the above rules.

Column I	Column II
1. E75044127B	A. 4, 1, 3, 2, 5
2. B96399104A	B. 4, 1, 2, 3, 5
3. B93939086A	C. 4, 3, 2, 5, 1
4. B47064465H	D. 3, 2, 5, 4, 1

In the simple question, the four serial numbers starting with B should be put before the serial number starting with E. The serial numbers starting with B and ending with A should be put before the serial number starting with B and ending with H. The three serial numbers starting with B and ending with A should be listed in numerical order, beginning with the lowest

2 (#1)

number. The correct way to arrange the serial numbers, therefore, is:
3. B93939086A
2. B96399104A
5. B99040922A
4. B47064465H
1. E75044127B

Since the order of arrangement is 3, 2, 5, 4, 1, the answer to the sample question is D.

	Column I	Column II	
1.	1. D89143888P 2. D98143838B 3. D89113883B 4. D89148338P 5. D89148388B	A. 3, 5, 2, 1, 4 B. 3, 1, 4, 5, 2 C. 4, 2, 3, 1, 5 D. 4, 1, 3, 5, 2	1._____
2.	1. W62455590E 2. W62455090F 3. W62405099E 4. V62455097F 5. V62405979E	A. 2, 4, 3, 1, 5 B. 3, 1, 5, 2, 4 C. 5, 3, 1, 4, 2 D. 5, 4, 3, 1, 2	2._____
3.	1. N74663826M 2. M74633286M 3. N76633228N 4. M76483686N 5. M74636688M	A. 2, 4, 5, 3, 1 B. 2, 5, 4, 1, 3 C. 1, 2, 5, 3, 4 D. 2, 5, 1, 4, 3	3._____
4.	1. P97560324B 2. R97663024B 3. P97503024E 4. R97563240E 5. P97652304B	A. 1, 5, 2, 3, 4 B. 3, 1, 4, 5, 2 C. 1, 5, 3, 2, 4 D. 1, 5, 2, 3, 4	4._____
5.	1. H92411165G 2. A92141465G 3. H92141165C 4. H92444165C 5. A92411465G	A. 2, 5, 3, 4, 1 B. 3, 4, 2, 5, 1 C. 3, 2, 1, 5, 4 D. 3, 1, 2, 5, 4	5._____
6.	1. X90637799S 2. N90037696S 3. Y90677369B 4. X09677693B 5. M09673699S	A. 4, 3, 5, 2, 1 B. 5, 4, 2, 1, 3 C. 5, 2, 4, 1, 3 D. 5, 2, 3, 4, 1	6._____

3 (#1)

	Column I	Column II	

7.
1. K78425174L
2. K78452714C
3. K78547214N
4. K78442774C
5. K78547724M

A. 4, 2, 1, 3, 5
B. 2, 3, 5, 4, 1
C. 1, 4, 2, 3, 5
D. 4, 2, 1, 5, 3

7.____

8.
1. P18736652U
2. P18766352V
3. T17686532U
4. T17865523U
5. P18675332V

A. 1, 3, 4, 5, 2
B. 1, 5, 2, 3, 4
C. 3, 4, 5, 1, 2
D. 5, 2, 1, 3, 4

8.____

9.
1. L51138101K
2. S51138001R
3. S51188222K
4. S51183110R
5. L51188100R

A. 1, 5, 3, 2, 4
B. 1, 3, 5, 2, 4
C. 1, 5, 1, 4, 3
D. 2, 5, 1, 4, 3

9.____

10.
1. J28475336
2. T28775363D
3. J27843566P
4. T27834563P
5. J2843553D

A. 5, 1, 2, 3, 4
B. 4, 3, 5, 1, 2
C. 1, 5, 2, 4, 3
D. 5, 1, 3, 2, 4

10.____

11.
1. S55126179E
2. R51336177Q
3. P55126177R
4. S55126178R
5. R55126180P

A. 1, 5, 2, 3, 4
B. 3, 4, 1, 5, 2
C. 3, 5, 2, 1, 4
D. 4, 3, 1, 5, 2

11.____

12.
1. T64217813Q
2. I64217817O
3. T64217818O
4. I64217811Q
5. T64217816Q

A. 4, 1, 3, 2, 4
B. 2, 4, 3, 1, 5
C. 4, 1, 5, 2, 3
D. 2, 3, 4, 1, 5

12.____

13.
1. B33886897B
2. B38386882B
3. D33389862B
4. D33336887D
5. B38888697D

A. 5, 1, 3, 4, 2
B. 1, 2, 5, 3, 4
C. 1, 2, 5, 4, 3
D. 2, 1, 4, 5, 3

13.____

14.
1. E11664554M
2. F11164544M
3. F11614455N
4. E11665454M
5. F16161545N

A. 4, 1, 2, 5, 3
B. 2, 4, 1, 5, 3
C. 4, 2, 1, 3, 5
D. 1, 4, 2, 3, 5

14.____

4 (#1)

    Column I   Column II

15. 1. C86611355W   A. 2, 4, 1, 5, 3   15.____
      2. C68631533V   B. 1, 2, 4, 3, 5
      3. G88631533V   C. 1, 2, 5, 4, 3
      4. C68833515V   D. 1, 2, 4, 3, 5
      5. G68833511W

16. 1. R73665312J   A. 3, 2, 1, 4, 5   16.____
      2. P73685512J   B. 2, 3, 5, 1, 4
      3. P73968511J   C. 2, 3, 1, 5, 4
      4. R73665321K   D. 3, 1, 5, 2, 4
      5. R63985211K

17. 1. X33661222U   A. 1, 4, 5, 2, 3   17..____
      2. Y83961323V   B. 4, 5, 1, 3, 2
      3. Y88991123V   C. 4, 5, 1, 2, 3
      4. X33691233U   D. 4, 1, 5, 2, 3
      5. X38691333U

18. 1. B22838847W   A. 4, 5, 2, 3, 1   18.____
      2. B28833874V   B. 4, 2, 5, 1, 3
      3. B22288344X   C. 4, 5, 2, 1, 3
      4. B28238374V   D. 4, 1, 5, 2, 3
      5. B28883347V

19. 1. H44477447G   A. 1, 3, 5, 4, 2   19.____
      2. H47444777G   B. 3, 1, 5, 2, 4
      3. H74777477C   C. 1, 4, 2, 3, 5
      4. H44747447G   D. 3, 5, 1, 4, 2
      5. H77747447C

20. 1. G11143447G   A. 3, 5, 1, 4, 2   20.____
      2. G15133388C   B. 1, 4, 3, 2, 5
      3. C15134378G   C. 5, 3, 4, 2, 1
      4. G11534477C   D. 4, 3, 1, 2, 5
      5. C15533337C

21. 1. J96693369F   A. 4, 3, 2, 5, 1   21.____
      2. J66939339F   B. 2, 5, 4, 1, 3
      3. J96693693E   C. 2, 5, 4, 3, 1
      4. J966T3933E   D. 3, 4, 5, 2, 1
      5. J69639363F

22. 1. L15567834Z   A. 3, 1, 5, 2, 4   22.____
      2. P11587638Z   B. 1, 3, 5, 4, 2
      3. M51567688Z   C. 1, 3, 5, 2, 4
      4. O55578784Z   D. 3, 1, 4, 4, 2
      5. N53588783Z

5 (#1)

	Column I	Column II	

23. 1. C83261824G   A. 2, 4, 1, 5, 3   23.____
     2. C78361822C   B. 4, 2, 1, 3, 5
     3. G83261732G   C. 3, 1, 5, 2, 4
     4. C88261823C   D. , 3, 5, 1, 4
     5. G83261743C

24. 1. A11710107H   A. 2, 1, 4, 3, 5   24.____
     2. H17110017A   B. 3, 1, 5, 2, 4
     3. A11170707A   C. 3, 4, 1, 5, 2
     4. H17170171H   D. 3, 5, 1, 2, 4
     5. A11710177A

25. 1. R26794821S   A. 3, 2, 4, 1, 5   25.____
     2. O26794821T   B. 3, 4, 2, 1, 5
     3. M26794821Z   C. 4, 2, 1, 3, 5
     4. Q26794821R   D. 5, 4, 1, 2, 3
     5. S26794821P

KEY (CORRECT ANSWERS)

1.	A	11.	C
2.	D	12.	B
3.	B	13.	B
4.	C	14.	D
5.	A	15.	A
6.	C	16.	C
7.	D	17.	A
8.	B	18.	B
9.	A	19.	D
10.	D	20.	C

21. A
22. B
23. A
24. D
25. A

TEST 2

Questions 1-5.

DIRECTIONS: Questions 1 through 5 consist of a set of letters and numbers located under Column I. For each question, pick the answer (A, B, C, or D) located under Column II which contains ONLY letters and numbers that appear in the question in Column II. *PRINT THE LETTER OF THE CORRECT ANSWER IN THE SPACE AT THE RIGHT.*

SAMPLE QUESTION

Column I

B-9-P-H-2-Z-N-8-4-M

Column II

A. B-4-C-3-R-9
B. 4-H-P-8-6-N
C. P-2-Z-8-M-9
D. 4-B-N-5-E-Z

Choice C is the correct answer because P,2,Z,8,M and 9 all appear in the sample question. All the other choices have at least one letter or number that is not in the question.

Column I

1. 1-7-6-J-L-T-3-S-A-2

2. C-0-Q-5-3-9-H-L-2-7

3. P-3-B-C-5-6-0-E-1-T

4. U-T-Z-2-4-S-8-6-B-3

5. 4-D-F-G-C-6-8-3-J-L

Column II

1. A. J-3-S-A-7-L
    B. T-S-A-2-6-5
    C. 3-7-J-L-S-Z
    D. A-7-4-J-L-1

2. A. F-9-T-2-7-Q
    B. 3-0-6-9-L-C
    C. 9-L-7-Q-C-3
    D. H-Q-4-5-9-7

3. A. B-4-6-1-3-T
    B. T-B-P-3-E-0
    C. 5-3-0-E-B-G
    D. 0-6-P-T-9-B

4. A. 2-4-S-V-Z-3
    B. B-Z-S-8-3-6
    C. 4-T-U-8-L-B
    D. 9-3-T-Z-1-2

5. A. T-D-6-8-4-J
    B. C-4-3-2-J-F
    C. 8-3-C-5-G-6
    D. C-8-6-J-G-L

Questions 6-12.

DIRECTIONS: Each of the questions numbered 6 through 12 consist of a long series of letters and numbers under Column I and four short series of letters and numbers under Column II. For each question, choose the short series of letters and numbers which is entirely and exactly the same as some part of the long series.

	Column I		Column II	
6.	IE227FE383L4700	A.	E27FE3	6.____
		B.	EF838L	
		C.	EL4700	
		D.	83LE70	
7.	77J646G54NPB318	A.	NPB318	7.____
		B.	J646J5	
		C.	4G54NP	
		D.	C54NPB	
8.	85887T358W24A93	A.	858887	8.____
		B.	W24A93	
		C.	858W24	
		D.	87T353	
9.	E104RY796B33H14	A.	04RY79	9.____
		B.	E14RYR	
		C.	96B3H1	
		D.	RY7996	
10.	W58NP12141DE07M	A.	8MP121	10.____
		B.	W58NP1	
		C.	14DEO7	
		D.	12141D	
11.	P473R365M442V5W	A.	P47365	11.____
		B.	73P365	
		C.	365M44	
		D.	5X42V5	
12.	865CG441V21SS59	A.	1V12SS	12.____
		B.	V21SS5	
		C.	5GC441	
		D.	894CG4	

KEY (CORRECT ANSWERS)

1.	A	7.	A
2.	C	8.	B
3.	B	9.	A
4.	B	10.	D
5.	D	11.	C
6	D	12.	B

TEST 3

DIRECTIONS: Each question from 1 through 8 consists of a set of letters and numbers. For each question, pick as your answer from the column to the right the choice has ONLY numbers and letters that are in the question you are answering.

To help you understand what to do, the following sample question is given:

SAMPLE: B-9-P-H-2-Z-N-8-4-M

    A. B-4-C-3-E-9
    B. 4-H-P-8-6-N
    C. P-2-Z-8-M-9
    D. 4-B-N-R-E-A

Choice C is the correct answer because P, 2, Z, 8, M-9 are in the sample question. All the other choices have at least one letter or number that is not in the question.

Questions 1 through 4 are based on Column I.

Column I

1. X-8-3-I-H-9-4-G-P-U   A. I-G-W-8-2-1   1._____

2. 4-1-2-X-U-B-9-H-7-3   B. U-3-G-9-P-8   2._____

3. U-I-G-2-5-4-W-P-3-B   C. 3-G-I-4-S-U   3._____

4. 3-H-7-G-4-5-1-U-B   D. 9-X-4-7-2-H   4._____

Questions 5 through 8 are based on Column II.

Column II

5. L-2-9-Z-R-8-Q-Y-5-7   A. 8-R-N-3-T-Z   5._____

6. J-L-9-N-Y-8-5-Q-Z-2   B. 2-L-R-5-7-Q   6._____

7. T-Y-3-3-J-Q-2-N-R-Z   C. J-2-8-Z-T-5   7._____

8. 8-Z-7-T-N-L-1-E-R-3   D. Z-8-9-3-L-5   8._____

KEY (CORRECT ANSWERS)

1. B   5. B
2. D   6. C
3. C   7. A
4. C   8. A

TEST 4

DIRECTIONS: Questions 1 through 5 have lines of letters and numbers. Each letter should be matched with its number in accordance with the following table.

Letter:	F	R	C	A	W	L	E	N	B	T
Matching Number:	0	1	2	3	4	5	6	7	8	9

From the table you can determine that the letter F has the matching number 0 below it, the letter R has the matching number 1 below it, etc.

For each question, compare each line of letters and numbers carefully to see if each letter has its correct matching number. If all the letters and numbers are matched correctly in none of the line of the question, mark your answer A; only one of the lines in the question, mark your answer B; only two of the lines of the question, mark your answer C; all three lines of the question, mark your answer D.

```
WBCR    4826
TLBF    9580
ATNE    3986
```

There is a mistake in the first line because the letter R should have its matching number 1 instead of the number 6. The second line is correct because each letter shown has the correct matching number.

There is a mistake in the third line because the letter N should have the matching number 7 instead of the number 8. Since all the letters and numbers are matched correctly in only one of the lines in the sample, the correct answer is B.

1.   EBCT   6829   1.____
      ATWR   3962
      NLBW   7584

2.   RNCT   1729   2.____
      LNCR   5728
      WAEB   5368

3.   STWB   7948   3.____
      RABL   1385
      TAEF   9360

4.   LWRB   5417   4.____
      RLWN   1647
      CBWA   2843

5.   ABTC   3792   5.____
      WCER   5261
      AWCN   3417

KEY (CORRECT ANSWERS)

1. C
2. B
3. D
4. B
5. A

TEST 5

DIRECTIONS: Assume that each of the capital letters in the table below represents the name of an employee enrolled in the city employees' retirement system. The number directly beneath the letter represents the agency for which the employee works, and the small letter directly beneath represents the code for the employee's account.

Name of Employee:	L	O	T	Q	A	M	R	N	C
Agency:	3	4	5	9	8	7	52	1	6
Account Code:	r	f	b	i	d	t	g	e	n

In each of the following Questions 1 through 10, the agency code numbers and the account code letters in Columns 2 and 3 should correspond to the capital letters in Column 1 and should be in the same consecutive order. For each question, look at each column carefully and mark your answer as follows:

if there are one or more errors in Column 2 only, mark your answer A;
if there are one or more errors in Column 3 only, mark your answer B;
if there are one or more error in Column 2 and one or more errors in Column 3, mark your answer C;
if there are NO errors in either column, mark your answer D.

The following sample question is given to help you understand the procedure.

Column 1	Column 2	Column 3
TQLMOC	583746	birtfn

In Column 2, the second agency code number (corresponding to letter Q) should be "9," not "8." Column 3 is coded correctly to Column 1. Since there is an error only in Column 2, the correct answer is A.

	Column 1	Column 2	Column 3	
1.	QLNRCA	931268	ifegnd	1.____
2.	NRMOTC	127546	egftbn	2.____
3.	RCTALM	265837	gndbrt	3.____
4.	TAMLON	578341	bdtrfe	4.____
5.	ANTROM	815427	debigt	5.____
6.	MRALON	728341	tgdrfe	6.____
7.	CTNQRO	657924	ndeigf	7.____
8.	QMROTA	972458	itgfbd	8.____

2 (#5)

	Column 1	Column 2	Column 3	
9.	RQMCOL	297463	gitnfr	9.____
10.	NOMRTQ	147259	eftgbi	10.____

KEY (CORRECT ANSWERS)

1. D 6. D
2. C 7. C
3. B 8. D
4. A 9. A
5. B 10. D

TEST 6

DIRECTIONS: Each of Questions 1 through 6 consist of three lines of code letters and numbers. The numbers on each line should correspond to the code letter on the same line in accordance with the table below.

Code Letter:	D	Y	K	L	P	U	S	R	A	E
Corresponding Number:	0	1	2	3	4	5	6	7	8	9

On some of the lines an error exists in the coding. Prepare the letters and numbers in each question carefully. If you find an error or errors on
    only one of the lines in the question, mark your answer A;
    any two lines in the question, mark your answer B;
    all three lines in the question, mark your answer C;
    none of the lines in the question, mark your answer D.

SAMPLE QUESTION
    KSRYELD   2671930
    SAPUEKL   6845913
    RYKADLP   5128034

In the above sample, the first line is correct since each code letter listed has the correct corresponding number. On the second line, an error exists because code letter R should have the number 2 instead of number 1. On the third line, an error exists because the code letter R should have the number 7 instead of the number 5. Since there are errors on two of the three lines, the correct answer is B.

Now answer the following questions using the same procedure.

1.   YPUSRLD   1456730   1.____
     UPSAEDY   5648901
     PREYDKS   4791026

2.   AERLPUS   8973456   2.____
     DKLYDPA   0231048
     UKLDREP   5230794

3.   DAPUSLA   0845683   3.____
     YKLDLPS   1230356
     PUSKYDE   4562101

4.   LRPUPDL   3745403   4.____
     SUPLEDR   6543907
     PKEYDLU   4291025

5.   KEYDESR   2910967   5.____
     PRSALEY   4678391
     LRAYSK   3687162

6. YESREYL   1967913
    PLPRAKY   4346821
    YLPSRDU   1346705

6.____

KEY (CORRECT ANSWERS)

1. A   4. A
2. D   5. B
3. C   6. A

NAME AND NUMBER COMPARISONS

COMMENTARY

This test seeks to measure your ability and disposition to do a job carefully and accurately, your attention to exactness and preciseness of detail, your alertness and versatility in discerning similarities and differences between things, and your power in systematically handling written language symbols.

It is actually a test of your ability to do academic and/or clerical work, using the basic elements of verbal (qualitative) and mathematical (quantitative) learning—words <u>and</u> numbers.

EXAMINATION SECTION

TEST 1

DIRECTIONS: In each line across the page there are three names or numbers that are much alike. Compare the three names or numbers and decide which ones are exactly alike. *PRINT IN THE SPACE AT THE RIGHT THE LETTER:*
- A. if all THREE names or numbers are exactly alike
- B. if only the FIRST and SECOND names or numbers are ALIKE
- C. if only the FIRST and THIRD names or numbers are alike
- D. if only the SECOND or THIRD names or numbers are alike
- E. if ALL THREE names or numbers are DIFFERENT

1.	Davis Hazen	David Hozen	David Hazen	1.____
2.	Lois Appel	Lois Appel	Lois Apfel	2.____
3.	June Allan	Jane Allan	Jane Allan	3.____
4.	10235	10235	10235	4.____
5.	32614	32164	32614	5.____

TEST 2

1.	2395890	2395890	2395890	1.____
2.	1926341	1926347	1926314	2.____
3.	E. Owens McVey	E. Owen McVey	E. Owen McVay	3.____
4.	Emily Neal Rouse	Emily Neal Rowse	Emily Neal Rowse	4.____
5.	H. Merritt Audubon	H. Merriott Audubon	H. Merritt Audubon	5.____

TEST 3

1.	6219354	6219354	6219354	1.____
2.	231793	2312793	2312793	2.____
3.	1065407	1065407	1065047	3.____
4.	Francis Ransdell	Frances Ramsdell	Francis Ramsdell	4.____
5.	Cornelius Detwiler	Cornelius Detwiler	Cornelius Detwiler	5.____

TEST 4

1.	6452054	6452564	6542054	1.____
2.	8501268	8501268	8501286	2.____
3.	Ella Burk Newham	Ella Burk Newnham	Elena Burk Newnham	3.____
4.	Jno. K. Ravencroft	Jno. H. Ravencroft	Jno. H. Ravencoft	4.____
5.	Martin Wills Pullen	Martin Wills Pulen	Martin Wills Pullen	5.____

TEST 5

1.	3457988	3457986	3457986	1.____
2.	4695682	4695862	4695682	2.____
3.	Stricklund Kaneydy	Sticklund Kanedy	Stricklund Kanedy	3.____
4.	Joy Harlor Witner	Joy Harloe Witner	Joy Harloe Witner	4.____
5.	R.M.O. Uberroth	R.M.O. Uberroth	R.N.O. Uberroth	5.____

TEST 6

1.	1592514	1592574	1592574	1.____
2.	2010202	2010202	2010220	2.____
3.	6177396	6177936	6177396	3.____
4.	Drusilla S. Ridgeley	Drusilla S. Ridgeley	Drusilla S. Ridgeley	4.____
5.	Andrei I. Tooumantzev	Andrei I. Tourmantzev	Andrei I. Toumantzov	5.____

TEST 7

1.	5261383	5261383	5261338	1.____
2.	8125690	8126690	8125609	2.____
3.	W.E. Johnston	W.E. Johnson	W.E. Johnson	3.____
4.	Vergil L. Muller	Vergil L. Muller	Vergil L. Muller	4.____
5.	Atherton R. Warde	Asheton R. Warde	Atherton P. Warde	5.____

TEST 8

1.	013469.5	023469.5	02346.95	1.____
2.	33376	333766	333766	2.____
3.	Ling-Temco-Vought	Ling-Tenco-Vought	Ling-Temco Vought	3.____
4.	Lorilard Corp.	Lorillard Corp.	Lorrilard Corp.	4.____
5.	American Agronomics Corporation	American Agronomics Corporation	American Agronomic Corporation	5.____

TEST 9

1.	436592864	436592864	436592864	1.____
2.	197765123	197755123	197755123	2.____
3.	Dewaay Cortvriendt International S.A.	Deway Cortvriendt International S.A.	Deway Corturiendt International S.A.	3.____
4.	Crédit Lyonnais	Crèdit Lyonnais	Crèdit Lyonais	4.____
5.	Algemene Bank Nederland N.V.	Algamene Bank Nederland N.V.	Algemene Bank Naderland N.V.	5.____

TEST 10

1.	00032572	0.0032572	00032522	1.____
2.	399745	399745	398745	2.____
3.	Banca Privata Finanziaria S.p.A.	Banca Privata Finanzaria S.P.A.	Banca Privata Finaziaria S.P.A.	3.____
4.	Eastman Dillon, Union Securities & Co.	Eastman Dillon, Union Securities Co.	Eastman Dillon, Union Securities & Co.	4.____
5.	Arnhold and S. Bleichroeder, Inc.	Arnhold & S. Bleichroeder, Inc.	Arnold and S. Bleichroeder, Inc.	5.____

TEST 11

DIRECTIONS: Answer the questions below on the basis of the following instructions: For each such numbered set of names, addresses, and numbers listed in Columns I and II, select your answer from the following options:
- A. The names in Columns I and II are different
- B. The addresses in Columns I and II are different
- C. The numbers in Columns I and II are different
- D. The names, addresses and numbers are identical

1. Francis Jones
   62 Stately Avenue
   96-12446

   Francis Jones
   62 Stately Avenue
   96-21446

   1.____

2. Julio Montez
   19 Ponderosa Road
   56-73161

   Julio Montez
   19 Ponderosa Road
   56-71361

   2.____

3. Mary Mitchell
   2314 Melbourne Drive
   68-92172

   Mary Mitchell
   2314 Melbourne Drive
   68-92172

   3.____

4. Harry Patterson
   25 Dunne Street
   14-33430

   Harry Patterson
   25 Dunne Street
   14-34330

   4.____

5. Patrick Murphy
   171 West Hosmer Street
   93-81214

   Patrick Murphy
   171 West Hosmer Street
   93-18214

   5.____

TEST 12

1. August Schultz
   816 St. Clair Avenue
   53-40149

   August Schultz
   816 St. Claire Avenue
   53-40149

   1.____

2. George Taft
   72 Runnymede Street
   47-04033

   George Taft
   72 Runnymede Street
   47-04023

   2.____

3. Angus Henderson
   1418 Madison Street
   81-76375

   Angus Henderson
   1418 Madison Street
   81-76375

   3.____

4. Carolyn Mazur
   12 Rivenlew Road
   38-99615

   Carolyn Mazur
   12 Rivervane Road
   38-99615

   4.____

5. Adele Russell
   1725 Lansing Lane
   72-91962

   Adela Russell
   1725 Lansing Lane
   72-91962

   5.____

TEST 13

DIRECTIONS: The following questions are based on the instructions given below. In each of the following questions, the 3-line name and address in Column I is the master-list entry, and the 3-line entry in Column II is the information to be checked against the master list.
If there is one line that is NOT exactly alike, mark your answer A.
If there are two lines NOT exactly alike, mark your answer B.
If there are three lines NOT exactly alike, mark your answer C.
If the lines ALL are exactly alike, mark your answer D.

1. Jerome A. Jackson
   1243 14th Avenue
   New York, N.Y. 10023

   Jerome A. Johnson
   1234 14th Avenue
   New York, N.Y. 10023

   1.____

2. Sophie Strachtheim
   33-28 Connecticut Ave.
   Far Rockaway, N.Y. 11697

   Sophie Strachtheim
   33-28 Connecticut Ave.
   Far Rockaway, N.Y. 11697

   2.____

3. Elisabeth NT. Gorrell
   256 Exchange St
   New York, N.Y. 10013

   Elizabeth NT. Correll
   256 Exchange St.
   New York, N.Y. 10013

   3.____

4. Maria J. Gonzalez
   7516 E. Sheepshead Rd.
   Brooklyn, N.Y. 11240

   Maria J. Gonzalez
   7516 N. Shepshead Rd.
   Brooklyn, N.Y. 11240

   4.____

5. Leslie B. Brautenweiler
   21-57A Seller Terr.
   Flushing, N.Y. 11367

   Leslie B. Brautenwieler
   21-75ASeiler Terr.
   Flushing, N.J. 11367

   5.____

KEY (CORRECT ANSWERS)

TEST 1	TEST 2	TEST 3	TEST 4	TEST 5	TEST 6	TEST 7
1. E	1. A	1. A	1. E	1. D	1. D	1. B
2. B	2. E	2. A	2. B	2. C	2. B	2. E
3. D	3. E	3. B	3. E	3. E	3. C	3. D
4. A	4. D	4. E	4. E	4. D	4. A	4. A
5. C	5. C	5. A	5. C	5. B	5. E	5. E

TEST 8	TEST 9	TEST 10	TEST 11	TEST 12	TEST 13
1. E	1. A	1. E	1. C	1. B	1. B
2. D	2. D	2. B	2. C	2. C	2. D
3. E	3. E	3. E	3. D	3. D	3. A
4. E	4. E	4. C	4. C	4. B	4. A
5. B	5. E	5. E	5. C	5. A	5. C

NAME AND NUMBER CHECKING
EXAMINATION SECTION
TEST 1

DIRECTIONS: Each question or incomplete statement is followed by several suggested answers or completions. Select the one that BEST answers the question or completes the statement. *PRINT THE LETTER OF THE CORRECT ANSWER IN THE SPACE AT THE RIGHT.*

Questions 1-10.

DIRECTIONS: Questions 1 through 10 below present the identification numbers, initials, and last names of employees enrolled in a city retirement system. You are to choose the option (A, B, C, or D) that has the identical identification number, initials, and last name as those given in each question.

SAMPLE QUESTION

B145695 JL Jones
- A. B146798 JL Jones
- B. B145698 JL Jonas
- C. P145698 JL Jones
- C. B145698 JL Jones

The correct answer is D. Only option D shows the identification number, initials, and last name exactly as they are in the sample question. Options A, B, and C have errors in the identification number or last name.

1. J297483 PL Robinson
   - A. J294783 PL Robinson
   - B. J297483 PL Robinson
   - C. K297483 PL Robinson
   - D. J297843 PL Robinson

2. S497662 JG Schwartz
   - A. S497662 JG Schwarz
   - B. S497762 JG Schwartz
   - C. S497662 JG Schwartz
   - D. S497663 JG Schwartz

3. G696436 LN Alberton
   - A. G696436 LM Alberton
   - B. G696436 LN Albertson
   - C. G696346 LN Albertson
   - D. G696436 LN Alberton

4. R774923 AD Aldrich
   - A. R774923 AD Aldrich
   - B. R744923 AD Aldrich
   - C. R774932 AP Aldrich
   - D. R774932 AD Allrich

5. N239638 RP Hrynyk
   - A. N236938 PR Hrynyk
   - B. N236938 RP Hrynyk
   - C. N239638 PR Hrynyk
   - D. N239638 RP Hrynyk

2 (#1)

6. R156949 LT Carlson
 A. R156949 LT Carlton
 B. R156494 LT Carlson
 C. R159649 LT Carlton
 D. R156949 LT Carlson

6.____

7. T524697 MN Orenstein
 A. T524697 MN Orenstein
 B. T524967 MN Orinstein
 C. T524697 NM Ornstein
 D. T524967 NM Orenstein

7.____

8. L346239 JD Remsen
 A. L346239 JD Remson
 B. L364239 JD Remsen
 C. L346438 JD Remsen
 D. L346239 JD Remsen

8.____

9. P966438 SB Rieperson
 A. P966438 SB Reiperson
 B. P966438 SB Reiperson
 C. R996438 SB Rieperson
 D. P966438 SB Rieperson

9.____

10. D749382 CD Thompson
 A. P749382 CD Thompson
 B. D749832 CD Thomsonn
 C. D749382 CD Thompson
 D. D749823 CD Thomspon

10.____

Questions 11-20.

DIRECTIONS: Each of Questions 11 through 20 gives the identification number and name of a person who has received treatment at a certain hospital. You are to choose the option (A, B, C, or D) which has EXACTLY the same identification number and name as those given in the question.

SAMPLE QUESTION

123765 Frank Y. Jones
 A. 123675 Frank Y. Jones
 B. 123765 Frank T. Jones
 C. 123765 Frank Y. Johns
 D. 123765 Frank Y. Jones

The correct answer is D. Only option D shows the identification number and name exactly as they are in the sample question. Option A has a mistake in the identification number. Option B has a mistake in the middle initial of the name. Option C has a mistake in the last name.

Now answer Questions 11 through 20 in the same manner.

11. 754898 Diane Malloy
 A. 745898 Diane Malloy
 B. 754898 Dion Malloy
 C. 754898 Diane Malloy
 D. 754898 Diane Maloy

11.____

12. 661818 Ferdinand Figueroa
 A. 661818 Ferdinand Figeuroa
 B. 661618 Ferdinand Figueroa
 C. 661818 Ferdnand Figueroa
 D. 661818 Ferdinand Figueroa

12.____

13. 100101 Norman D. Braustein
    A. 100101 Norman D. Braustein
    B. 101001 Norman D. Braustein
    C. 100101 Norman P. Braustien
    D. 100101 Norman D. Bruastein

14. 838696 Robert Kittredge
    A. 838969 Robert Kittredge
    B. 838696 Robert Kittredge
    C. 388696 Robert Kittredge
    D. 838696 Robert Kittridge

15. 243716 Abraham Soletsky
    A. 243716 Abrahm Soletsky
    B. 243716 Abraham Solestky
    C. 243176 Abraham Soletsky
    D. 243716 Abraham Soletsky

16. 981121 Phillip M. Maas
    A. 981121 Phillip M. Mass
    B. 981211 Phillip M. Maas
    C. 981121 Phillip M. Maas
    D. 981121 Phillip N. Maas

17. 786556 George Macalusso
    A. 785656 George Macalusso
    B. 786556 George Macalusso
    C. 786556 George Maculasso
    D. 786556 George Macluasso

18. 639472 Eugene Weber
    A. 639472 Eugene Weber
    B. 639472 Eugene Webre
    C. 693472 Eugene Weber
    D. 639742 Eugene Weber

19. 724936 John J. Lomonaco
    A. 724936 John J. Lomanoco
    B. 724396 John J. Lomonaco
    C. 724936 John J. Lomonaco
    D. 724936 John J. Lamonaco

20. 899868 Michael Schnitzer
    A. 899868 Micheal Schnitzer
    B. 898968 Michael Schnizter
    C. 899688 Michael Schnitzer
    D. 899868 Michael Schnitzer

Questions 21-28.

DIRECTIONS: Questions 21 through 28 consist of lines of names, dates, and numbers which represent the names, membership dates, social security numbers, and members of the retirement system. For each question you are to choose the option (A, B, C, or D) which exactly matches the information in the question.

SAMPLE QUESTION

Crossen 12/23/56 173568929 25349
   A. Crossen 2/23/56 173568929 253492
   B. Crossen 12/23/56 173568719 253492
   C. Crossen 12/23/56 173568929 253492
   D. Crossan 12/23/56 173568929 258492

The correct answer is C. Only option C shows the name, date, and numbers exactly as they are in Column I. Option A has a mistake in the date. Option B has a mistake in the social security number. Option D has a mistake in the name and in the membership number.

21. Figueroa 1/15/64 119295386
    A. Figueroa 1/5/64 119295386 147563
    B. Figueroa 1/15/64 119295386 147563
    C. Figueroa 1/15/64 119295836 147563
    D. Figueroa 1/15/64 119295886 147563

21.____

22. Goodridge 6/19/59 106237869 128352
    A. Goodridge 6/19/59 106287869 128332
    B. Goodrigde 6/19/59 106237869 128352
    C. Goodridge 6/9/59 106237869 128352
    D. Goodridge 6/19/59 106237869 128352

22.____

23. Balsam 9/13/57 109652382 116938
    A. Balsan 9/13/57 109652382 116938
    B. Balsam 9/13/57 109652382 116938
    C. Balsom 9/13/57 109652382 116938
    D. Balsalm 9/13/57 109652382 116938

23.____

24. Mackenzie 2/16/49 127362513 101917
    A. Makenzie 2/16/49 127362513 101917
    B. Mackenzie 2/16/49 127362513 101917
    C. Mackenzie 2/16/49 127362513 101977
    D. Mackenzie 2/16/49 127862513 101917

24.____

25. Halpern 12/2/73 115205359 286070
    A. Halpern 12/2/73 115206359 286070
    B. Halpern 12/2/73 113206359 286070
    C. Halpern 12/2/73 115206359 206870
    D. Halpern 12/2/73 115206359 286870

25.____

26. Phillips 4/8/66 137125516 192612
    A. Phillips 4/8/66 137125516 196212
    B. Philipps 4/8/66 137125516 192612
    C. Phillips 4/8/66 137125516 192612
    D. Phillips 4/8/66 137122516 192612

26.____

27. Francisce 11/9/63 123926037 152210
    A. Francisce 11/9/63 123826837 152210
    B. Francisce 11/9/63 123926037 152210
    C. Francisce 11/9/63 123936037 152210
    D. Franscice 11/9/63 123926037 152210

27.____

28. Silbert 7/28/54 118421999 178514
    A. Silbert 7/28/54 118421999 178544
    B. Silbert 7/28/54 184421999 178514
    C. Silbert 7/28/54 118421999 178514
    D. Siblert 7/28/54 118421999 178514

28.____

KEY (CORRECT ANSWERS)

1.	B	11.	C	21.	B
2.	C	12.	D	22.	D
3.	D	13.	A	23.	B
4.	A	14.	B	24.	B
5.	D	15.	D	25.	A
6.	D	16.	C	26.	C
7.	A	17.	B	27.	B
8.	D	18.	A	28.	C
9.	D	19.	C		
10.	C	20.	D		

TEST 2

DIRECTIONS: Each question or incomplete statement is followed by several suggested answers or completions. Select the one that BEST answers the question or completes the statement. *PRINT THE LETTER OF THE CORRECT ANSWER IN THE SPACE AT THE RIGHT.*

Questions 1-3.

DIRECTIONS: Items 1 through 3 are a test of your proofreading ability. Each item consists of Copy I and Copy II. You are to assume that Copy I in each item is correct. Copy II, which is meant to be a duplicate of Copy I, may contain some typographical errors. In each item, compare Copy II with Copy I and determine the number of errors in Copy II. If there are:
no errors, mark your answer A;
1 or 2 errors, mark your answer B;
3 or 4 errors, mark your answer C;
5 or 6 errors, mark your answer D;
7 errors or more, mark your answer E.

1. 1.____

COPY I
The Commissioner, before issuing any such license, shall cause an investigation to be made of the premises named and described in such application, to determine whether all the provisions of the sanitary code, building code, state industrial code, state minimum wage law, local laws, regulations of municipal agencies, and other requirements of this article are fully observed. (Section B32-169.0 of Article 23.)

COPY II
The Commissioner, before issuing any such license shall cause an investigation to be made of the premises named and described in such application, to determine whether all the provisions of the sanitary code, bilding code, state industrial code, state minimum wage laws, local laws, regulations of municipal agencies, and other requirements of this article are fully observed. (Section E32-169.0 of Article 23.)

2. 2.____

COPY I
Among the persons who have been appointed to various agencies are John Queen, 9 West 55th Street, Brooklyn; Joseph Blount, 2497 Durward Road, Bronx; Lawrence K. Eberhardt, 3194 Bedford Street, Manhattan; Reginald L. Darcy, 1476 Allerton Drive, Bronx; and Benjamin Ledwith, 177 Greene Street, Manhattan.

COPY II
Among the persons who have been appointed to various agencies are John Queen, 9 West 56th Street, Brooklyn, Joseph Blount, 2497 Dureward Road, Bronx: Lawrence K. Eberhart, 3194 Belford Street, Manhattan; Reginald L. Barcey, 1476 Allerton drive, Bronx; and Benjamin Ledwith, 177 Green Street, Manhattan.

3. 3.____

COPY I
Except as hereinafter provided, it shall be unlawful to use, store or have on hand any inflammable motion picture film in quantities greater than one standard or two sub-standard reels, or aggregating more than two thousand feet in length, or more than ten pounds in weight without the permit required by this section.

COPY II
Except as herinafter provided, it shall be unlawful to use, store or have on hand any inflamable motion picture film, in quantities greater than one standard or two substandard reels or aggregating more than two thousand feet in length, or more than ten pounds in weight without the permit required by this section.

Questions 4-6.

DIRECTIONS: Items 4 through 6 are a test of your proofreading ability. Each question consists of Copy I and Copy II. You are to assume that Copy I in each question is correct. Copy II, which is meant to be a duplicate of Copy I, may contain some typographical errors. In each question, compare Copy II with Copy I and determine the number of errors in Copy II. If there are:
no errors, mark your answer A;
1 or 2 errors, mark your answer B;
3 or 4 errors, mark your answer C;
5 or 6 errors or more, mark your answer D;

4. 4.____

COPY I
It shall be unlawful to install wires or appliances for electric light, heat or power, operating at a potential in excess of seven hundred fifty volts, in or on any part of a building, with the exception of a central station, sub-station, transformer, or switching vault, or motor room; provided, however, that the Commissioner may authorize the use of radio transmitting apparatus under special conditions.

COPY II
It shall be unlawful to install wires or appliances for electric light, heat or power, operating at a potential in excess of seven hundred fifty volts, in or on any part of a building, with the exception of a central station, sub-station, transformer, or switching vault, or motor room, provided, however, that the Commissioner may authorize the use of radio transmitting apperatus under special conditions.

5.

COPY I
The grand total debt service for the fiscal year 2006-27 amounts to $350,563,718.63, as compared with $309,561,347.27 for the current fiscal year, or an increase of $41,002,371.36. The amount payable from other sources in 2006-07 shows an increase of $13,264,165.47, resulting in an increase of $27,733,205.89 payable from tax levy funds.

COPY II
The grand total debt service for the fiscal year 2006-07 amounts to $350,568,718.63, as compared with $309,561,347.27 for the current fiscel year, or an increase of $41,002,371.36. The amount payable from other sources in 2006-07 show an increase of $13,264,165.47 resulting in an increase of $27,733,295.89 payable from tax levy funds.

6.

COPY I
The following site proposed for the new building is approximately rectangular in shape and comprises an entire block, having frontages of about 721 feet on 16th Road, 200 feet on 157th feet, 721 on 17th Avenue and 200 feet on 154th Street, with a gross area of about 144,350 square feet. The 2006-07 assessed valuation is $28,700,000 of which $6,000,000 is for improvements.

COPY II
The following site proposed for the new building is approximately rectangular in shape and comprises an entire block, having frontage of about 721 feet on 16th Road, 200 feet on 157th Street on 17th Avenue, and 200 feet on 134th Street, with a gross area of about 114,350 square feet. The 2006-07 assessed valuation is $28,700,000 of which $6,000,000 is for improvements.

KEY (CORRECT ANSWERS)

1. D
2. E
3. E
4. B
5. D
6. C

TEST 3

DIRECTIONS: Each question or incomplete statement is followed by several suggested answers or completions. Select the one that BEST answers the question or completes the statement. *PRINT THE LETTER OF THE CORRECT ANSWER IN THE SPACE AT THE RIGHT.*

Questions 1-8.

DIRECTIONS: Each of the questions numbered 1 through 8 consists of three sets of names and name codes. In each question, the two names and name codes on the same line are supposed to be exactly the same.
Look carefully at each set of names and cods and mark your answer
A. if there are mistakes in all three sets
B. if there are mistakes in two of the sets
C. if there is a mistake in only one set
D. if there are no mistakes in any of the sets

SAMPLE QUESTION

The following sample question is given to help you understand the procedure.

Macabe, John N. – V53162	Macade, John N. – V53162
Howard, Joan S. – J24791	Howard, Joan S. – J24791
Ware, Susan B. – A45068	Ware, Susan B. – A45968

In the above sample question, the names and name codes of the first set are not exactly the same because of the spelling of the last name (Macabe – Macade). The names and name codes of the second set are exactly the same. The names and name codes of the third set are not exactly the same because the two name codes are different (A45068 – A45968). Since there are mistakes in only 2 of the sets, the answer to the sample question is B.

1. Powell, Michael C. – 78537F   Powell, Michael C. – 78537F   1.____
   Martinez, Pablo J. – 24435P   Martinez, Pablo J. – 24435P
   MacBane, Eliot M. – 98674E   MacBane, Eliot M. – 98674E

2. Fitz-Kramer Machines, Inc. – 259090   Fitz-Kramer Machines, Inc. – 259090   2.____
   Marvel Cleaning Service – 482657   Marvel Cleaning Service – 482657
   Donato, Carl G. – 637418   Danato, Carl G. - 687418

3. Martin Davison Trading Corp –   Martin Davidson Trading Corp. –   3.____
      43108T   43108T
   Cotwald Lighting Fixtures -76065L   Cotwald Lighting Fixtures – 70056L
   R. Crawford Plumbers – 23157C   R. Crawford Plumbers – 23157G

4. Fraiman Engineering Corp. – M4773   Friaman Engineering Corp. – M4773   4.____
   Neuman, Walter B. – N7745   Neumen, Walter B. – N7745
   Pierce, Eric M. – W6304   Pierce, Eric M. – W6304

159

2 (#3)

5. Constable, Eugene – B64837 Comstable, Eugene – B6437 5.____
   Derrick, Paul – H27119 Derrik, Paul – H27119
   Heller, Karen – S4966 Heller, Karen – S46906

6. Hernando Delivery Service Co. - D7456 Hernando Delivery Service Co. – D7456 6.____
   Barettz Electrical Supplies - N5392 Barettz Electrical Supplies – N5392
   Tanner, Abraham – M4798 Tanner, Abraham – M4798

7. Kalin Associates – R38641 Kaline Associates – R38641 7.____
   Sealey, Robert E. – P63533 Sealey, Robert E. – P63553
   Seals! Office Furniture – R36742 Seals! Office Furniture – R36742

8. Janowsky, Philip M. – 742213 Janowsky, Philip M. – 742213 8.____
   Hansen, Thomas H. – 934816 Hanson, Thomas H. – 934816
   L. Lester and Son Inc. – 294568 L. Lester and Son Inc. - 294568

Questions 9-13.

DIRECTIONS: Each of the questions numbered 9 through 13 consists of three sets of names and building codes. In each question, the two names and building codes on the same line are supposed to be exactly the same.
If you find an error or errors on only one of the sets in the question, mark your answer A; any two of the sets in the question, mark your answer B; all three of the sets in the question, mark your answer C; none of the sets, mark your answer D.

SAMPLE QUESTION

Column I
Duvivier, Anne P. – X52714
Dyrborg, Alfred – B4217
Dymnick, JoAnne – P482596

Column II
Duviver, Anne P. – X52714
Dyrborg, Alfred – B4267
Dymnick, JoAnne – P482596

In the above sample question, the first set of names and building codes is not exactly the same because the last names are spelled differently (Duvivier – Duviver). The second set of names and building codes is not exactly the same because the building codes are different (B4217 – B4267). The third set of names and building codes is exactly the same. Since there are mistakes in two of the sets of names and building codes, the answer to the sample question is B.

Now answer the questions using the same procedure.

Column I
9. Lautmann, Gerald G. – C2483
   Lawlor, Michael – W44639
   Lawrence, John J. – H1358

Column II
Lautmann, Gerald C. – C2483
Lawler, Michael – W44639
Lawrence, John J. – H1358

9.____

3 (#3)

Column I	Column II	
10. Mittmann, Howard – J4113 Mitchell, William T. – M75271 Milan, T. Thomas – Q67553	Mittmann, Howard – J4113 Mitchell, William T. – M75721 Milan, T. Thomas – Q67553	10.____
11. Quarles, Vincent – J34760 Quinn, Alan N. – S38813 Quinones, Peter W. – B87467	Quarles, Vincent – J34760 Quinn, Alan N. – S38813 Quinones, Peter W. – B87467	11.____
12. Daniels, Harold H. – A26554 Dantzler, Richard – C35780 Davidson, Martina – E62901	Daniels, Harold H – A26544 Dantzler, Richard – 035780 Davidson, Martin – E62901	12.____
13. Graham, Cecil J. – I20244 Granger, Deborah – T86211 Grant, Charles L. – G5788	Graham, Cecil J. – I20244 Granger, Deborah – T86211 Grant, Charles L. – G5788	13.____

KEY (CORRECT ANSWERS)

1.	D	6.	D	11.	D
2.	C	7.	B	12.	C
3.	A	8.	C	13.	D
4.	B	9.	B		
5.	A	10.	A		

TEST 4

DIRECTIONS: In Questions 1 through 10 there are five pairs of numbers or letters and numbers. Compare each pair and decide how many pairs are exactly alike. *PRINT THE LETTER OF THE CORRECT ANSWER IN THE SPACE AT THE RIGHT.*
- A. if only one pair is exactly alike
- B. if only two pairs are exactly alike
- C. if only three pairs are exactly alike
- D. if only four pairs are exactly alike
- E. if all five pairs are exactly alike.

1. 73-F.....F-73   FF-73.....FF-73   1._____
   F-7373.....F-7373   373-FF.....337-FF
   F-733.....337-F

2. 0-17158.....0-17158   0-71518.....0-71518   2._____
   0-11758.....0-11758   0-15817.....0-15817

3. 1A-7908.....1A-7908   7A-8901.....7A-8091   3._____
   71-891.....7A-891   1A-9078.....1A-9708
   9A-7018.....9A-7081

4. 2V-6426.....2V-6246   2N-6246.....2N-6246   4._____
   2V-6426.....2N-6426   2N-6624.....2N-6624
   2V-6462.....2V-6562

5. 3NY-56.....3NY-65   5NY-356.....3NY-356   5._____
   6NY-3566.....3NY-3566 5NY-6536.....5NY-6536
   3NY-5663.....5NY-3663

6. COB-065.....COB-065   BCL-506.....BCL-506   6._____
   LBC-650.....LBC-650   DLB-560.....DLB-560
   CDB-056.....COB-065

7. 4KQ-9130.....4KQ-9130   4KQ-9310.....4KQ-9130   7._____
   4KQ-9031.....4KQ-9301   4KQ-9301.....4KQ-9301
   4KQ-9013.....4KQ-9013

8. MK-89.....MK-98   98-MK.....89-MK   8._____
   MSK-998.....MSK-998   MOSK.....MOKS
   SMK-899.....SMK-899

9. 8MD-2104.....SMD-2014   2MD-8140.....2MD-8140   9._____
   814-MD.....814-MD   4MD-8201.....4MD-8201
   MD-281.....MD-481

10. 161-035.....161-035   150-316.....150-316   10._____
    315-160.....315-160   131-650.....131-650
    165-301.....165-301

KEY (CORRECT ANSWERS)

1. B   6. D
2. E   7. D
3. B   8. B
4. C   9. C
5. A   10. E

TEST 5

DIRECTIONS: Each question or incomplete statement is followed by several suggested answers or completions. Select the one that BEST answers the question or completes the statement. *PRINT THE LETTER OF THE CORRECT ANSWER IN THE SPACE AT THE RIGHT.*

Questions -5.

DIRECTIONS: Questions 1 through 5, inclusive, consist of groups of four displays representing license identification plates. Examine each group of plates and determine the number of plates in each group which are identical. Mark your answer sheets as follows:
    If only two plates are identical, mark answer A.
    If only three plates are identical, mark answer B.
    If all four plates are identical, mark answer C.
    If the plates are all different, mark answer D.

EXAMPLE
ABC123   BCD123   ABC123   BCD235

Since only two plates are identical, the first and third, the correct answer is A.

1.   PBV839   PVB839   PVB839   PVB839   1.____

2.   WTX083   WTX083   WTX083   WTX083   2.____

3.   B73609   D73906   BD7396   BD7906   3.____

4.   AK7423   AK7423   AK1423   A81324   4.____

5.   583Y10   683Y10   583701   583710   5.____

Questions 6-10.

DIRECTIONS: Questions 6 through 10 consist of groups of numbers and letters similar to those which might appear on license plates. Each group of numbers and letters will be called a license identification. Choose the license identification lettered A, B, C, or D that EXACTLY matches the license identification shown next to the question number.

SAMPLE
NY 1977
ABC-123

A. NY 1976   B. NY 1977   C. NY 1977   D. NY 1977
   ABC-123   ABC-132   CBA-123   ABC-123

2 (#5)

The license identification given is NY 1977.
ABC-123
The only choice that exactly matches it is the license identification next to the letter D. The correct answer is therefore D.

6. NY 1976
QLT-781

   A. NJ 1976 QLT-781
   B. NY 1975 QLT-781
   C. NY 1976 QLT-781
   D. NY 1977 QLT-781

6.____

7. FLA 1977
2-7LT58J

   A. FLA 1977 2-7TL58J
   B. FLA 1977 2-7LTJ58
   C. FLA 1977 2-7LT58J
   D. LA 1977 2-7LT58J

7.____

8. NY 1975
OQC383

   A. NY 1975 OQC383
   B. NY 1975 OQC833
   C. NY 1975 QCQ383
   D. NY 1977 OCQ383

8.____

9. MASS 1977
B-8DK02

   A. MISS 1977 B-8DK02
   B. MASS 1977 B-8DK02
   C. MASS 1976 B-8DK02
   D. MASS 1977 B-80KD2

9.____

10. NY 1976
ZV0586

   A. NY 1976 2V-0586
   B. NY 1977 ZV0586
   C. NY 1975 ZV0586
   D. NY 1976 ZU0586

10.____

KEY (CORRECT ANSWERS)

1.	B	6.	C
2.	C	7.	C
3.	D	8.	A
4.	A	9.	B
5.	A	10.	C

TEST 6

DIRECTIONS: Assume that each of the capital letters in the table below represent the name of an employee enrolled in the city employees' retirement system. The number directly beneath the letter represents the agency for which the employee works, and the small letter directly beneath represents the code for the employee's account.

Name of Employee	L	O	T	Q	A	M	R	N	C
Agency	3	4	5	9	8	7	2	1	6
Account Code	r	f	b	i	d	t	g	e	n

In each of the following questions 1 through 3, the agency code numbers and the account code letters in Columns 2 and 3 should correspond to the capital letters in Column 1 and should be in the same consecutive order. For each question, look at each column carefully and mark your answer as follows:
If there are one or more errors in Column 2 only, mark your answer A.
If there are one or more errors in Column 3 only, mark your answer B.
If there are one or more errors in Column 2 and one or more errors in Column 3, mark your answer C.
If there are NO errors in either column, mark your answer D.
The following sample question is given to help you understand the procedure.

Column 1	Column 2	Column 3
TQLMOC	583746	birtfn

In Column 2, the second agency code number (corresponding to letter Q) should be "9", not "8". Column 3 is coded correctly to Column 1. Since there is an error only in Column 2, the correct answer is A.

	Column 1	Column 2	Column 3	
1.	QLNRCA	931268	iregnd	1.____
2.	NRMOTC	127546	egftbn	2.____
3.	RCTALM	265837	gndbrt	3.____

KEY (CORRECT ANSWERS)

1. D
2. C
3. B

ADDRESS CHECKING

EXAMINATION SECTION
TEST 1

DIRECTIONS: This test is designed to measure your speed and accuracy. You are urged to work both quickly and accurately and to do correctly as many lists as you can in the time allowed. The test consists of lists of pairs of addresses. Circle the letter *A* on your answer sheet if the two addresses are exactly ALIKE in every way. Circle the letter *D* if they are DIFFERENT.

CIRCLE CORRECT ANSWER

1. 405 Winter Rd NW	405 Winter Rd NW	A	D
2. 607 S Calaveras Rd	607 S Calaveras Rd	A	D
3. 8406 La Casa St	8406 La Cosa St	A	D
4. 121 N Rippon St	121 N Rippon St	A	D
5. Wideman Ar	Wiseman Ar	A	D
6. Sodus NY 14551	Sodus NY 14551	A	D
7. 3429 Hermosa Dr	3429 Hermoso Dr	A	D
8. 3628 S Zeeland St	3268 S Zeeland St	A	D
9. 1330 Cheverly Ave NE	1330 Cheverly Ave NE	A	D
10. 1689 N Derwood Dr	1689 N Derwood Dr	A	D
11. 3886 Sunrise Ct	3886 Sunrise Ct	A	D
12. 635 La Calle Mayor	653 La Calle Mayor	A	D
13. 2560 Lansford Pl	2560 Lansford St	A	D
14. 4631 Central Ave	4631 Central Ave	A	D
15. Mason City Ia 50401	Mason City Ia 50401	A	D
16. 758 Los Arboles Ave SE	758 Los Arboles Ave SW	A	D
17. 3282 E Downington St	3282 E Dunnington St	A	D
18. 7117 N Burlingham Ave	7117 N Burlingham Ave	A	D
19. 32 Oaklawn Blvd	32 Oakland Blvd	A	D
20. 1274 Manzana Rd	1274 Manzana Rd	A	D

KEY (CORRECT ANSWERS)

1. A	6. A	11. A	16. D
2. A	7. D	12. D	17. D
3. D	8. D	13. D	18. A
4. A	9. A	14. A	19. D
5. D	10. A	15. A	20. A

TEST 2

DIRECTIONS: This test is designed to measure your speed and accuracy. You are urged to work both quickly and accurately and to do correctly as many lists as you can in the time allowed. The test consists of lists of pairs of addresses. Circle the letter *A* on your answer sheet if the two addresses are exactly ALIKE in every way. Circle the letter *D* if they are DIFFERENT.

CIRCLE CORRECT ANSWER

1.	4598 E Kenilworth Dr	4598 E Kenilworth Dr	A	D
2.	Dayton Ok 73449	Dagton Ok 73449	A	D
3.	1172 W 83rd Ave	1127 W 83rd Ave	A	D
4.	6434 E Pulaski St	6434 E Pulaski Ct	A	D
5.	2764 N Rutherford Pl	2764 N Rutherford Pl	A	D
6.	565 Greenville Blvd SW	565 Greenview Blvd SE	A	D
7.	3824 Massasoit St	3824 Massasoit St	A	D
8.	22 Sagnaw Pkwy	22 Saganaw Pkwy	A	D
9.	Byram Ct 10573	Byram Ct 10573	A	D
10.	1928 S Fairfield Ave	1928 S Fairfield St	A	D
11.	36218 Overhills Dr	36218 Overhills Dr	A	D
13.	516 Avenida de Las Americas NW	516 Avenida de Las Americas NW	A	D
14.	7526 Naraganset Pl SW	7526 Naraganset Pl SW	A	D
15.	52626 W Ogelsby Dr	52626 W Ogelsby Dr	A	D
16.	1003 Winchester Rd	1003 Westchester Rd	A	D
17.	3478 W Cavanaugh Ct	3478 W Cavenaugh Ct	A	D
18.	Kendall Ca 90551	Kendell Ca 90551	A	D
19.	225 El Camino Blvd	225 El Camino Av	A	D
20.	7310 Via de los Pisos	7310 Via de los Pinos	A	D

KEY (CORRECT ANSWERS)

1. A	6. D	11. D	16. D
2. D	7. D	12. A	17. D
3. D	8. A	13. A	18. D
4. D	9. D	14. A	19. D
5. A	10. A	15. A	20. D

TEST 3

DIRECTIONS: This test is designed to measure your speed and accuracy. You are urged to work both quickly and accurately and to do correctly as many lists as you can in the time allowed. The test consists of lists of pairs of addresses. Circle the letter *A* on your answer sheet if the two addresses are exactly ALIKE in every way. Circle the letter *D* if they are DIFFERENT.

			CIRCLE CORRECT ANSWER	
1.	1987 Wellington Ave SW	1987 Wellington Ave SW	A	D
2.	3124 S 71st St	3142 S 71st St	A	D
3.	729 Lincolnwood Blvd	729 Lincolnwood Blvd	A	D
4.	1166 N Beaumont Dr	1166 S Beaumont Dr	A	D
5.	3224 W Winecona Pl	3224 W Winecona Pl	A	D
6.	608 La Calle Bienvenida	607 La Calle Bienvenida	A	D
7.	La Molte Ia 52045	La Molte Ia 52045	A	D
8.	8625 Armitage Ave NW	8625 Armitage Ave NW	A	D
9.	2343 Broadview Ave	2334 Broadview Ave	A	D
10.	4279 Sierra Grande -Ave NE	427-9 Sierra Grande Dr NE	A	D
11.	165 32d Ave	165 32d Ave	A	D
12.	12742 N Deerborn St	12724 N Deerborn St	A	D
13.	114 Estancia Ave	141 Estancia Ave	A	D
14.	351 S Berwyn Rd	351 S Berwyn Pl	A	D
15.	7732 Avenida Manana SW	7732 Avenida Manana SW	A	D
16.	6337 C St SW	6337 G St SW	A	D
17.	57895 E Drexyl Ave	58795 E Drexyl Ave	A	D
18.	Altro Tx 75923	Altra Tx 75923	A	D
19.	3465 S Nashville St	3465 N Nashville St	A	D
20.	1226 Odell Blvd NW	1226 Oddell Blvd NW	A	D

KEY (CORRECT ANSWERS)

1. A	6. D	11. A	16. D
2. D	7. A	12. D	17. D
3. A	8. A	13. D	18. D
4. D	9. D	14. D	19. D
5. A	10. D	15. A	20. D

TEST 4

DIRECTIONS: This test is designed to measure your speed and accuracy. You are urged to work both quickly and accurately and to do correctly as many lists as you can in the time allowed. The test consists of lists of pairs of addresses. Circle the letter *A* on your answer sheet if the two addresses are exactly ALIKE in every way. Circle the letter *D* if they are DIFFERENT.

CIRCLE CORRECT ANSWER

1.	94002 Chappel Ct	94002 Chappel Ct	A	D
2.	512 La Vega Dr	512 La Veta Dr	A	D
3.	8774 W Winona Pl	8774 E Winona Pl	A	D
4.	6431 Ingleside St SE	6431 Ingleside St SE	A	D
5.	2270 N Leanington St	2270 N Leanington St	A	D
6.	235 Calle de Los Vecinos	235 Calle de Los Vecinos	A	D
7.	3987 E Westwood Ave	3987 W Westwood Ave	A	D
8.	Skamokawa Wa	Skamohawa Wa	A	D
9.	2674 E Champlain Cir	2764 E Champlain Cir	A	D
10.	8751 Elmhurst Blvd	8751 Elmwood Blvd	A	D
11.	6649 Solano Dr	6649 Solana Dr	A	D
12.	4423 S Escenaba St	4423 S Escenaba St	A	D
13.	1198 N St NW	1198 M St NW	A	D
14.	Sparta Ga	Sparta Va	A	D
15.	96753 Wrightwood Ave	96753 Wrightwood Ave	A	D
16.	2445 Sangamow Ave SE	2445 Sangamow Ave SE	A	D
17.	5117 E 67 Pl	5171 E 67 Pl	A	D
18.	847 Mesa Grande Pl	847 Mesa Grande Ct	A	D
19.	1100 Cermaken St	1100 Cermaker St	A	D
20.	321 Tijeras Ave NW	321 Tijeras Ave NW	A	D

KEY (CORRECT ANSWERS)

1. A	6. A	11. D	16. A
2. D	7. D	12. A	17. D
3. D	8. D	13. D	18. D
4. A	9. D	14. D	19. D
5. A	10. D	15. A	20. A

———

TEST 5

DIRECTIONS: This test is designed to measure your speed and accuracy. You are urged to work both quickly and accurately and to do correctly as many lists as you can in the time allowed. The test consists of lists of pairs of addresses. Circle the letter A on your answer sheet if the two addresses are exactly ALIKE in every way. Circle the letter D if they are DIFFERENT.

CIRCLE CORRECT ANSWER

1.	3405 Prospect St	3405 Prospect St	A	D
2.	6643 Burlington Pl	6643 Burlingtown Pl	A	D
3.	851 Esperanza Blvd	851 Esperanza Blvd	A	D
4.	Jenkinjones WV	Kenkinjones W	A	D
5.	1008 Pennsylvania Ave SE	1008 Pennsylvania Ave SW	A	D
6.	2924 26th St N	2929 26th St N	A	D
7.	7115 Highland Dr	7115 Highland Dr	A	D
8.	Chaptico Md	Chaptica Md	A	D
9.	3508 Camron Mills Rd	3508 Camron Mills Rd	A	D
10.	67158 Capston Dr	67158 Capston Dr	A	D
11.	3613 S Taylor Av	3631 S Taylor Av	A	D
12.	2421 Menokin Dr	2421 Menokin Dr	A	D
13.	3226 M St NW	3226 N St NW	A	D
14.	1201 S Court House Rd	1201 S Court House Rd	A	D
15.	Findlay Ohio 45840	Findley Ohio 45840	A	D
16.	17 Bennett St	17 Bennet St	A	D
17.	7 Vine Bowl Dr	7 Vine Bowl Pl	A	D
18.	126 McKinley Av	126 MacKinley Av	A	D
19.	384 Nepperhan Rd	387 Nepperhan Rd	A	D
20.	1077 Contreras Av NW	1077 Contreras Av NW	A	D

KEY (CORRECT ANSWERS)

1. A	6. D	11. D	16. D
2. D	7. A	12. A	17. D
3. A	8. D	13. D	18. D
4. D	9. A	14. A	19. D
5. D	10. A	15. D	20. A

TEST 6

DIRECTIONS: This test is designed to measure your speed and accuracy. You are urged to work both quickly and accurately and to do correctly as many lists as you can in the time allowed. The test consists of lists of pairs of addresses. Circle the letter *A* on your answer sheet if the two addresses are exactly ALIKE in every way. Circle the letter *D* if they are DIFFERENT.

CIRCLE CORRECT ANSWER

1.	239 Summit Pl NE	239 Summit Pl NE	A	D
2.	152 Continental Pkwy	152 Continental Blvd	A	D
3.	8092 13th Rd S	8029 13th Rd S	A	D
4.	3906 Queensbury Rd	3906 Queensbury Rd	A	D
5.	4719 Linnean Av NW	4719 Linnean Av NE	A	D
6.	Bradford Me	Bradley Me	A	D
7.	Parrott Ga 31777	Parrott Ga 31177	A	D
8.	4312 Lowell Lane	4312 Lowell Lane	A	D
9.	6929 W 135th Place	6929 W 135th Plaza	A	D
10.	5143 Somerset Cir	5143 Somerset Cir	A	D
11.	8501 Kennedy St	8501 Kennedy St	A	D
12.	2164 E McLean Av	2164 E McLean Av	A	D
13.	7186 E St NW	7186 F St NW	A	D
14.	2121 Beechcrest Rd	2121 Beechcroft Rd	A	D
15.	324 S Alvadero St	324 S Alverado St	A	D
17.	2908 Plaza de las Estrellas	2908 Plaza de las Estrellas	A	D
18.	223 Great Falls Rd SE	223 Great Falls Dr SE	A	D
19.	Kelton SC 29354	Kelton SC 29354	A	D
20.	3201 Landover Rd	3201 Landover Rd	A	D

KEY (CORRECT ANSWERS)

1. A	6. D	11. A	16. D
2. D	7. D	12. A	17. A
3. D	8. A	13. D	18. D
4. A	9. D	14. D	19. A
5. D	10. A	15. A	20. A

TEST 7

DIRECTIONS: This test is designed to measure your speed and accuracy. You are urged to work both quickly and accurately and to do correctly as many lists as you can in the time allowed. The test consists of lists of pairs of addresses. Circle the letter *A* on your answer sheet if the two addresses are exactly ALIKE in every way. Circle the letter *D* if they are DIFFERENT.

CIRCLE CORRECT ANSWER

1.	111 Caroline Pl Armnk	111 Caroline Pl Armnk	A	D
2.	21 Grnleaf Rye	121 Grnleaf Rye	A	D
3.	245 Rumsy Rd Ynkrs	245 Rumsey Rd Ynkrs	A	D
4.	927 South Peekskl	927 South Pekskl	A	D
5.	44 Monro Av Lrchmt	44 Monroe Av Lrchmt	A	D
6.	39 Andrea Ln Scrsdl	39 Andrea La Scrsdl	A	D
7.	Ruland Wy 62143	Ruland Wy 62143	A	D
8.	51 Cyprs Rd Tukaho	51 Cyprs Rd Tuckaho	A	D
9.	213 Shore Lane Rd Mahopc	213 Shore Lane Av Mahopc	A	D
10.	189 Colmbs Av Lk Oscawna	189 Columbus Av Lk Oscawna	A	D
11.	124 West Stationery Rd	124 West Stationary Rd	A	D
12.	Purdy Vt 03124	Purdy Vt 03124	A	D
13.	129 Tewksbury Rd	129 Twksbury Rd	A	D
14.	Gallow Hill Rd SW	Gallow Hill Rd	A	D
15.	234 Myrtle Av	234 Myrtl Av	A	D
16.	35 Chase Pl NE	35 Chse Pl NE	A	D
17.	14 Terace Av	41 Terace Av	A	D
18.	Collins Pt Rd SE	Colins Pt Rd SE	A	D
19.	164 Sagmor Ct	164 Sagmor Ct	A	D
20.	117 Warburtn Dr NE	117 Wrburtn Dr NE	A	D

KEY (CORRECT ANSWERS)

1. A	6. D	11. D	16. D
2. D	7. A	12. A	17. D
3. D	8. D	13. D	18. D
4. D	9. D	14. D	19. A
5. D	10. D	15. D	20. D

ARITHMETIC

EXAMINATION SECTION
TEST 1

DIRECTIONS: Each question or incomplete statement is followed by several suggested answers or completions. Select the one that BEST answers the question or completes the statement. *PRINT THE LETTER OF THE CORRECT ANSWER IN THE SPACE AT THE RIGHT.*

1. From 30983 subtract 29998. The answer should be 1.____
   A. 985   B. 995   C. 1005   D. 1015

2. From $2537.75 subtract $1764.28. The answer should be 2.____
   A. $763.58   B. $773.47   C. $774.48   D. $873.58

3. From 254211 subtract 76348. The answer should be 3.____
   A. 177863   B. 177963   C. 187963   D. 188973

4. Divide 4025 by 35. The answer should be 4.____
   A. 105   B. 109   C. 115   D. 125

5. Multiply 0.35 by 2764. The answer should be 5.____
   A. 997.50   B. 967.40   C. 957.40   D. 834.40

6. Multiply 1367 by 0.50. The answer should be 6.____
   A. 6.8350   B. 68.350   C. 683.50   D. 6835.0

7. Multiply 841 by 0.01. The answer should be 7.____
   A. 0.841   B. 8.41   C. 84.1   D. 841

8. Multiply 1962 by 25. The answer should be 8.____
   A. 47740   B. 48460   C. 48950   D. 49050

9. Multiply 905 by 0.05. The answer should be 9.____
   A. 452.5   B. 45.25   C. 4.525   D. 0.4525

10. Multiply 8.93 by 4.7. The answer should be 10.____
    A. 41.971   B. 40.871   C. 4.1971   D. 4.0871

11. Multiply 25 by 763. The answer should be 11.____
    A. 18075   B. 18875   C. 19075   D. 20965

12. Multiply 2530 by 0.10. The answer should be 12.____
    A. 2.5300   B. 25.300   C. 253.00   D. 2530.0

13. Multiply 3053 by 0.25. The answer should be   13._____
    A. 76.325   B. 86.315   C. 763.25   D. 863.15

14. Multiply 6204 by 0.35. The answer should be   14._____
    A. 2282.40   B. 2171.40   C. 228.24   D. 217.14

15. Multiply $.35 by 7619. The answer should be   15._____
    A. $2324.75   B. $2565.65   C. $2666.65   D. $2756.75

16. Multiply 6513 by 45. The answer should be   16._____
    A. 293185   B. 293085   C. 292185   D. 270975

17. Multiply 3579 by 70. The answer should be   17._____
    A. 25053.0   B. 240530   C. 250530   D. 259530

18. A class had an average of 24 words correct on a spelling test. The class average on this spelling test was 80%.   18._____
    The AVERAGE number of words missed on this test was
    A. 2   B. 4   C. 6   D. 8

19. In which one of the following is 24 renamed as a product of primes?   19._____
    A. 2 x 6 x 2   B. 8 x 3 x 1
    C. 2 x 2 x 3 x 2   D. 3 x 4 x 2

Questions 20-23.

DIRECTIONS: In answering Questions 20 through 23, perform the indicated operation. Select the BEST answer from the choices below.

20. Add: 7068   20._____
           2807
           9434
           6179
    A. 26,488   B. 24,588   C. 25,488   D. 25,478

21. Divide: 75√45555   21._____
    A. 674   B. 607.4   C. 6074   D. 60.74

22. Multiply: 907   22._____
              x806
    A. 73,142   B. 13,202   C. 721,042   D. 731,042

23. Subtract: 60085   23._____
              -47194
    A. 12,891   B. 13,891   C. 12,991   D. 12,871

24. A librarian reported that 1/5% of all books taken out last school year had not been returned.
If 85,000 books were borrowed from the library, how many were not returned?

   A. 170   B. 425   C. 1,700   D. 4,250

25. At 40 miles per hour, how many minutes would it take to travel 12 miles?

   A. 30   B. 18   C. 15   D. 20

KEY (CORRECT ANSWERS)

1. A
2. B
3. A
4. C
5. B

6. C
7. B
8. D
9. B
10. A

11. C
12. C
13. C
14. B
15. C

16. B
17. C
18. C
19. C
20. C

21. B
22. D
23. A
24. A
25. B

SOLUTIONS TO PROBLEMS

1. 30,983 - 29,998 = 985

2. $2537.75 - $1764.28 = $773.47

3. 254,211 - 76,348 = 177,863

4. 4025 ÷ 35 = 115

5. (.35)(2764) = 967.4

6. (1367)(.50) = 683.5

7. (841)(.01) = 8.41

8. (1962)(25) = 49,050

9. (905)(.05) = 45.25

10. (8.93)(4.7) = 41.971

11. (25)(763) = 19,075

12. (2530)(.10) = 253

13. (3053)(.25) = 763.25

14. (6204)(.35) = 2171.4

15. ($.35)(7619) = $2666.65

16. (6513)(45) = 293,085

17. (3579)(70) = 250,530

18. 24 ÷ .80 = 30. Then, 30 - 24 = 6 words

19. 24 = 2 x 2 x 3 x 2, where each number is a prime.

20. 7068 ÷ 2807 + 9434 + 6179 = 25,488

21. 45,555 ÷ 75 = 607.4

22. (907)(806) = 731,042

23. 60,085 - 47,194 = 12,891

24. (1/5%)(85,000) = (.002)(85,000) = 170 books

25. Let x = number of minutes. Then, $\dfrac{40}{60} = \dfrac{12}{x}$. Solving, x = 18

TEST 2

DIRECTIONS: Each question or incomplete statement is followed by several suggested answers or completions. Select the one that BEST answers the question or completes the statement. *PRINT THE LETTER OF THE CORRECT ANSWER IN THE SPACE AT THE RIGHT.*

1. The sum of 57901 + 34762 is   1.____
   A. 81663   B. 82663   C. 91663   D. 92663

2. The sum of 559 + 448 + 362 + 662 is   2.____
   A. 2121   B. 2031   C. 2021   D. 1931

3. The sum of 36153 + 28624 + 81379 is   3.____
   A. 136156   B. 146046   C. 146146   D. 146156

4. The sum of 742 + 9197 + 8972 is   4.____
   A. 19901   B. 18911   C. 18801   D. 17921

5. The sum of 7989 + 8759 + 2726 is   5.____
   A. 18455   B. 18475   C. 19464   D. 19474

6. The sum of $111.55 + $95.05 + $38.80 is   6.____
   A. $234.40   B. $235.30   C. $245.40   D. $254.50

7. The sum of 1302 + 46187 + 92610 + 4522 is   7.____
   A. 144621   B. 143511   C. 134621   D. 134521

8. The sum of 47953 + 58041 + 63022 + 22333 is   8.____
   A. 170248   B. 181349   C. 191349   D. 200359

9. The sum of 76563 + 43693 + 38521 + 50987 + 72723 is   9.____
   A. 271378   B. 282386   C. 282487   D. 292597

10. The sum of 85923 + 97211 + 11333 + 4412 + 22533 is   10.____
    A. 209302   B. 212422   C. 221412   D. 221533

11. The sum of 4299 + 54163 + 89765 + 1012 + 38962 is   11.____
    A. 188201   B. 188300   C. 188301   D. 189311

12. The sum of 48526 + 709 + 11534 + 80432 + 6096 is   12.____
    A. 135177   B. 139297   C. 147297   D. 149197

13. The sum of $407.62 + $109.01 + $68.44 + $378.68 is   13.____
    A. $963.75   B. $964.85   C. $973.65   D. $974.85

14. From 40614 subtract 4697. The answer should be

    A. 35917   B. 35927   C. 36023   D. 36027

15. From 81773 subtract 5717. The answer should be

    A. 75964   B. 76056   C. 76066   D. 76956

16. From $1755.35 subtract $1201.75. The answer should be

    A. $542.50   B. $544.50   C. $553.60   D. $554.60

17. From $2402.10 subtract $998.85. The answer should be

    A. $1514.35   B. $1504.25   C. $1413.25   D. $1403.25

18. Add: 12 1/2
           2 1/2
           3 1/2

    A. 17   B. 17 1/4   C. 17 3/4   D. 18

19. Subtract: 150
               -80

    A. 70   B. 80   C. 130   D. 150

20. After cleaning up some lots in the city dump, five cleanup crews loaded the following amounts of garbage on trucks:
    Crew No. 1 loaded 2 1/4 tons
    Crew No. 2 loaded 3 tons
    Crew No. 3 loaded 1 1/4 tons
    Crew No. 4 loaded 2 1/4 tons
    Crew No. 5 loaded 1/2 ton.
    The TOTAL number of tons of garbage loaded was

    A. 8 1/4   B. 8 3/4   C. 9   D. 9 1/4

21. Subtract: 17 3/4
                -7 1/4

    A. 7 1/2   B. 10 1/2   C. 14 1/4   D. 17 3/4

22. Yesterday, Tom and Bill each received 10 leaflets about rat control. They were supposed to distribute one leaflet to each supermarket in the neighborhood. When the day was over, Tom had 8 leaflets left. Bill had no leaflets left.
    How many supermarkets got leaflets yesterday?

    A. 8   B. 10   C. 12   D. 18

23. What is 2/3 of 1 1/8?

    A. 1 11/16   B. 3/4   C. 3/8   D. 4 1/3

24. A farmer bought a load of 120 bushels of corn.
    After he fed 45 bushels to his hogs, what fraction of his supply remained?

    A. 5/8   B. 3/5   C. 3/8   D. 4/7

25. In the numeral 3,159,217, the 2 is in the _____ column.   25._____

   A.   hundreds   B.   units   C.   thousands   D.   tens

KEY (CORRECT ANSWERS)

1. D
2. B
3. D
4. B
5. D

6. C
7. A
8. C
9. C
10. C

11. A
12. C
13. A
14. A
15. B

16. C
17. D
18. D
19. A
20. D

21. B
22. C
23. B
24. A
25. A

SOLUTIONS TO PROBLEMS

1. 57,901 + 34,762 = 92,663

2. 559 + 448 + 362 + 662 = 2031

3. 36,153 + 28,624 + 81,379 = 146,156

4. 742 + 9197 + 8972 = 18,911

5. 7989 + 8759 + 2726 = 19,474

6. $111.55 + $95.05 + $38.80 = $245.40

7. 1302 + 46,187 + 92,610 + 4522 = 144,621

8. 47,953 + 58,041 + 63,022 + 22,333 = 191,349

9. 76,563 + 45,693 + 38,521 + 50,987 + 72,723 = 282,487

10. 85,923 + 97,211 + 11,333 + 4412 + 22,533 = 221,412

11. 4299 + 54,163 + 89,765 + 1012 + 38,962 = 188,201

12. 48,526 + 709 + 11,534 + 80,432 + 6096 = 147,297

13. $407.62 + $109.01 + $68.44 + $378.68 = $963.75

14. 40,614 - 4697 = 35,917

15. 81,773 - 5717 = 76,056

16. $1755.35 - $1201.75 = $553.60

17. $2402.10 - $998.85 = $1403.25

18. 12 1/2 + 2 1/4 + 3 1/4 = 17 4/4 = 18

19. 150 - 80 = 70

20. 2 1/4 + 3 + 1 1/4 + 2 1/4 + 1/2 = 8 5/4 = 9 1/4 tons

21. 17 3/4 - 7 1/4 = 10 2/4 = 10 1/2

22. 10 + 10 - 8 - 0 = 12 supermarkets

23. $(\frac{2}{3})(1\frac{1}{8}) = (\frac{2}{3})(\frac{9}{8}) = \frac{18}{24} = \frac{3}{4}$

24. 120 - 45 = 75. Then, $\frac{75}{120} = \frac{5}{8}$

25. The number 2 is in the hundreds column of 3,159,217

TEST 3

DIRECTIONS: Each question or incomplete statement is followed by several suggested answers or completions. Select the one that BEST answers the question or completes the statement. *PRINT THE LETTER OF THE CORRECT ANSWER IN THE SPACE AT THE RIGHT.*

1. The distance covered in three minutes by a subway train traveling at 30 mph is _____ mile(s).

   A. 3   B. 2   C. 1 1/2   D. 1

   1._____

2. A crate contains 3 pieces of equipment weighing 73, 84, and 47 pounds, respectively. The empty crate weighs 16 pounds.
   If the crate is lifted by 4 trackmen, each trackman lifting one corner of the crate, the AVERAGE number of pounds lifted by each of the trackmen is

   A. 68   B. 61   C. 55   D. 51

   2._____

3. The weight per foot of a length of square-bar 4" x 4" in cross-section, as compared with one 2" x 2" in cross-section, is _____ as much.

   A. twice   B. 2 1/2 times
   C. 3 times   D. 4 times

   3._____

4. An order for 360 feet of 2" x 8" lumber is shipped in 20-foot lengths.
   The MAXIMUM number of 9-foot pieces that can be cut from this shipment is

   A. 54   B. 40   C. 36   D. 18

   4._____

5. If a trackman gets $10.40 per hour and time and one-half for working over 40 hours, his gross salary for a week in which he worked 44 hours should be

   A. $457.60   B. $478.40   C. $499.20   D. $514.80

   5._____

6. If a section of ballast 6'-0" wide, 8'-0" long, and 2'-6" deep is excavated, the amount of ballast removed is _____ cu. feet.

   A. 96   B. 104   C. 120   D. 144

   6._____

7. The sum of 7'2 3/4", 0'-2 7/8", 3'-0", 4'-6 3/8", and 1'-9 1/4" is

   A. 16'-8 1/4"   B. 16'-8 3/4"   C. 16'-9 1/4"   D. 16'-9 3/4"

   7._____

8. The sum of 3 1/16", 4 1/4", 2 5/8", and 5 7/16" is

   A. 15 3/16"   B. 15 1/4"   C. 15 3/8"   D. 15 1/2"

   8._____

9. Add: $51.79, $29.39, and $8.98.
   The CORRECT answer is

   A. $78.97   B. $88.96   C. $89.06   D. $90.16

   9._____

10. Add: $72.07 and $31.54. Then subtract $25.75.
    The CORRECT answer is

    A. $77.86   B. $82.14   C. $88.96   D. $129.36

    10._____

2 (#3)

11. Start with $82.47. Then subtract $25.50, $4.75, and 35¢. 11.____
    The CORRECT answer is

    A. $30.60   B. $51.87   C. $52.22   D. $65.25

12. Add: $19.35 and $37.75. Then subtract $9.90 and $19.80. 12.____
    The CORRECT answer is

    A. $27.40   B. $37.00   C. $37.30   D. $47.20

13. Add: $153   13.____
            114
            210
           +186

    A. $657   B. $663   C. $713   D. $757

14. Add: $64.91   14.____
            13.53
            19.27
            20.00
           +72.84

    A. $170.25   B. $178.35   C. $180.45   D. $190.55

15. Add: 1963   15.____
            1742
           +2497

    A. 6202   B. 6022   C. 5212   D. 5102

16. Add: 206   16.____
            709
            1342
           +2076

    A. 3432   B. 3443   C. 4312   D. 4333

17. Subtract: $190.76   17.____
              -    .99

    A. $189.97   B. $189.87   C. $189.77   D. $189.67

18. From 99876 subtract 85397. The answer should be   18.____

    A. 14589   B. 14521   C. 14479   D. 13589

19. From $876.51 subtract $92.89. The answer should be   19.____

    A. $773.52   B. $774.72   C. $783.62   D. $784.72

20. From 70935 subtract 49489. The answer should be   20.____

    A. 20436   B. 21446   C. 21536   D. 21546

21. From $391.55 subtract $273.45. The answer should be   21.____
    A. $118.10   B. $128.20   C. $178.10   D. $218.20

22. When 119 is subtracted from the sum of 2016 + 1634, the answer is   22.____
    A. 2460   B. 3531   C. 3650   D. 3769

23. Multiply 35 x 65 x 15. The answer should be   23.____
    A. 2275   B. 24265   C. 31145   D. 34125

24. Multiply: 4.06   24.____
              x.031
    A. 1.2586   B. .12586   C. .02586   D. .1786

25. When 65 is added to the result of 14 multiplied by 13, the answer is   25.____
    A. 92   B. 182   C. 247   D. 16055

KEY (CORRECT ANSWERS)

1. C   11. B
2. C   12. A
3. D   13. B
4. C   14. D
5. B   15. A

6. C   16. D
7. C   17. C
8. C   18. C
9. D   19. C
10. A   20. B

21. A
22. B
23. D
24. B
25. C

SOLUTIONS TO PROBLEMS

1. Let x = distance. Then, $\dfrac{30}{60} = \dfrac{x}{3}$ Solving, x = 1 1/2 miles

2. (73 + 84 + 47 + 16) ÷ 4 = 55 pounds

3. (4 x 4) ÷ (2 x 2) = a ratio of 4 to 1.

4. 20 ÷ 9 = 2 2/9, rounded down to 2 pieces. Then, (360 ÷ 20)(2) = 36

5. Salary =($10.40)(40) + ($15.60)(4) = $478.40

6. (6)(8)(2 1/2) = 120 cu.ft.

7. $7'2\tfrac{3}{4}" + 0'2\tfrac{7}{8}" + 3'0" + 4'6\tfrac{3}{8}" + 1'9\tfrac{1}{4}" = 15'19\tfrac{18}{8}" = 15'21\tfrac{1}{4}" = 16'9\tfrac{1}{4}"$

8. $3\tfrac{1}{16}" + 4\tfrac{1}{4}" + 2\tfrac{5}{8}" + 5\tfrac{7}{16}" = 14\tfrac{22}{16}" = 15\tfrac{3}{8}"$

9. $51.79 + $29.39 + $8.98 = $90.16

10. $72.07 + $31.54 = $103.61. Then, $103.61 - $25.75 = $77.86

11. $82.47 - $25.50 - $4.75 - $0.35 = $51.87

12. $19.35 + $37.75 = $57.10. Then, $57.10 - $9.90 - $19.80 = $27.40

13. $153 + $114 + $210 + $186 = $663

14. $64.91 + $13.53 + $19.27 + $20.00 + $72.84 = $190.55

15. 1963 + 1742 + 2497 = 6202

16. 206 + 709 + 1342 + 2076 = 4333

17. $190.76 - .99 = $189.77

18. 99,876 - 85,397 = 14,479

19. $876.51 - $92.89 = $783.62

20. 70,935 - 49,489 = 21,446

21. $391.55 - $273.45 = $118.10

22. (2016 + 1634) - 119 = 3650 - 119 = 3531

23. (35)(65)(15) = 34,125

24. (4.06)(.031) = .12586

25. 65 + (14)(13) = 65 + 182 = 247

ARITHMETIC
EXAMINATION SECTION

DIRECTIONS: Each question or incomplete statement is followed by several suggested answers or completions. Select the one that BEST answers the question or completes the statement. *PRINT THE LETTER OF THE CORRECT ANSWER IN THE SPACE AT THE RIGHT.*

1. The sum of 53632 + 27403 + 98765 + 75424 is 1.____
   A. 19214   B. 215214   C. 235224   D. 255224

2. The sum of 76342 + 49050 + 21206 + 59989 is 2.____
   A. 196586   B. 206087   C. 206587   D. 234487

3. The sum of $452.13 + $963.45 + $621.25 is 3.____
   A. $1936.83   B. $2036.83   C. $2095.73   D. $2135.73

4. The sum of 36392 + 42156 + 98765 is 4.____
   A. 167214   B. 177203   C. 177313   D. 178213

5. The sum of 40125 + 87123 + 24689 is 5.____
   A. 141827   B. 151827   C. 151937   D. 161947

6. The sum of 2379 + 4015 + 6521 + 9986 is 6.____
   A. 22901   B. 22819   C. 21801   D. 21791

7. From 50962 subtract 36197.
   The answer should be 7.____
   A. 14675   B. 14765   C. 14865   D. 24765

8. From 90000 subtract 31928.
   The answer should be 8.____
   A. 58072   B. 59062   C. 68172   D. 69182

9. From 63764 subtract 21548.
   The answer should be 9.____
   A. 42216   B. 43122   C. 45126   D. 85312

10. From $9605.13 subtract $2715.96.
    The answer should be 10.____
    A. $12,321.09   B. $8,690.16   C. $6,990.07   D. $6,889.17

11. From 76421 subtract 73101.
    The answer should be 11.____
    A. 3642   B. 3540   C. 3320   D. 3242

12. From $8.25 subtract $6.50.
    The answer should be
    A. $1.25   B. $1.50   C. $1.75   D. $2.25

13. Multiply 563 by 0.50.
    The answer should be
    A. 281.50   B. 28.15   C. 2.815   D. 0.2815

14. Multiply 0.35 by 1045.
    The answer should be
    A. 0.36575 B. 3.6575   C. 36.575   D. 365.75

15. Multiply 25 by 2513.
    The answer should be
    A. 62825   B. 62725   C. 60825   D. 52825

16. Multiply 423 by 0.01.
    The answer should be
    A. 0.0423   B. 0.423   C. 4.23   D. 42.3

17. Multiply 6.70 by 3.2.
    The answer should be
    A. 2.1440   B. 21.440   C. 214.40   D. 2144.0

18. Multiply 630 by 517.
    The answer should be
    A. 325,710 B. 345,720 C. 362,425 D. 385,660

19. Multiply 35 by 846.
    The answer should be
    A. 4050   B. 9450   C. 18740   D. 29610

20. Multiply 823 by 0.05.
    The answer should be
    A. 0.4115   B. 4.115   C. 41.15   D. 411.50

21. Multiply 1690 by 0.10.
    The answer should be
    A. 0.169   B. 1.69   C. 16.90   D. 169.0

22. Divide 2765 by 35.
    The answer should be
    A. 71   B. 79   C. 87   D. 93

23. From $18.55 subtract $6.80.
    The answer should be
    A. $9.75   B. $10.95   C. $11.75   D. $25.35

24. The sum of 2.75 + 4.50 + 3.60 is 24._____
    A. 9.75   B. 10.85   C. 11.15   D. 11.95

25. The sum of 9.63 + 11.21 + 17.25 is 25._____
    A. 36.09   B. 38.09   C. 39.92   D. 41.22

26. The sum of 112.0 + 16.9 + 3.84 is 26._____
    A. 129.3   B. 132.74   C. 136.48   D. 167.3

27. When 65 is added to the result of 14 multiplied by 13, the answer is 27._____
    A. 92   B. 182   C. 247   D. 16055

28. From $391.55 subtract $273.45.
    The answer should be 28._____
    A. $118.10 B. $128.20 C. $178.10 D. $218.20

29. When 119 is subtracted from the sum of 2016 + 1634, the answer is 29._____
    A. 2460   B. 3531   C. 3650   D. 3769

30. What is $367.20 + $510.00 + $402.80? 30._____
    A. $1,276.90 B. $1,277.90 C. $1,279.00 D. $1,280.00

31. Multiply 35 x 65 x 15.
    The answer should be 31._____
    A. 2275   B. 24265   C. 31145   D. 34125

32. Multiply 40 x 65 x 10.
    The answer should be 32._____
    A. 26000   B. 28000   C. 25200   D. 22300

33. The total amount of money represented by 43 half-dollars, 26 quarters, and 71 dimes is 33._____
    A. $28.00 B. $35.10   C. $44.30   D. $56.60

34. The total amount of money represented by 132 quarters, 97 dimes, and 220 nickels is 34._____
    A. $43.70 B. $44.20   C. $52.90   D. $53.70

35. The total amount of money represented by 40 quarters, 40 dimes, and 20 nickels is 35._____
    A. $14.50 B. $15.00   C. $15.50   D. $16.00

36. The sum of $29.61 + $101.53 + $943.64 is 36._____
    A. $983.88 B. $1074.78 C. $1174.98 D. $1341.42

37. The sum of $132.25 + $85.63 + $7056.44 is 37._____
    A. $1694.19 B. $7274.32 C. $8464.57 D. $9346.22

38. The sum of 4010 + 1271 + 23 + 838 is   38.____

    A. 6142   B. 6162   C. 6242   D. 6362

39. What is the value of 3 twenty dollar bills, 5 ten dollar bills, 13 five dollar bills, and 43 one   39.____
    dollar bills?

    A. $218.00   B. $219.00   C. $220.00   D. $221.00

40. What is the value of 8 twenty dollar bills, 13 ten dollar bills, 27 five dollar bills, 3 two dollar   40.____
    bills, and 43 one dollar bills?

    A. $364.00   B. $374.00   C. $474.00   D. $485.00

41. What is the value of 6 twenty dollar bills, 8 ten dollar bills, 19 five dollar bills, and 37 one   41.____
    dollar bills?

    A. $232.00   B. $233.00   C. $332.00   D. $333.00

42. What is the value of 13 twenty dollar bills, 17 ten dollar bills, 24 five dollar bills, 7 two dol-   42.____
    lar bills, and 55 one dollar bills?

    A. $594.00   B. $599.00   C. $609.00   D. $619.00

43. What is the value of 7 half dollars, 9 quarters, 23 dimes, and 17 nickels?   43.____

    A. $7.80   B. $7.90   C. $8.80   D. $8.90

44. What is the value of 3 one dollar coins, 3 half dollars, 7 quarters, 13 dimes, and 27 nick-   44.____
    els?

    A. $7.80   B. $8.70   C. $8.80   D. $8.90

45. What is the value of 73 quarters?   45.____

    A. $18.25   B. $18.50   C. $18.75   D. $19.00

46. What is the value of 173 nickels?   46.____

    A. $8.55   B. $8.65   C. $8.75   D. $8.85

47. In checking a book of consecutively numbered Senior Citizen tickets, you find there are   47.____
    no tickets between number 13,383 and 13,833.
    How many tickets are missing?

    A. 448   B. 449   C. 450   D. 451

48. A ticket clerk begins her shift with 2,322 tickets. How many tickets will she have at the   48.____
    end of her shift if she sells 1,315 and collects 1,704 from the turnstiles during her shift?

    A. 2,687   B. 2,693   C. 2,711   D. 2,722

49. A ticket clerk has three books of tickets. One contains 273 tickets, one contains 342 tick-   49.____
    ets, and one contains 159 tickets. The clerk combines the contents of the three books
    and then sells 217 tickets.
    How many tickets are left?

    A. 556   B. 557   C. 568   D. 991

50. A ticket clerk has a quantity of consecutively numbered tickets. The number on the ticket having the lowest number is 27,069. The number on the ticket having the highest number is 27,154.
How many tickets does the clerk have?

   A. 84   B. 85   C. 86   D. 87

50.____

KEY (CORRECT ANSWERS)

1. D	11. C	21. D	31. D	41. C
2. C	12. C	22. B	32. A	42. D
3. B	13. A	23. C	33. B	43. D
4. C	14. D	24. B	34. D	44. D
5. C	15. A	25. B	35. B	45. A
6. A	16. C	26. B	36. B	46. B
7. B	17. B	27. C	37. B	47. B
8. A	18. A	28. A	38. A	48. C
9. A	19. D	29. B	39. A	49. B
10. D	20. C	30. D	40. C	50. C

6 (#1)

SOLUTIONS TO PROBLEMS

1. 53,632 + 27,403 + 98,765 + 75,424 = 255,224

2. 76,342 + 49,050 + 21,206 + 59,989 = 206,587

3. $452.13 + $963.83 + $621.25 = $2037.21

4. 36,392 + 42,156 + 98,765 = 177,313

5. 40,125 + 87,123 + 24,689 = 151,937

6. 2379 + 4015 + 6521 + 9986 = 22901

7. 50,962 - 36,197 = 14,765

8. 90,000 - 31,928 = 58,072

9. 63,764 - 21,548 = 42,216

10. $9605.13 - $2715.96 = $6889.17

11. 76,421 - 73,101 = 3320

12. $8.25 - $6.50 = $1.75

13. (563)(.50) = 281.50

14. (.35)(1045) = 365.75

15. (25)(2513) = 62,825

16. (423)(.01) = 4.23

17. (6.70)(3.2) = 21.44

18. (630)(517) = 325,710

19. (35)(846) = 29,610

20. (823)(.05) = 41.15

21. (1690)(.10) = 169

22. 2765 / 35 = 79

23. $18.55 - $6.80 = $11.75

24. 2.75 + 4.50 + 3.60 = 10.85

25. 9.63 + 11.21 + 17.25 = 38.09

26. 112.0 + 16.9 + 3.84 = 132.74

27. 65 + (14)(13) = 247

28. $391.55 - $273.45 = $118.10

29. 2016 + 1634 - 119 = 3531

30. $367.20 + $510.00 + $402.80 = $1280.00

31. (35)(65)(15) = 34,125

32. (40)(65)(10) - 26,000

33. (43)(.50) + (26)(.25) + (71)(.10) = $35.10

34. (132)(.25) + (97)(.10) + (220)(.05) = $53.70

35. (40)(.25) + (40)(.10) + (20)(.05) = $15.00

36. $29.61 + $101.53 + $943.64 = $1074.78

37. $132.25 + $85.63 + $7056.44 = $7274.32

38. 4010 + 1271 + 23 + 838 = 6142

39. (3)($20) + (5)($10) + (13)($5) + (43)($1) + $218.00

40. (8)($20) + (13)($10) + (27)($5) + (3)($2) + (43)($1) = $474.00

41. (6)($20) + (8)($10) + (19)($5) + (37)($1) = $332.00

42. (13)($20) + (17)($10) + (24)($5) + (7)($2) + (55)($1) = $619.00

43. (7)(.50) + (9)(.25) + (23)(.10) + (17)(.05) = $8.90

44. (3)($1) + (3)(.50) + (7)(.25) + (13)(.10) + (27)(.05) = $8.90

45. (73)(.25) = $18.25

46. (173)(.05) = $8.65

47. The missing tickets are numbered 13,384 through 13,832. This represents 13,832 - 13,384 + 1 = 449 tickets.

48. 2322 - 1315 + 1704 = 2711 tickets left.

49. 273 + 342 + 159 - 217 = 557 tickets left

50. 27,154 - 27,069 + 1 = 86 tickets

ARITHMETIC

EXAMINATION SECTION
TEST 1

DIRECTIONS: Each question or incomplete statement is followed by several suggested answers or completions. Select the one that BEST answers the question or completes the statement. *PRINT THE LETTER OF THE CORRECT ANSWER IN THE SPACE AT THE RIGHT.*

1. The sum of 76342 + 49050 + 21206 + 59989 is 1._____
   A. 196586   B. 206087   C. 206587   D. 234487

2. The sum of $452.13 + $963.83 + $621.25 is 2._____
   A. $1936.83   B. $2037.21   C. $2095.73   D. $2135.73

3. The sum of 36392 + 42156 + 98765 is 3._____
   A. 167214   B. 177203   C. 177313   D. 178213

4. The sum of 40125 + 87123 + 24689 is 4._____
   A. 141827   B. 151827   C. 151937   D. 161947

5. The sum of 2379 + 4015 + 6521 + 9986 is 5._____
   A. 22901   B. 22819   C. 21801   D. 21791

6. From 50962 subtract 36197. The answer should be 6._____
   A. 14675   B. 14765   C. 14865   D. 24765

7. From 90000 subtract 31928. The answer should be 7._____
   A. 58072   B. 59062   C. 68172   D. 69182

8. From 63764 subtract 21548. The answer should be 8._____
   A. 42216   B. 43122   C. 45126   D. 85312

9. From $9605.13 subtract $2715.96. The answer should be 9._____
   A. $12,321.09   B. $8,690.16
   C. $6,990.07   D. $6,889.17

10. From 76421 subtract 73101. The answer should be 10._____
    A. 3642   B. 3540   C. 3320   D. 3242

11. From $8.25 subtract $6.50. The answer should be 11._____
    A. $1.25   B. $1.50   C. $1.75   D. $2.25

12. Multiply 563 by 0.50. The answer should be 12._____
    A. 281.50   B. 28.15   C. 2.815   D. 0.2815

13. Multiply 0.35 by 1045. The answer should be   13._____
    A. 0.36575   B. 3.6575   C. 36.575   D. 365.75

14. Multiply 25 by 2513. The answer should be   14._____
    A. 62825   B. 62725   C. 60825   D. 52825

15. Multiply 423 by 0.01. The answer should be   15._____
    A. 0.0423   B. 0.423   C. 4.23   D. 42.3

16. Multiply 6.70 by 3.2. The answer should be   16._____
    A. 2.1440   B. 21.440   C. 214.40   D. 2144.0

17. Multiply 630 by 517. The answer should be   17._____
    A. 325,710   B. 345,720   C. 362,425   D. 385,660

18. Multiply 35 by 846. The answer should be   18._____
    A. 4050   B. 9450   C. 18740   D. 29610

19. Multiply 823 by 0.05. The answer should be   19._____
    A. 0.4115   B. 4.115   C. 41.15   D. 411.50

20. Multiply 1690 by 0.10. The answer should be   20._____
    A. 0.169   B. 1.69   C. 16.90   D. 169.0

21. Divide 2765 by 35. The answer should be   21._____
    A. 71   B. 79   C. 87   D. 93

22. From $18.55 subtract $6.80. The answer should be   22._____
    A. $9.75   B. $10.95   C. $11.75   D. $25.35

23. The sum of 2.75 + 4.50 + 3.60 is   23._____
    A. 9.75   B. 10.85   C. 11.15   D. 11.95

24. The sum of 9.63 + 11.21 + 17.25 is   24._____
    A. 36.09   B. 38.09   C. 39.92   D. 41.22

25. The sum of 112.0 + 16.9 + 3.84 is   25._____
    A. 129.3   B. 132.74   C. 136.48   D. 167.3

KEY (CORRECT ANSWERS)

1.	C	11.	C
2.	B	12.	A
3.	C	13.	D
4.	C	14.	A
5.	A	15.	C
6.	B	16.	B
7.	A	17.	A
8.	A	18.	D
9.	D	19.	C
10.	C	20.	D

21. B
22. C
23. B
24. B
25. B

SOLUTIONS TO PROBLEMS

1. 76,342 + 49,050 + 21,206 + 59,989 = 206,587

2. $452.13 + $963.83 + $621.25 = $2037.21

3. 36,392 + 42,156 + 98,765 = 177,313

4. 40,125 + 87,123 + 24,689 = 151,937

5. 2379 + 4015 + 6521 + 9986 = 22901

6. 50,962 - 36,197 = 14,765

7. 90,000 - 31,928 = 58,072

8. 63,764 - 21,548 = 42,216

9. $9605.13 - $2715.96 = $6889.17

10. 76,421 - 73,101 = 3320

11. $8.25 - $6.50 = $1.75

12. (563)(.50) = 281.50

13. (.35)(1045) = 365.75

14. (25)(2513) = 62,825

15. (423)(.01) = 4.23

16. (6.70)(3.2) = 21.44

17. (630)(517) = 325,710

18. (35)(846) = 29,610

19. (823)(.05) = 41.15

20. (1690)(.10) = 169

21. 2765 ÷ 35 = 79

22. $18.55 - $6.80 = $11.75

23. 2.75 + 4.50 + 3.60 = 10.85

24. 9.63 + 11.21 + 17.25 = 38.09

25. 112.0 + 16.9 + 3.84 = 132.74

TEST 2

Questions 1-10.

DIRECTIONS: Questions 1 through 10 refer to the arithmetic examples shown in the boxes below. Be sure to refer to the proper box when answering each question.

23.3 - 5.72	$491.26 -127.47	$7.95 ÷ $0.15	4758 1639 2075 864 23	27.6 179.47 8.73 46.5
BOX 1	BOX 2	BOX 3	BOX 4	BOX 5
243 x57	57697 -9748	23.65 x 9.7	3/4 260	25/1975
BOX 6	BOX 7	BOX 8	BOX 9	BOX 10

1. The difference between the two numbers in Box 1 is
   A. 17.42   B. 17.58   C. 23.35   D. 29.02

2. The difference between the two numbers in Box 2 is
   A. $274.73   B. $363.79   C. $374.89   D. $618.73

3. The result of the division indicated in Box 3 is
   A. $0.53   B. $5.30   C. 5.3   D. 53

4. The sum of the five numbers in Box 4 is
   A. 8355   B. 9359   C. 9534   D. 10359

5. The sum of the four numbers in Box 5 is
   A. 262.30   B. 272.03   C. 372.23   D. 372.30

6. The product of the two numbers in Box 6 is
   A. 138.51   B. 1385.1   C. 13851   D. 138510

7. The difference between the two numbers in Box 7 is
   A. 67445   B. 48949   C. 47949   D. 40945

8. The product of the two numbers in Box 8 is
   A. 22.9405   B. 229.405   C. 2294.05   D. 229405

9. The product of the two numbers in Box 9 is
   A. 65   B. 120   C. 195   D. 240

1. ____
2. ____
3. ____
4. ____
5. ____
6. ____
7. ____
8. ____
9. ____

10. The result of the division indicated in Box 10 is   10.____

    A. 790   B. 379   C. 179   D. 79

Questions 11-20.

DIRECTIONS: Questions 11 through 20 refer to the arithmetic examples shown in the boxes below. Be sure to refer to the proper box when answering each question.

3849 728 3164 773 32	18.70 268.38 17.64 9.40	66788 -8639	154 x48	32.56 x 8.6
BOX 1	BOX 2	BOX 3	BOX 4	BOX 5
34/2890	32.49 - 8.7	$582.17 -38.58	$6.72 ÷ $0.24	3/8 x 264
BOX 6	BOX 7	BOX 8	BOX 9	BOX 10

11. The sum of the five numbers in Box 1 is   11.____

    A. 7465   B. 7566   C. 8465   D. 8546

12. The sum of the four numbers in Box 2 is   12.____

    A. 341.21   B. 341.12   C. 314.21   D. 314.12

13. The difference between the two numbers in Box 3 is   13.____

    A. 75427   B. 74527   C. 58149   D. 57149

14. The product of the two numbers in Box 4 is   14.____

    A. 1232   B. 6160   C. 7392   D. 8392

15. The product of the two numbers in Box 5 is   15.____

    A. 28.016   B. 280.016   C. 280.16   D. 2800.16

16. The result of the division indicated in Box 6 is   16.____

    A. 85   B. 850   C. 8.5   D. 185

17. The difference between the two numbers in Box 7 is   17.____

    A. 23.79   B. 21.53   C. 19.97   D. 18.79

18. The difference between the two numbers in Box 8 is   18.____

    A. $620.75   B. $602.59   C. $554.75   D. $543.59

19. The result of the division indicated in Box 9 is   19.____

    A. .0357   B. 28.0   C. 280   D. 35.7

20. The product of the two numbers in Box 10 is						20.____
    A. 9.90		B. 89.0		C. 99.0		D. 199.

21. When 2597 is added to the result of 257 multiplied by 65, the answer is		21.____
    A. 16705		B. 19302		C. 19392		D. 19402

22. When 948 is subtracted from the sum of 6527 + 324, the answer is		22.____
    A. 5255		B. 5903		C. 7151		D. 7799

23. When 736 is subtracted from the sum of 3191 + 1253, the answer is		23.____
    A. 2674		B. 3708		C. 4444		D. 5180

24. Divide 6 2/3 by 2 1/2.							24.____
    A. 2 2/3		B. 16 2/3		C. 3 1/3		D. 2 1/2

25. Add: 1/2 + 2 1/4 + 2/3							25.____
    A. 3 1/4		B. 2 7/8		C. 4 1/4		D. 3 5/12

KEY (CORRECT ANSWERS)

1.	B		11.	D
2.	B		12.	D
3.	D		13.	C
4.	B		14.	C
5.	A		15.	B
6.	C		16.	A
7.	C		17.	A
8.	B		18.	D
9.	C		19.	B
10.	D		20.	C

21. B
22. B
23. B
24. A
25. D

SOLUTIONS TO PROBLEMS

1. 23.3 - 5.72 = 17.58

2. $491.26 - $127.47 = $363.79

3. $7.95 $.15 = 53

4. 4758 + 1639 + 2075 + 864 + 23 = 9359

5. 27.6 + 179.47 + 8.73 + 46.5 = 262.3

6. (243)(57) = 13,851

7. 57,697 - 9748 = 47,949

8. (23.65X9.7) = 229.405

9. $(\frac{3}{4})(260) = 195$

10. 1975 ÷ 25 = 79

11. 3849 + 728 + 3164 + 773 + 32 = 8546

12. 18.70 + 268.38 + 17.64 + 9.40 = 314.12

13. 66,788 - 8639 = 58,149

14. (154)(48) = 7392

15. (32.56)(8.6) = 280.016

16. 2890 34 = 85

17. 32.49 - 8.7 = 23.79

18. $582.17 - $38.58 = $543.59

19. $6.72 ÷ $.24 = 28

20. $(\frac{3}{8})(264) = 99$

21. 2597 + (257)(65) = 2597 + 16,705 = 19,302

22. (6527 + 324) - 948 = 6851 - 948 = 5903

5 (#2)

23. (3191 + 1253) - 736 = 4444 - 736 = 3708

24. $6\frac{2}{3} \div 2\frac{1}{2} = (\frac{20}{3})(\frac{2}{5}) = \frac{40}{15} = 2\frac{2}{3}$

25. $\frac{1}{2} + 2\frac{1}{4} + \frac{2}{3} = \frac{6}{12} + 2\frac{3}{12} + \frac{8}{12} = 2\frac{17}{12} = 3\frac{5}{12}$

———

TEST 3

Questions 1-10.

DIRECTIONS: Questions 1 through 10 refer to the arithmetic examples shown in the boxes below. Be sure to refer to the proper box when answering each item.

8462 2974 5109 763 47 BOX 1	14/1890 BOX 2	182 x63 BOX 3	27412 -8426 BOX 4	$275.15 -162.28 BOX 5
2/3 x 246 BOX 6	14.36 x 7.2 BOX 7	14.6 9.22 143.18 27.1 BOX 8	$6.45 ÷ $0.15 BOX 9	16.6 - 7.91 BOX 10

1. The sum of the five numbers in Box 1 is

   A. 16245   B. 16355   C. 17245   D. 17355

2. The result of the division indicated in Box 2 is

   A. 140   B. 135   C. 127 6/7   D. 125

3. The product of the two numbers in Box 3 is

   A. 55692   B. 16552   C. 11466   D. 1638

4. The difference between the two numbers in Box 4 is

   A. 18986   B. 19096   C. 35838   D. 38986

5. The difference between the two numbers in Box 5 is

   A. $103.87   B. $112.87   C. $113.97   D. $212.87

6. The product of the two numbers in Box 6 is

   A. 82   B. 123   C. 164   D. 369

7. The product of the two numbers in Box 7 is

   A. 103.492   B. 103.392   C. 102.392   D. 102.292

8. The sum of the four numbers in Box 8 is

   A. 183.00   B. 183.10   C. 194.10   D. 204.00

9. The result of the division indicated in Box 9 is

   A. $0.43   B. 4.3   C. 43   D. $4.30

10. The difference between the two numbers in Box 10 is   10._____
    A. 8.69   B. 8.11   C. 6.25   D. 3.75

11. Add $4.34, $34.50, $6.00, $101.76, and $90.67. From the result, subtract $60.54 and   11._____
    $10.56.
    A. $76.17   B. $156.37   C. $166.17   D. $300.37

12. Add 2,200, 2,600, 252, and 47.96. From the result, subtract 202.70, 1,200, 2,150, and   12._____
    434.43.
    A. 1,112.83   B. 1,213.46   C. 1,341.51   D. 1,348.91

13. Multiply 1850 by .05 and multiply 3300 by .08. Then, add both results.   13._____
    A. 242.50   B. 264.00   C. 333.25   D. 356.50

14. Multiply 312.77 by .04. Round off the result to the nearest hundredth.   14._____
    A. 12.52   B. 12.511   C. 12.518   D. 12.51

15. Add 362.05, 91.13, 347.81, and 17.46. Then, divide the result by 6.   15._____
    The answer rounded off to the nearest hundredth is
    A. 138.409   B. 137.409   C. 136.41   D. 136.40

16. Add 66.25 and 15.06. Then, multiply the result by 2 1/6. The answer is MOST NEARLY   16._____
    A. 176.18   B. 176.17   C. 162.66   D. 162.62

17. Each of the following options contains three decimals. In which case do all three deci-   17._____
    mals have the same value?
    A. .3; .30; .03   B. .25; .250; .2500
    C. 1.9; 1.90; 1.09   D. .35; .350; .035

18. Add 1/2 the sum of (539.84 and 479.26) to 1/3 the sum of (1461.93 and 927.27). Round   18._____
    off the result to the nearest whole number.
    A. 3408   B. 2899   C. 1816   D. 1306

19. Multiply $5,906.09 by 15%. Then, divide the result by 3.   19._____
    A. $295.30   B. $885.91   C. $8,859.14   D. $29,530.45

20. A team has won 10 games, lost 4, and has 6 games yet to play.   20._____
    How many of these remaining games MUST be won if the team is to win 65% of its
    games for the season?
    A. One   B. Two
    C. Four   D. None of the above

21. If a certain candy sells at the rate of $1 for 2 1/2 ounces, what is the price per pound?   21._____
    (Do not include tax.)
    A. $2.50   B. $6.40   C. $8.50   D. $4.00

22. Which is the SMALLEST of the following numbers? 22.____

    A. .3980   B. .3976   C. .39752   D. .399

23. A tank can be filled by one pipe in 10 minutes and by another in 15 minutes. 23.____
    How long will it take to fill the tank if both pipes are opened?
    _____ min.

    A. 4   B. 5   C. 6   D. 7.5

24. If $17.60 is to be divided between two people so that one person receives one and three- 24.____
    fourths as much as the other, how much should each receive?

    A. $6.40 and $11.20   B. $5.50 and $12.10
    C. $6.60 and $11.20   D. $6.00 and $11.60

25. Mr. Burns owns a block of land which is exactly 320 ft. long and 140 ft. wide. 25.____
    At 40¢ per square foot, how much will it cost to build a 4 foot cement walk around this
    land, bound by its outer edge?

    A. $1420.80   B. $1472   C. $368   D. $1446.40

KEY (CORRECT ANSWERS)

1. D   11. C
2. B   12. A
3. C   13. D
4. A   14. D
5. B   15. C

6. C   16. B
7. B   17. B
8. C   18. D
9. C   19. A
10. A   20. D

21. B
22. C
23. C
24. A
25. D

SOLUTIONS TO PROBLEMS

1. 8462 + 2974 + 5109 + 763 + 47 = 17,355

2. 1890 ÷ 14 = 135

3. (182)(63) = 11,466

4. 27,412 - 8426 = 18,986

5. $275.15 - $162.28 = $112.87

6. $(\frac{2}{3})(246) = 164$

7. (14.36)(7.2) = 103.392

8. 14.6 + 9.22 + 143.18 + 27.1 = 194.1

9. $6.45 $.15 = 43

10. 16.6 - 7.91 = 8.69

11. ($4.34 + $34.50 + $6.00 + $101.76 + $90.67) - ($60.54 + $10.56) = $237.27 - $71.10 = $166.17

12. (2200 + 2600 + 252 + 47.96) - (202.70 + 1200 + 2150 + 434.43) = 5099.96 - 3987.13 = 1112.83

13. (1850)(.05) + (3300X.08) = 92.5 + 264 = 356.5

14. (312.77)(.04) = 12.5108 = 12.51 rounded off to nearest hundredth

15. (362.05 + 91.13 + 347.81 + 17.46) 6 = 818.45 6 = 136.4083" = 136.41 rounded off to nearest hundredth

16. $(66.25 + 15.06)(2\frac{1}{6}) = (81.31)(2\frac{1}{6}) \approx 176.17$

17. .25 = .250 = .2500

18. 1/2(539.84 + 479.26) + 1/3(1461.93 + 927.27) = 509.55 + 796.4 = 1305.95 = 1306 rounaed off to nearest whole number

19. $($5906.09)(.15)(\frac{1}{3}) = $295.3045 = 295.30 rounded off to 2 places

5 (#3)

20. (.65)(20) = 13 games won. Thus, the team must win 3 more games.

21. Let x = price per pound. Then, $\dfrac{1.00}{x} = \dfrac{2\frac{1}{2}}{16}$. Solving, x = 6.40

22. .39752 is the smallest of the numbers.

23. Let x = required minutes. Then, $\dfrac{x}{10} + \dfrac{x}{15} = 1$. So, 3x + 2x = 30. Solving, x = 6.

24. Let x, 1.75x represent the two amounts. Then, x + 1.75x = $17.60. Solving, x = $6.40 and 1.75x = $11.20.

25. Area of cement walk = (320)(140) - (312)(132) = 3616 sq.ft. Then, (3616)(.40) = $1446.40.

TEST 4

DIRECTIONS: Each question or incomplete statement is followed by several suggested answers or completions. Select the one that BEST answers the question or completes the statement. *PRINT THE LETTER OF THE CORRECT ANSWER IN THE SPACE AT THE RIGHT.*

1. Subtract: 10,376
   -8,492

   A. 1834   B. 1884   C. 1924   D. 2084

   1.____

2. Subtract: $155.22
   - 93.75

   A. $61.47   B. $59.33   C. $59.17   D. $58.53

   2.____

3. Subtract: $22.50
   -13.78

   A. $9.32   B. $9.18   C. $8.92   D. $8.72

   3.____

4. Multiply: 485
   x32

   A. 13,350   B. 15,520   C. 16,510   D. 17,630

   4.____

5. Multiply: $3.29
   x 14

   A. $41.16   B. $42.46   C. $44.76   D. $46.06

   5.____

6. Multiply: 106
   x318

   A. 33,708   B. 33,632   C. 33,614   D. 33,548

   6.____

7. Multiply: 119
   x1.15

   A. 136.85   B. 136.94   C. 137.15   D. 137.34

   7.____

8. Divide: 432 by 16

   A. 37   B. 32   C. 27   D. 24

   8.____

9. Divide: $115.65 by 5

   A. $24.25   B. $23.13   C. $22.83   D. $22.55

   9.____

10. Divide: 18,711 by 63

    A. 267   B. 273   C. 283   D. 297

    10.____

11. Divide: 327.45 by .15

    A. 1,218   B. 2,183   C. 2,243   D. 2,285

    11.____

12. The sum of 637.894, 8352.16, 4.8673, and 301.5 is MOST NEARLY   12._____

    A. 8989.5   B. 9021.35   C. 9294.9   D. 9296.4

13. If 30 is divided by .06, the result is   13._____

    A. 5   B. 50   C. 500   D. 5000

14. The sum of the fractions 1/3, 4/6, 3/4, 1/2, and 1/12 is   14._____

    A. 3 1/4   B. 2 1/3   C. 2 1/6   D. 1 11/12

15. If 96934.42 is divided by 53.496, the result is MOST NEARLY   15._____

    A. 181   B. 552   C. 1812   D. 5520

16. If 25% of a number is 48, the number is   16._____

    A. 12   B. 60   C. 144   D. 192

17. The average number of reports filed per day by a clerk during a five-day week was 720.   17._____
    He filed 610 reports the first day, 720 reports the second day, 740 reports the third day,
    and 755 reports the fourth day.
    The number of reports he filed the fifth day was

    A. 748   B. 165   C. 775   D. 565

18. The number 88 is 2/5 of   18._____

    A. 123   B. 141   C. 220   D. 440

19. If the product of 8.3 multiplied by .42 is subtracted from the product of 156 multiplied by 19._____
    .09, the result is MOST NEARLY

    A. 10.6   B. 13.7   C. 17.5   D. 20.8

20. The sum of 284.5, 3016.24, 8.9736, and 94.15 is MOST NEARLY   20._____

    A. 3402.9   B. 3403.0   C. 3403.9   D. 4036.1

21. If 8394.6 is divided by 29.17, the result is MOST NEARLY   21._____

    A. 288   B. 347   C. 2880   D. 3470

22. If two numbers are multiplied together, the result is 3752. If one of the two numbers is 56, 22._____
    the other number is

    A. 41   B. 15   C. 109   D. 67

23. The sum of the fractions 1/4, 2/3, 3/8, 5/6, and 3/4 is   23._____

    A. 20/33   B. 1 19/24   C. 2 1/4   D. 2 7/8

24. The fraction 7/16 expressed as a decimal is   24._____

    A. .1120   B. .2286   C. .4375   D. .4850

25. If .10 is divided by 50, the result is   25._____

    A. .002   B. .02   C. .2   D. 2

KEY (CORRECT ANSWERS)

1. B
2. A
3. D
4. B
5. D

6. A
7. A
8. C
9. B
10. D

11. B
12. D
13. C
14. B
15. C

16. D
17. C
18. C
19. A
20. C

21. A
22. D
23. D
24. C
25. A

SOLUTIONS TO PROBLEMS

1. 10,376 - 8492 = 1884

2. $155.22 - $93.75 = $61.47

3. $22.50 - $13.78 = $8.72

4. (485)(32) = 15,520

5. ($3.29)(14) = $46.06

6. (106)(318) = 33,708

7. (119)(1.15) = 136.85

8. 432 ÷ 16 = 27

9. $115.65÷5=$23.13

10. 18,711÷63=297

11. 327.45 ÷ .15 = 2183

12. 637.894 + 8352.16 + 4.8673 + 301.5 = 9296.4213 ≈ 9296.4

13. 30 ÷ .06 = 500

14. $\frac{1}{3}+\frac{4}{6}+\frac{3}{4}+\frac{1}{2}+\frac{1}{12}=\frac{4}{12}+\frac{8}{12}+\frac{9}{12}+\frac{6}{12}+\frac{1}{12}=\frac{28}{12}=2\frac{1}{3}$

15. 96,934.42 ÷ 53.496 ≈ 1811.99 ≈ 1812

16. Let x = number. Then, .25x = 48. Solving, x = 192.

17. Let x = number of reports on 5th day. Then, (610 + 720 + 740 + 755 + x)/5 = 720. Simplifying, 2825 + x = 3600, so x = 775.

18. $88 \div \frac{2}{5} = 220$

19. (156)(.09) - (8.3)(.42) = 10.554 ≈ 10.6

20. 284.5 + 3016.24 + 8.9736 + 94.15 = 3403.8636 ≈ 3403.9

5 (#4)

21. 8394.6 ÷ 29.17 ≈ 287.78 ≈ 288

22. The other number = 3752 ÷ 56 = 67

23. $\dfrac{1}{4}+\dfrac{2}{3}+\dfrac{3}{8}+\dfrac{5}{6}+\dfrac{3}{4}=\dfrac{6}{24}+\dfrac{16}{24}+\dfrac{9}{24}+\dfrac{20}{24}+\dfrac{18}{24}=\dfrac{69}{24}=2\dfrac{7}{8}$

24. $\dfrac{7}{16}=.4375$

25. .10÷50=.002

www.ingramcontent.com/pod-product-compliance
Lightning Source LLC
Chambersburg PA
CBHW082035300426
44117CB00015B/2485